TUSCAN SPACES:
LITERARY CONSTRUCTIONS OF PLACE

Tuscany has long had an important place in the literary productions of writers both Italian and non-Italian. The reasons for the region's cultural impact are many and stem from its distinctive geography, history, and unique contribution not only to the development of the Italian language but also to Western literature and art. These diverse traits have been recorded in a wide range and large volume of literary and artistic works.

Tuscan Spaces examines verbal and visual narratives by modern and contemporary Italian authors who are native to or have great familiarity with the region, as well as by foreign writers who have travelled to or taken up residence in Tuscany. Silva Ross focuses on aspects of the literary construction of Tuscan space in works by several modern Italian authors, such as Aldo Palazzeschi, Vasco Pratolini, Elena Gianini Belotti, and Federigo Tozzi, as well as by foreign authors such as Stendhal, E.M. Forster, and Frances Mayes. She examines how these and other writers portray either a sense of belonging to or exclusion from place, society, and culture, be it in autobiographical or fictional terms. In addition to the interrogation of the local/foreign opposition, Ross explores how Tuscan space functions as an indicator of a particular writer's poetics, background, and experience. Ideas and ideals of culture, geography, history, space, travel, and narrative provide a conceptual framework for her consideration of the dualisms commonly employed in writings about Tuscany, such as country/city, nature/culture, self/other. Wide-ranging and theoretically informed, *Tuscan Spaces* offers a richly rewarding perspective on this archetypal region, its writers, and its literary representations.

SILVIA ROSS is a senior lecturer in the Department of Italian at University College Cork.

SILVIA ROSS

Tuscan Spaces

Literary Constructions of Place

UNIVERSITY OF TORONTO PRESS
Toronto Buffalo London

© University of Toronto Press 2010
Toronto Buffalo London
utorontopress.com

Reprinted in paperback 2021

ISBN 978-1-4426-3998-0 (cloth)
ISBN 978-1-4875-2626-9 (paper)

Toronto Italian Studies.

Cataloguing in Publication information available from Library and Archives Canada.

This book has been published with the help of a grant from the Canadian Federation for the Humanities and Social Sciences, through the Aid to Scholarly Publications Programme, using funds provided by the Social Sciences and Humanities Research Council of Canada.

University of Toronto Press acknowledges the financial assistance to its publishing program of the Canada Council for the Arts and the Ontario Arts Council, an agency of the Government of Ontario.

Canada Council for the Arts   Conseil des Arts du Canada

ONTARIO ARTS COUNCIL
CONSEIL DES ARTS DE L'ONTARIO
an Ontario government agency
un organisme du gouvernement de l'Ontario

Funded by the Government of Canada   Financé par le gouvernement du Canada   Canadä

for Mark, David, and Isabella

Contents

List of Illustrations ix

Acknowledgments xi

Introduction 3

1 The Country and the City: Vertigo and Legendary Psychasthenia in Tozzi's Tuscany 19

2 Palazzeschi's Spaces of Difference: The Materassi Sisters at the Window 44

3 Vasco Pratolini's Florentine Spaces of Exclusion 67

4 The Stendhal Syndrome, or The Horror of Being Foreign in Florence 90

5 'Going Native': Tuscan Houses and Italian Others in Contemporary American Travel Writing 120

6 The Tuscan Countryside: Nature and the (Non)Domestic in Elena Gianini Belotti 142

Afterword: Further Tuscan Spaces of Alterity 164

Notes 171

Works Cited 201

Index 215

Illustrations

1 Tozzi's Farm at Castagneto, outside Siena, 1995   21
2 Siena, rooftops   30
3 Workers leaving the Officine Galileo, Viale Morgagni, 1963   72
4 Ivory, *A Room with a View*, Lucy and George near the Arno River, the Torre di Arnolfo in the background   106
5 Argento, *La sindrome di Stendhal*, Anna Manni in the Uffizi Gallery   113
6 Images of Mayes's house and garden, Bramasole, Cortona, from *In Tuscany*   136

Acknowledgments

Portions of chapter 4 previously appeared as 'Forster's Florence and the Stendhal Syndrome,' in *The Poetics of Place: Florence Imagined*, edited by Irene Marchegiani Jones and Thomas Haeussler (Florence: Olschki, 2001), 125–42. An earlier version of chapter 5 appeared as 'Home and Away: Mayes, Leavitt, and Mitchell's Tuscany and the Italian "Other,"' *Studies in Travel Writing* 13.1 (2009) 43–58.

All translations into English are my own, unless otherwise indicated.

The Research Fund and the Publication Fund of the College of Arts, Celtic Studies and Social Sciences of University College Cork, as well as the National University of Ireland Publication Fund and the Aid to Scholarly Publications Programme of the Canadian Federation for the Humanities and Social Sciences, provided crucial grants which made the realization of this book possible. The Sabbatical Leave Committee of University College Cork granted me six months' leave in 2007, which allowed me to make immense progress on the research and writing of the manuscript.

Many people gave me considerable help and support, both professional and personal, throughout the writing of this book. Elena Rossi read and commented enthusiastically and constructively on most of the chapters, including the translations, and also provided practical help unstintingly: *grazie infinite*. Michael Ross patiently went through the entire manuscript, in its different versions, and supplied copious and invaluable suggestions, of which I am most appreciative. Lorraine York gave useful input, especially in the earliest phases of the project. Eduardo Saccone, mentor, colleague, and friend, read several chapters and generously provided insightful critique; he is greatly missed. Stefano Odorico cheerfully provided expert help in assembling and formatting the images included in the book. Ron Schoeffel of University of Toronto Press was unfailingly reassuring and most helpful throughout, and John St James's painstaking copy-editing is also greatly appreciated. I am indebted to Silvia Tozzi for allowing me to visit her properties outside Siena and to take photographs of her grandfather's haunts in 1995, and to Francesca Vicario for facilitating the meeting and kindly agreeing to accompany me. Elena Gianini Belotti has given liberally of her time and has provided dynamic and stimulating feedback on my research on her texts. I also gratefully acknowledge the Archivio FLOG, for giving me permission to use an image (figure 3) from their archive on the Galileo Factory, and Frances Mayes, for allowing me to include photographs (from *In Tuscany*) which she took herself (figure 6).

Friends lent a hand, gave advice and encouragement for the entire duration of the project, and good-naturedly put up with my reclusiveness during the writing and revising of the manuscript, among them Kathleen and Freddie Butler, Alessia Li Causi, Aisling O'Leary, Nuala Finnegan, Louise Sheehan, Claire O'Driscoll, Sinéad McSweeney, Gina Cogan, and Johanna Cagney. And finally, my husband and colleague, Mark Chu, provided constructive input, constant support, and affirmation, and kept the home fires burning throughout the entire process: for all this, a most heartfelt 'thank you.'

TUSCAN SPACES:
LITERARY CONSTRUCTIONS OF PLACE

Introduction

The Significance of Tuscany

Tuscany has long played an important part in the literary production of writers both Italian and non-Italian. The reasons for the region's cultural impact are numerous and derive from its distinctive geography, its singular history, and its unique contribution not only to the development of Italian language but also to Western literature and art. Throughout different epochs, Tuscany has constituted the locus of major socio-historical and economic trends: from the Middle Ages onwards it was a key mercantile hub, subsequently it was known as the epicentre of the Renaissance, and, later still, under Unification – in part because of its exceptional cultural heritage – its dialect was definitively selected as the basis for the formulation of standard Italian. In more recent times it has assumed further guises, from mass tourist destination, to upscale vacation-property opportunity for members of the elite such as Tony Blair or Sting, to manufacturing centre.

These diverse traits of the region have been recorded – and in some cases subverted – in a wide range and large volume of literary and artistic works. Even during the period of the revising of this manuscript, several more titles associated with Tuscany have appeared in print (the most significant probably being Salman Rushdie's *The Enchantress of Florence*, 2008), evidence that the region's fascination persists. This book therefore examines verbal and visual narratives by modern and contemporary Italian authors who have great familiarity with the region, as well as by those foreign writers who have travelled to or chosen a more permanent migration in Tuscany, all of whom have felt compelled – for whatever reason – to engage textually with the renowned milieu.

Beginning with a summary of some salient elements that have contributed to Tuscany's geographical and historical importance and its impact on Western culture, I will then move on to describe my own 'situatedness' with respect to the region and to the present study. Thereafter, I provide an examination of key terms that underpin my analysis, namely 'space' and 'place,' within a theoretical framework. I then discuss the specific texts that constitute the focus of my interpretation, and their interplay around the core notions of region, space, and alterity.

Geography

To classify any region can prove a problematic exercise, given the complexities of distinguishing borders[1] and of pinning down the concept of region itself.[2] Despite this difficulty in establishing territorial boundaries, the region conventionally denoted as 'Tuscany' can be viewed as encompassing certain geographical and cultural features and as having relatively specific borders. Mori describes the configuration of Tuscany when first designated a region in the late nineteenth century as 'quella porzione di territorio italiano a forma grossolanamente triangolare collocata fra l'alto Tirreno, l'Appennino centrale ed una convenzionale linea di confine con il vecchio Stato pontificio' (Mori 5–6) [that roughly triangular portion of Italian territory located between the upper Tyrrhenian, the central Apennines and the conventional border with the old papal State]. While the Central Italian region comprises geographical variety, from mountainous zones, to rolling hills, to coastal areas, its remarkably fertile terrain possesses a common agricultural tradition based on the production of typical crops (olives and grapes, among others) and cultivation techniques, as well as on a shared history of property and labour organization, namely, the system of *mezzadria*, or sharecropping.

The Tuscan landscape, perhaps to a greater degree than most, is said to epitomize the relationship between humans and their environment: the impact of agricultural practices and edificial development on the topography is clearly visible, and many would consider the aesthetic result particularly harmonious. To this end, an effort to establish and maintain a 'Tuscan' landscape endures, with regional and local governments attempting to protect their heritage through the legislation of limitations on building and industrial expansion, the success of which is debatable, given the visible presence of large factories and the resultant ecological damage in many areas; one need only think, for instance, of certain polluted zones of the Arno valley.³ Nonetheless, the emblematic panorama of the Renaissance Tuscan villa, situated on a sunny hilltop surrounded by vineyards, olive groves, and cypress trees, remains etched in the mind's eye of those who have actually gazed upon such territorial arrangements, as well as those who have never been there. The aim of this book, however, is to transcend such established visions of Tuscan environs, to question the 'myth of Tuscany,'⁴ and to encompass a variety of textual portrayals of place, ranging from the highly idealized to the abject, bearing in mind the authorial positioning, psychology, and ideology that have elicited his or her individuated rendition of locale.

History

Just as stereotypical and romanticized notions of a 'Tuscan landscape' have been instrumental in the establishment of the region's 'distinct' identity, so too has the region's role in Italian culture singled it out as a 'special case' in intellectual, literary, and artistic perceptions. That Tuscany's terrain should be seen to incarnate the human–nature relationship is perhaps not surprising, given its long, uninterrupted history of settlement, a fact attested by the archaeological evidence of the presence of the Etruscans (from roughly the eighth to the third century BC) and the Romans (from about the third century BC until the fall of the empire) in various areas throughout the region. Furthermore, Tuscany's urban development owes much to the growth of a mercantile class in the Middle Ages and the Renaissance, with a resulting affluence concentrated in specific centres which spawned architectural and artistic creations that have come to define Tuscan towns and cities as centres of note.⁵ The burgeoning trade and the institution of banking in Florence and neighbouring cities provided the economic climate and, in some cases, the patronage for major cultural figures who would make their mark on Western thought and literary and artistic production: the *tre corone* (three crowns) of Italian letters, Dante, Petrarca, and Boccaccio, thinkers such as humanists Leonardo Bruni or Coluccio Salutati, and later Machiavelli, as well as artists and architects ranging from Giotto to Brunelleschi, Botticelli, da Vinci, and Michelangelo – all were born or spent significant and formative stages in Tuscany – and these names are only a few of the host of notable figures who gravitated around the region's intellectual and artistic nuclei in these periods.

Florence thus became synonymous with the birth of the Renaissance, a status emblematized by its iconic skyline, its landmark churches, bridges, and *palazzi*.[6] The influence of ruling families – in particular the Medicis – has been the object of much scholarship, with some of their leaders, Lorenzo the Magnificent (1449–92), for instance, fostering a unique cultural atmosphere in which major thinkers (Marsilio Ficino, Pico della Mirandola, and Agnolo Poliziano, among others) were to operate.[7] At the same time, the Tuscan capital is characterized by its history of factionalism, from the Guelph-Ghibelline and Bianchi-Neri conflicts, which constitute a significant part of the backdrop to Dante's *Divina commedia*, to other notorious political upheavals, including the revolt of the Ciompi (1378), the Pazzi conspiracy (1478), and the burning at the stake of Savonarola (1498).[8]

With the works of Dante, Petrarca, and Boccaccio achieving canonical status, the Tuscan idiom heavily influenced the development of the Italian language. In particular, the recognized literary figure and later senator under the newly formed Italian state, Alessandro Manzoni, deliberately chose to employ the Tuscan vernacular in his cornerstone historical novel *I promessi sposi* (The Betrothed), transposed from its earlier Lombard version and re-published in 1840–2. This decision was partly responsible for standard Italian being modelled on the Tuscan tongue, thanks to the novel's success and to the author's own influence on language policy under Italian unification.

In recognition of its cultural and linguistic contribution, Florence became the Italian capital shortly after unification, from 1865–70. It was during and after this period that the city's configuration was radically altered in order to modernize its profile, with the demolition of central medieval neighbourhoods so as to create the spacious Piazza della Repubblica (formerly Piazza Vittorio Emanuele II) and the construction of wide avenues and the panoramic Piazzale Michelangelo. It was also during the nineteenth century that the English-speaking community became fully established in Tuscany with eminent writers such as Shelley, Trollope, Robert Browning, and Elizabeth Barrett Browning, among others, taking up residence there either temporarily or permanently.[9]

Florence continued its role as cultural hub throughout the nineteenth and twentieth centuries, with writers and artists, both Italian as well as foreign, residing there and frequenting its *caffé letterari*, the most famous of which is the *Giubbe rosse*. The resulting interactions spawned many journals. Indeed, some of the authors discussed in this study had close ties with these Tuscan literary groups in different periods; Federigo

Tozzi (with Domenico Giuliotti), for instance, in 1913 formed his own, short-lived journal *La Torre*, based in Siena, and had great familiarity with other *letterati* of these Tuscan circles. Aldo Palazzeschi, in particular through his involvement with the Futurists in the years leading up to the First World War, frequented Florentine cultural circles along with artists such as Ardengo Soffici or Carlo Carrà, as did Vasco Pratolini in the interwar period when he came into contact with other notable figures, both Tuscan and non-Tuscan, of the Italian literary scene, for example, Carlo Bo, Mario Luzi, and Elio Vittorini.[10]

During the Second World War Tuscany found itself yet again embroiled in political conflict, with Resistance fighters combating Nazi and Fascist soldiers during the German occupation on those very streets where its artistic treasures and architectural landmarks are located; such struggles have been portrayed in both fictional narrative and cinema, such as the classic Florence episode of Rossellini's *Paisà* (1946). Many areas in the countryside and in urban quarters were also devastated by the occupiers, the signs of which are still legible in certain Florentine neighbourhoods, for instance, in the reconstruction of via Por Santa Maria or Borgo San Jacopo, north and south of the Ponte Vecchio, respectively.

Post-war Tuscany did not undergo the same seismic shifts in productivity and migration that characterized the industrial centres of Milan, Turin, or Genova. Nonetheless, significant effects of the *miracolo economico*, or Economic Miracle (circa 1958–63), can be recognized in the increase in manufacturing in the Florentine peripheries as well as in other zones, and in the change in demographics and the rise in construction in these areas. Indeed, the region's wealth has been bolstered in more recent decades by the policy of industrial expansion in restricted zones and, significantly, by the onset of mass tourism. This is not to ignore the fact that Tuscany has known deprivation, and that the agricultural gains, industrial enlargement, and hospitality industry have developed at the expense of impoverished labourers and workers. At the same time, Tuscany maintains its seemingly almost antithetical activities of artisanal workmanship and industrial production.

Tuscany's complex history and its richness as a cultural environment have thus attracted countless authors, from the Middle Ages until today. The wealth of existing literature about the region presents particular challenges for writers, namely, that of formulating an original contribution to an ever-increasing bibliography. Consequently, literary criticism of 'Tuscan' texts is also on the rise. Surprisingly few scholarly studies of the region and its literary output, however, take into account the texts of more than a single nationality, and none, to my knowledge, concentrate on the spatiality of Tuscany in a comparative, analytical context.[11]

Personal Place / Subjective Space

I have attempted thus far to provide an explanation of Tuscany's import for artists and writers, basing my overview on commonly accepted notions of its socio-historical and cultural significance both for Italy but also for Western civilization more generally. Yet writers who represent the region clearly have their own personal motivations for doing so, and I, too, as critic, am drawn to it on grounds related to my own biography. My cultural provenance (I was born in North America to a Florentine mother) has undoubtedly in some ways contributed to my fascination with Tuscany, an attraction intensified by my ongoing familiarity with the place and the local idiom, having lived and studied there for extensive periods both as a child and as an adult. Furthermore, my own formation as an Italianist who studied the *questione della lingua*, as well as the medieval canon of the Tuscan *tre corone*, Tuscany's historical role in the Renaissance, and the region's more modern literary production, has fostered my ongoing interest in this locale. My concern with Tuscany as a location began earlier in my career with the analysis of literary landscapes, but has since expanded to include the multi-dimensional and fruitful notions of space and place as related to the region.

Furthermore, my awareness of questions of alterity – a core concept which subtends my study – also stems most likely from my gender as woman, but also from my own hybrid ethnic and cultural identity (Canadian/American/Italian, now residing in Ireland), which has made me feel constantly on the border between insider and outsider, cognizant of the fact that identity is very much a social and cultural construct and is, almost by definition, fluctuating and unstable. For these and other reasons, I find the interplay between Italian and anglophone writers' depictions of this same region particularly stimulating and worthy of investigation. I am convinced, moreover, that the textual analysis of the interaction between people and place constitutes a fundamental component of the study of identity. With this in mind, it is important to reflect on the theoretical underpinning of concepts fundamental to my analysis – space, place, and, to a lesser extent, landscape – as I set out to do in the next section.

Space/Place

While my enquiry centres on the textual representation of a curtailed geographical zone, it explores a deliberately loosely defined notion of 'space.' For the purposes of my analysis, space implies the environment or the surroundings in which human subjects find themselves. The types of space examined are multifarious: they can be interiors (such as the domestic sphere) or external locations, urban or rural environments, artificial or natural zones, cultivated or wild areas; at the same time, it must be recognized that such oppositions are in themselves by no means clear-cut.

Furthermore, theoretical interpretations of space versus place vary greatly.[12] For de Certeau, the difference between place and space boils down essentially to that between stasis and movement. Place (*lieu*), according to de Certeau, is

> the order (of whatever kind) in accord with which elements are distributed in relationships of coexistence. It thus excludes the possibility of two things being in the same location (*place*). The law of the 'proper' rules in the place: the elements taken into consideration are *beside* one another, each situated in its own 'proper' and distinct location, a location it defines. A place is thus an instantaneous configuration of positions. It implies an indication of stability. (117)

Space, by contrast,

> exists when one takes into consideration vectors of direction, velocities, and time variables. Thus space is composed of intersections of mobile elements. It is in a sense actuated by the ensemble of movements deployed within it. Space occurs as the effect produced by the operations that orient it, situate it, temporalize it, and make it function in a polyvalent unity of conflictual programs or contractual proximities. (117)

Thus, place is related to positionality and location, whereas space is a 'practiced place' within which people and objects operate, move (117); de Certeau's own particular interest lies in examining these terms as defined by narrative actions or stories.[13]

For W.J.T. Mitchell, the place-space dyad should expand to include a third term, 'landscape': 'One might think, then, of space, place, and landscape as a dialectical triad, a conceptual structure that may be activated from several different angles. If a place is a specific location, a space is a "practiced place," a site activated by movements, actions, narratives, and signs, and a landscape is that site encountered as image or "sight"' (Mitchell x). Landscapes, too, enter into play in the present study of literary depictions of Tuscany, but within the more general context of space and localization. In any case, the scope of landscape theory is vast and much of it concerns questions of aesthetics that diverge from the primary focus of this project.[14]

What does emerge in the diverse theoretical understandings of place and space is an increasing acknowledgment that these concepts must perforce be analysed in relation to subjectivity:

> Deliberate stress is given to the crucial role played by human beings 'out there' in the 'real world' as people perceiving, interpreting and shaping the human geography of their surroundings ... It is vital to notice the concern shown ... by humanistic geographers to *place* – to the myriad ways in which people 'relate' to the places around them where they work, rest and play – and to register that all manner of questions about people and their places have now spilled over from humanistic geography to energise human-geographical inquiry more generally.[15]

Thus, when interpreting space, it becomes necessary to ask questions such as: Who perceives? How do the actions of the subject produce space? How does the subject experience space?

The subject's perception of the external environment is thus a core issue in considering spatial dynamics. The geographer Yi-Fu Tuan elucidates the relationship between human experience and the outside world:

> Experience is a cover-all term for the various modes through which a person knows and constructs a reality. These modes range from the more direct and passive senses of smell, taste, and touch to active visual perception and the indirect mode of symbolization ... Experience is directed to the external world. Seeing and thinking clearly reach out beyond the self. (Tuan, *Space* 8–9)

What reaction, then, do these Tuscan spaces elicit in the writers examined? Obviously Tuscany, while encompassing some common geographical, botanical, and climatic features can also be quite varied. Yet, in some instances, an identical locale can generate quite diverse responses. For example, Florence's main civic square, the Piazza della Signoria, for some writers triggers a sense of delight, for others, anxiety, terror, or a complete mental breakdown, depending on the author and on the circumstances depicted. Rural locations, too, can elicit diverse reactions: the prototypical Tuscan villa for some instils a sense of respect for the natural surroundings, for others, the desire to control the land while denigrating the local residents. Moreover, while Tuscany is renowned for its beauty, authors can choose to ignore it, extol it, or revile it.

The human experiential element of a given geography is, therefore, as important as the inanimate surroundings. Bearing this in mind, another fundamental question raised in the analysis of these texts anchored in Tuscany is that of the relationship between place, identity, and alterity. For Harvey, space – of its very nature – invariably elicits the Self–Other relation:

> Space and time, once they are set, are a primary means to individuate and identify objects, people, relations, processes, and events ... Space and time appear, however, not to be of equal significance to individuation. Many individuals can occupy the same moment in most social (as opposed to personalized) accounts of time, but none of us can occupy exactly the same space at that moment of time without becoming 'the other.' If the difference of horizons and perspectives between two people is annihilated, notes Bakhtin ..., then those two people would have 'to merge into one, to become one and the same person.' The relations between 'self' and 'other' from which a certain kind of cognition of social affairs emanates is always, therefore, a spatio-temporal construction. This is a crucial issue for understanding how identities (personal and political) get formed. Changes in spatio-temporal frame affect self-other relations (by, for example, either dissolving the self-other distinction entirely or redefining who are or are not significant others in assigning value to the self). (264)

My analysis interrogates, therefore, how the specific writers in question contend with the Self-Other opposition within the spatial context of Tuscany. It examines how these authors choose to represent the Other, an Other predicated on some criterion of difference such as ethnicity, gender, or sexuality. In tandem with these issues, a related question must also be raised: How do these authors communicate a sense of being 'Othered' or alienated themselves?

Place invariably elicits these fundamental concerns regarding belonging and can provoke oppositions between native and foreigner,

Self and Other. The marginalization or even negation of an Other, for instance, can serve to reinforce one's own sense of identity: in the attempt to determine that which one is not, one endeavours to establish that which one is: 'For a person to develop a self-identity, he or she must generate *discourses of* both *difference and similarity* and must reject and embrace specific identities. The external Other should thus be considered as a range of positions within a system of difference' (Riggins 4). My study of texts set in Tuscan spaces highlights how writers portray either a sense of belonging to, or an exclusion from, place, society, and culture – be it in autobiographical or fictional terms – and how locale affects the Self-Other dichotomy.

It follows, too, that literary and cinematic constructions of space must be considered in light of their localization in either the city or the country and the opposition (or even lack thereof) between urban and rural is one which informs this monograph.[16] The texts explored here represent a range of Tuscan settings, from the agricultural to the highly developed, yet in many cases the lines between these two culturally constructed polarities are blurred, leading to insights on the urban-rural condition, and enabling the exploration of areas as diverse as Florence's industrial peripheries or the domesticated countryside outside Cortona. Furthermore, the nature/culture dualism – along with many others – is one that needs to be critiqued and undermined, as Plumwood explains:

> What is at issue here is not the distinctions between women/men, and human/nature, but their dualistic construction. The concept of the human has a masculine bias (among others) because the male/female and human/nature dualisms are intertwined, so much that neither can be fully understood in isolation from the other. The dualistic distortion of culture and the historical inferiority of women and nature in the west have been based ... on a network of assumptions involving a range of closely related dualistic contrasts, especially the dualism of reason and nature, or (in a virtually equivalent formulation), of humanity and culture on the one side and nature on the other. (Plumwood 33)

Plumwood raises our awareness that oppositions such as country/city, nature/culture, female/male, are all part and parcel of Western society's formulation of place and gender, and the feminist philosopher reminds us that such dualisms must be interrogated, along with others, such as body/mind, innocence/corruption, often associated with the country/city dyad.

Just as the country and city locations in this examination are diverse and evade narrow denotations, so, too, is genre not restricted to one particular category, such as the narrowly defined 'regional novel.'[17] The texts analysed span a range of genres, from the travelogue, to the memoir, the novel, the short story, to film. These heterogeneous works all confront the question of the individual's relationship to Tuscan space, and for each of them the issue of alterity constitutes a crucial consideration. The texts chosen are representative of particular reactions found in modern and contemporary literature, but by no means constitute an exhaustive overview of the literary depictions of Tuscany; instead, they serve to illustrate, more generally, the complex nature of spatial constructions and alterity in literature and film. The varied chapters take into account, then, both 'place' in terms of specific toponymical reference to setting and its classification (or undermining thereof) as rural or urban, and 'space' in the wider sense, meaning the subject's interaction with his or her surroundings, be they a domestic or an external environment, or both. Overall, my investigation explores the importance of space within the texts examined so as to ascertain just how space functions as an indicator of the writer's poetics and the key problematics she or he develops in the text.

Textual Spaces

The opening chapter explores an especially striking literary example of the interplay between the subject and his or her surroundings, whereby the standard dividing lines between the body and the environment are eroded. The literary production of the Tuscan Federigo Tozzi (1883–1920) portrays characters who have problematic relationships not only with the community, but also with their spatial environs. While Tozzi the author was an autochthonous resident of the Sienese area, the location produces a sense of alienation, indeed persecution, in his characters. Tuscan environments – both rural and urban – provoke extreme reactions in the Tozzian subject: she or he commonly experiences a sense of vertigo in the face of Sienese or Florentine architecture, as well as in more bucolic settings, the country-city dualism being undermined by this writer who deals regularly with both contexts. This vertigo, I posit, is symptomatic of psychasthenia, the sensation of a human's melding with the external environment, and an indicator of a troubled relationship between the subject and his or her surroundings. These distinctive yet enigmatic relations between the human and the environment in Tozzi's oeuvre testify, furthermore, to his modernity.

While in Tozzi's case the subject's spatial 'dysfunction' reflects a personalized sense of alienation that exhibits itself in psychological terms, for Aldo Palazzeschi (1885–1974) the interplay between space and difference is related primarily to questions of sexuality. The second chapter centres on the Florentine's novel *Sorelle Materassi* (The Sisters Materassi), published in 1934, and explores the writer's depiction of liminal spaces, namely, that of the window as a threshold between interior and exterior and as a symbol for the writer's own conceptualization of sexuality as fluid, of gender as a performance. Through the personae of two aging 'spinsters' and their unacknowledged attraction to their young nephew – an elusive figure who represents certain traits of the Fascist male – Palazzeschi both masks and sublimates his own homosexual desire. The writer situates this sisterly pairing of characters who trouble heteronormative sexuality within particularly symbolic surroundings; not only does the window play an important metaphorical role, but so, too, does the house itself, as well as the neighbourhood in which it is located, Santa Maria a Coverciano, an area in Florence's outskirts which defies classification as either city or country.

In-between zones feature prominently in another work set in a different Florentine periphery, the industrial and residential area of Rifredi, the setting for *La costanza della ragione* (The Constancy of Reason, 1962), a novel by the third native Tuscan examined, Vasco Pratolini (1913–91), and the subject of chapter 3. Unlike Pratolini's earlier fiction, which is located primarily in working-class neighbourhoods in the city centre, the industrialized suburb of Rifredi emblematizes concerns that dominate this text set during the *miracolo economico*. Labile, rural-urban spaces, which can be classified as 'heterotopias' in their emphasis on figures of marginalization or exclusion, feature heavily in the novel, and indicate the author's growing concern with the socio-economic situation of the time. Yet Pratolini's project has dubious outcomes; he constructs a morally ambiguous protagonist, Bruno, who endorses industrialization and rejects the Florence of the past, its monuments and landmarks – hallmarks of canonical notions of architectural beauty – but also displays prejudice towards those he perceives as Others on the basis of gender, sexuality, or ethnicity, rendering him an equivocal hero with whom readers cannot wholly empathize.

The Florentine city-centre constitutes the principal setting for an exploration in chapter 4 of the problematics of encounters with cultural or ethnic alterity as situated in place; this is manifested in a phenomenon known as the 'Stendhal Syndrome,' a psychosomatic response to the city's richness of art, architecture, and culture. When tourists visit Florence they can be overcome by this excess of art and experience physical and mental symptoms denoting a crisis or breakdown, in an extreme manifestation of cultural clash. The Stendhal Syndrome encapsulates the dangers of confronting both cultural alterity and the sublime, and spans almost two centuries. It manifests itself both in literature and in actual cases of patients treated at the hospital of Santa Maria Nuova, as the psychologist Graziella Magherini has outlined in her book *La sindrome di Stendhal* (1989). This illness hearkens back to Stendhal's own experience, which he describes in his travel narrative of 1826, *Rome, Naples et Florence*, and manifests itself, I maintain, in E.M. Forster's *A Room with a View* (1908) and in its cinematic adaptation by Merchant and Ivory (1985). Dario Argento's movie *La sindrome di Stendhal* (1996) also investigates the syndrome, and his film depicts a Florence characterized by the terrible, the horrific: reactions associated with a visual overdose of this city's culture.

Recent textual constructions of ethnic otherness within a rural environment constitute the focus of the analysis in chapter 5 of American travel writing set in a Tuscan milieu. Frances Mayes's *Under the Tuscan Sun* (1996) and *In Maremma* (2001) by David Leavitt and Mark Mitchell narrate the authors' experiences of buying and restoring houses in Tuscany. Both travelogues demonstrate the writers' penchant for stereotyping Italians while simultaneously endeavouring to assimilate to the indigenous culture. The figure of the house and domestic space are of cardinal importance in the writers' attempts to root themselves, yet their proclivity for Italian interior decoration and cuisine is not matched by a similar interest in Italian social issues such as questions of class or the country's political situation. These travel writers abide in Tuscany in a kind of cultural vacuum that capitalizes on consumer trends such as those found in gourmet magazines or in home-improvement television programs, all the while perpetuating stereotypes about Italians that do not challenge readers' preconceptions about place. The Tuscany they present is an idealized, sophisticated construction of the countryside that ignores ethical issues in favour of extolling the *dolce vita* lifestyle.

A rural locale in southern Tuscany constitutes the site of another text that narrates the experience of residing in a reconstructed house, but this time as recounted by an Italian, Elena Gianini Belotti, in her memoir *Voli* (Flights, 2001). Unlike Mayes or Leavitt and Mitchell, Belotti pays less attention to her residence and its restoration, highlighting instead her relationship to nature and animals in the surrounding area through an eco-feminist lens.[18] Her text focuses on her interactions with local wildlife, narrated with close observation and true interest in the zoological Other. Her portrayal of place demonstrates a sensitivity to local cultural and socio-economic conditions, but when confronted with situations she perceives as threatening, she does on occasion resort to stereotyping the locals. Belotti's blanket statements are, however, few and far between, and in actuality serve to shed light on her own 'otherness,' as her status of single-woman homeowner runs counter to standard practice in an area dominated by traditional family structures. Unlike Mayes and Leavitt/Mitchell, however, Belotti does not see the house as a means through which she can 'buy' herself a local identity.

Thus, many of these writers, while setting their texts in Tuscany, choose to portray locations which deviate from prevailing, touristic images of the region that for the majority of readers might be ingrained, and allow them to develop particular concerns. Palazzeschi's Florentine neighbourhood of Santa Maria a Coverciano, neither pure countryside nor wholly town, illustrates the writer's engagement with labile categorizations and difference, while Pratolini's industrialized suburb enables him to explore zones of marginalization and to highlight the climate of the Italian Economic Miracle. Other writers might depict better- (as well as lesser-) known locales, yet the ways in which these are perceived by their subjects constitute a novel depiction of a toponymically designated place. Tozzi's urban locations such as Siena and, to some extent, Florence may, in some instances, depict famous attractions (e.g., the Loggia dei Lanzi), but the manner in which they are experienced undermines preconceived notions, with the Tozzian subject frequently perceiving place as menacing and succumbing to vertigo and a collapsing of barriers between the self and the outside world. Other writers, such as Stendhal and Forster, draw on the iconography of such renowned Florentine landmarks as Piazza Santa Croce or Piazza della Signoria and the Palazzo Vecchio, but the characters' reactions of feeling overpowered by this architecture of the sublime lead to surprising outcomes, and these monuments can even connote the terrible or the terrifying, to the extent that Argento has seen fit to base an entire horror film on such psychosomatic experiences.

The Tuscan rural environs, on the other hand, have elicited less insightful portrayals of place in the American travel writers who choose to depict their resettlement within that context. Mayes's house outside Cortona and Leavitt and Mitchell's in Maremma furnish the authors with shelter but not with particularly innovative perceptions of local culture and inhabitants, despite their adept and fluid prose styles. In contrast, Gianini Belotti's property outside Trequanda provides her with the opportunity to observe and interact with the wildlife in the area, an activity that, for her, gives meaning to her residing in that specific locale.

The house, furthermore, is a fundamental spatial trope in several of the texts examined, and its construction, on the one hand, indicates the socio-economic status of its occupants, while at the same time raising a host of other questions. While for Gianini Belotti the four walls imply a means of communicating with nature and a breaking down of borders between interiors and exteriors, for Mayes and for Leavitt and Mitchell the abode is more about decor, or even conspicuous consumption, and signifies a way of attempting to acquire roots in a newly adopted community. For Palazzeschi, in contrast, the eclectic dwelling of the Materassi sisters becomes a metaphorical figure that indicates the social standing and financial position of its inhabitants, but also, via the icon of the window, denotes a kind of permeability between inside and outside, a symbol of the writer's flexible conceptualization of sexuality.

All these authors in one way or another inflect space (and specifically Tuscan space) to communicate their poetics, and for this reason a careful reading of these depictions can help shed light on a text's mechanisms, as Gelley explains:

> I would analyze an author's representation of places and objects for those modifications, let us say, those deformations of natural perception that often represent the unspoken but controlling laws of his [sic] fictional world ... It is the reader himself [sic], not empirically but as the intended goal of the fictional project, who is capable of registering and organizing such modifications of natural perception. The task of criticism, then, would be to probe into the principle of these modifications, to analyze in each work how the means of representation solicit a distinctive form of participation. (194–5)

Gelley rightly points out that each author in some way adapts a vision of place, and that it is the reader's undertaking to analyze what modifications are indeed effected by the writer. This does not necessarily imply that a standard model (be it literary or visual) of any given locale exists, but at the same time common portrayals or stereotypes both about a place and its inhabitants can emerge, especially when the location under consideration is a remarkably celebrated one, such as Tuscany, with its Medieval and Renaissance cities and its inimitable landscapes. This volume therefore aims to interpret how the writers in question textually construct and explore both place and space – above all in terms of alterity – and in doing so it assesses whether or not they make an original contribution to the depiction of this archetypal Italian region.

1 The Country and the City: Vertigo and Legendary Psychasthenia in Tozzi's Tuscany

Descriptions of place constitute an integral element of Federigo Tozzi's poetics of alienation and the subject's perception of space denotes a sense of dis-ease with the external world. For Williams, landscapes imply a division between the human and the natural: 'The very idea of landscape implies separation and observation' (120). Yet when Tozzian characters observe their surroundings, their interactions with them belie such a statement as Williams's, since their rapport with their environment is characterized precisely by a breaking down of barriers, an intermingling, between the subject and space.

While some critics have labelled his descriptive passages 'digressions' because they do not contribute directly to the advancement of plot, in reality Tozzi's delineations of place function as important interpretive markers and serve to denote key dynamics within the Sienese writer's texts. In past years, limited attention has been paid to the question of setting in Tozzi's prose, beginning with such studies as his son Glauco's 'I luoghi tozziani di Siena' (Tozzian Locations in Siena, which focuses on the actual topography around Siena where the author chose to locate much of his fiction), Cassola's 'Alla ricerca di Federigo Tozzi' (In Search of Federigo Tozzi), Schippisi's 'Il paesaggio di Tozzi' (Tozzi's Landscape), or Barzanti's 'Senso e immagine della città in Federigo Tozzi' (Sense and Image of the City in Federigo Tozzi). More recently, *Paysages: Essai sur la description de Federigo Tozzi* (Landscapes: An Essay on Federigo Tozzi's Descriptions), a comprehensive if predominantly descriptive overview of Tozzi's landscapes, has been penned by Fratnik, and the proceedings of the 2002 conference (edited by Grignani) contain a number of articles dedicated to the subject of description or place. While this latest scholarship on Tozzi's spatial configurations can be considered symptomatic of a more generalized current critical interest in questions of representation, at the same time it indicates a heightened awareness of the crucial significance of landscape depiction in this particular writer's work.

Tozzi's spatial representations of Siena, Florence, and the Tuscan countryside are complex and give rise to various interpretive possibilities. Yet the most fascinating aspect of Tozzi's textual construction of locale is that it demonstrates his protagonists' troubled rapport with reality and the problematic of subject–object relations in his oeuvre. His settings can be excessively idealized or, alternately – sometimes even simultaneously – menacing, to the extent that certain features of place seem to foreshadow textual events. This chapter will discuss the depiction of rural and urban Tuscan settings in Tozzi, and will focus on two distinct phenomena associated with spatial configurations in the writer's work: namely, the sense of vertigo elicited by place, and the frequently concomitant notion of legendary psychasthenia as it affects the Tozzian subject.

The Country and the City

Both urban and rural environments abound in Tozzi's novels, such as *Con gli occhi chiusi* (With Eyes Shut, 1919), *Tre croci* (Three Crosses, 1920), *Il podere* (The Farm, 1921), *Ricordi di un impiegato* (Memoirs of a Clerk, 1920), and *Adele* (posthumously published in 1979), in his prose passages of *Bestie* (Beasts, 1917), as well as in his short stories. The places portrayed derive largely from those where Tozzi lived, namely, the two farms his family owned outside Siena, at Pecorile and Castagneto (see figure 1). His fiction also reflects his knowledge of urban areas, as in his portrayal of Sienese streets in proximity to via de' Rossi, where the family's *trattoria* and apartment were located. It remains difficult and perhaps even futile to categorize a rigid country/city division, especially as regards their affective value, in Tozzi's works, since the two environments feature so prominently and can evoke both positive as well as negative associations; furthermore, the peculiar textual mechanisms I investigate in this chapter manifest themselves equally in both settings.

Superficially, for instance, Tozzi's rural settings might seem to serve primarily as instruments of the pathetic fallacy, apparently mirroring the characters' mood or situation,[1] or appear idealized, even

Figure 1 Tozzi's farm at Castagneto, outside Siena, 1995

bucolic; yet on closer examination the countryside often contains some menacing element, eliciting a sense of foreboding and hinting at negative outcomes. A classic example of this sort of dynamic takes place in the following passage from *Il podere*, where Remigio Selmi, the young man who on the death of his father has inherited a farm which he is incapable of managing, falls into rapture when observing his georgic surroundings shortly after an unpleasant exchange with his stepmother:

> Fuori c'era un bel sole; e si sentì subito meglio. Nel cielo, che pareva più alto del solito, le nuvole passavano silenziose. Un uccello nero svolazzava sopra la casa; senza avvicinarcisi mai. Un calabrone, con le ali di un nero luccicante e turchino, cadde nell'acqua; facendo lo stesso rumore d'una pietruzza; una delle anatre accorse nuotando e lo inghiottì; poi, scosse il becco goccioloso.
>   Egli pensò, come se sognasse: 'Sono giovane!' (341)

[Outside the sun was shining; and immediately he felt better. The clouds passed by silently in the sky, which seemed higher than usual. A black bird was flying around above the house; without ever getting close to it. A hornet, with shiny, blue-black wings, fell into the water; making the same noise as a pebble; one of the ducks swam over and swallowed it; then, shook its dripping beak.

As if in a dream, he thought: 'I am young!']

Remigio stares at his surroundings, his reverie undisturbed, despite the drama played out between the duck and the hornet that takes place before his (unseeing) eyes. Notwithstanding the situation of increasing debt and the farm workers' resentment towards him, Remigio continues to resort to escapism, his dream-like states reflecting his incapacity to perceive reality. Rossi and Saccone point out that the scene depicted above can be read as having a premonitory function (Rossi 29–32 and Saccone, *Conclusioni* 85–6, both cited by Fratnik 10), the *analogon* of the hornet essentially prefiguring the death of the protagonist of *Il podere*.

Fratnik, in making her case for the supposed uselessness of attempting to ascribe meaning to Tozzian landscapes, cites this specific passage and contrasts Luperini's interpretation of it with Saccone's, illustrating how they are diametrically opposed. Therefore, she reasons, semiotic analyses of the writer's landscapes are ineffectual, since just about any meaning can be attributed to Tozzian spatial configurations; their significance, she claims, lies elsewhere, and she proceeds to conduct a survey of the various modes of description found in Tozzi's texts.[2] Yet her conclusion is per force flawed, since the assignation of meaning to any textual element (be it part of a description or otherwise) is a core concept of interpretation, and the debatable nature of, for example, a particular line from Dante's *Commedia*, is precisely what constitutes fruitful scholarly exchange. The same holds, too, for Tozzi's multifaceted, indeed puzzling, spatial depictions, and in many ways they epitomize the writer's interest in representing the unexplained, for what fascinates him, he declares in 'Come leggo io' [The Way I Read], an essay that is key in interpreting his poetics, is 'un qualsiasi misterioso atto nostro' (1325) [any random mysterious act of ours]. His spatial delineations, therefore, contribute to the mysteriousness, and indeed the modernity, of his prose, and constitute fertile interpretive terrain.

While Remigio continually seeks to idealize the rural landscape around him, he is an inept landowner, unskilled in agricultural techniques and unable to exert authority on the farm labourers or *mezzadri* in the efficient and advantageous running of the farm.[3] His reaction (or lack thereof) is clearly a response to his recently deceased father's excessive exertion of power, and, as if to underscore his rejection of paternal control, he takes solace in the comforting, feminized forms of the land, in a kind of return to the womb:[4]

> Andò a una specie di nascondiglio, che s'era trovato su la greppa della Tressa: come dentro un letto di erba; dove con il corpo aveva fatto ormai una buca.
> Sopra l'acqua limpida, un velo di sudicio si spezzava; trascinato via dalla corrente: un velo biancastro, che bucavano e tagliavano certi insetti galleggiando con la punta delle zampe alte. In mezzo a un prato, dall'altra parte della Tressa, c'era steso in terra il tronco di un melo, nero e marcio; che però aveva messo alcune foglie stente e di un verde patito. (389–90)
>
> [He went to a sort of hiding place, which he had found for himself on the bank of the Tressa: like a kind of grassy bed, which by now he had hollowed out with his body.
> On the clear water, a film of dirt was breaking up; dragged away by the current: a kind of whitish veil, punctured and cut by the tips of the long legs of some insects as they floated along. In the middle of a field, on the other side of the Tressa, the trunk of an apple tree was lying on the ground, black and rotten, which had however managed to sprout a few weak leaves of a sickly green colour.]

Clearly Remigio's retreat to the landscape constitutes an effort to reconnect not only with the maternal, but also with nature and his surroundings, a common tendency in Tozzi's characters. Yet while Remigio's withdrawal to the 'uterine' terrain should presumably provide him some reassurance, in reality several elements of the scene – the dirty scum on the water, the insects floating on the stream, the blackened tree trunk – can all be construed as ominous, as critics have noted. In fact, Remigio's rest is interrupted by Ilda, who announces the arrival of a letter that turns out to be from his lawyer.

Thus Remigio holds an idealized view of the land, but in actuality his well-being is directly linked to the *podere* in terms of its practical aspects, namely, its fertility (again, a concept correlated to the maternal topographical forms). Remigio's livelihood, and that of the labourers, depends precisely on the material success of the farm, on thriving livestock and the positive outcome of crops. The *podere* represents capital, and all those around Remigio wish to get their hands on it, from his father's lover Giulia, to his stepmother Luigia, to his lawyer's clerk. Remigio's ineptitude at managing the property compromises his own finances while causing resentment in the farmhands and others who judge him undeserving of such an inheritance. At the same time, the omnipresence of malevolence in the characters depicted in the novel seems disproportionate, rendering it unclear as to why the protagonist should merit such persecution, and reiterating the Tozzian hero's sense of separation from society.

Not only rural environments but cities, too, conjure up feelings of persecution and alienation for the Tozzian subject. Tozzi's explorations of alterity derive primarily from his characters' own sense of difference and estrangement from the world around them, as typified by the author's depiction of *inetti*, or inept, maladjusted characters. These perceptions are superimposed on to people, nature, and architecture, whereby the subject's own sense of difference and marginalization can be read in his or her surroundings. Architecture frequently connotes sensations of oppression, as witnessed, for example, in Siena's conglomerations of houses, one piled up on top of the other to the extent that they seem on the verge of toppling. The *topos* of the hero's exclusion in the city is a trait common to much literature of the late nineteenth and early twentieth century, as Burton Pike observes:

> Weak heroes and artists are intensely involved with cities. Their creators use the city thematically to represent the isolation or alienation of the individual within the culture. Joyce, Kafka, and Musil, for instance, present isolated individuals moving within cities which for most of the other characters are communities. The protagonists are excluded from these communities and feel their exclusion, although at the same time they may reject the communities as inferior or ignorant. (101)

This dynamic does indeed seem applicable to the case of Tozzi's *inetti*, who yearn for acceptance in an openly hostile atmosphere. Tozzi the writer's own ambivalence towards his native city is easily traced in his letters to his fiancée (later wife) Emma Palagi, in *Novale* (1925; new edition published in 1984), and is repeatedly noted by his biographer, Paolo Cesarini. Pike's mention of Kafka, too, is not irrelevant, since critics have posited parallels between his thematics and those found in Tozzi (see, for example, Debenedetti 248–55).

This alienation of the individual in society, then, would seem a typically modernist response to an urban setting. Castellana, too, has noted this tendency in Tozzi, saying that 'il cronotopo della città è ... sempre caratterizzato negativamente nella narrativa di Tozzi: è nella città, non a caso quasi sempre descritta *in assenza* della figura umana, che si forma, traumaticamente, l'esperienza del Moderno' (Castellana 67–8) [the chronotope of the city is ... always characterized negatively in Tozzi's fiction: it is in the city, almost always described not un-coincidentally in the absence of human figures, that the experience of the Modern is formed, traumatically]. According to Castellana, people do not feature prominently in many of Tozzi's cityscapes; in reality, however, they do appear recurrently and denote the individual's separation from the community. In fact, Tozzi's cities are replete with disturbing human images, people whom Castellana sees as having undergone a 'deumanizzazione' (68). Yet rather than being 'dehumanized,' they – in their intimidating difference – more likely function, like so many other figures (human and non-) in Tozzi's works, as markers of the Tozzian subject's own disjunction from the external world.

A scene that typifies this dynamic takes place in Florence's Piazza della Signoria, where, in *Ricordi di un impiegato*, the young Leopoldo Gradi recalls his reaction to the Loggia dei Lanzi or, more precisely, to the people found within this repository of celebrated Renaissance sculpture:

Quanti occhi e quanti sguardi io rivedo ancora, che fecero tremare e sgomentare la mia anima!
C'era, poi, un uomo con i piedi deformi e ripiegati in dentro che andava a sedersi, tutto il giorno, sotto le Logge dei Lanzi. Appoggiava le grucce al muro e stava lì a chiacchierare con certi uomini ... Me ne ricordo tre. Un uomo, un poco gobbo e la barba nera; un altro con i baffi bianchi e le braccia tatuate; un altro, bassetto, con i baffi neri e il vestito doventato verde, sempre lo stesso.
Quello con le grucce, che non poteva lavorare, mi guardava sempre in un modo che io avevo preso ad odiarlo. Egli guardava le mie gambe come per volermele stroncare.
Quando il sole non era più da quella parte, andavano a sedersi su le scale del Palazzo Vecchio. C'era anche un giovinotto, scemo, che passava con il corbello pieno di trucioli su le spalle. Era magro e il mento aguzzo: gli occhi di un verde nero. Mi dava sempre noia, e una volta mi prese per un braccio. (420–1)

[I can still see so many eyes, so many gazes that made my soul tremble, striking fear in it!

Then there was a man with deformed feet turned inward who sat every day under the Loggia dei Lanzi. He would lean his crutches against the wall and would hang around there chatting with certain men ... I remember three of them. One man, a bit hunched and with a black beard; another with a white moustache and tattooed arms; and another, rather short, with a black moustache and a suit which had turned green, always the same.

The one with crutches who couldn't work always looked at me in such a way that I had come to hate him. He looked at my legs as if he wanted to tear them off.

When the sun was no longer on that side, they would sit on the steps of the Palazzo Vecchio. There was also a stupid young man who would pass by with a basket full of wood shavings on his shoulders. He was thin and had a pointed chin: his eyes were a blackish green. He always annoyed me, and once he grabbed me by the arm.]

In a manner typical of Tozzi's perennially diffident protagonists, Leopoldo's eyes focus on beings marked by physical difference or some kind of deformity, perceiving them as malevolent. Leopoldo's viewpoint is anything but a 'tourist gaze' (Urry, *Tourist Gaze*) and contrasts, as will be seen in chapter 4, with that of Forster's heroine, Lucy Honeychurch, as she wanders through the same square in *A Room with a View*. Rather than viewing the landmark sights and studying famous monuments such as the Palazzo Vecchio and the statues housed in the Loggia dei Lanzi, Leopoldo – a native Florentine – homes in on the human figures that populate the scene.[5] At the same time, parallels can be drawn with Forster's heroine, since as she enters the square she is feeling ill at ease with the Florentine milieu, overwhelmed, and soon after witnesses a gruesome murder which causes her to faint. In Lucy's case these sensations and events are symptomatic of an encounter with cultural difference; for Tozzi, by contrast, the alterity which is emphasized is that of the subject himself, an attitude transposed on to those around him. Indeed, a case can be made for people being as integral a part of landscape as buildings and vegetation, as the Tozzian protagonist's eyes are frequently drawn to the human inhabitants of space, considering his fellow citizens sources of ill will, corporeal representations of his own persecution.

Vertigo

Tozzi's heroes' rapport not only with people but also with the external world is clearly fraught. These problematic subject–object relations can be interpreted as deriving from a situation of mental instability resulting primarily from difficult family dynamics, in particular the father-son dyad. One of the key indicators of the subject's troubled interaction with the outside world, not to mention one of the more intriguing aspects of spatial relationships in Tozzi, is the sensation of vertigo that recurs time and again in virtually all of the author's works. In *Con gli occhi chiusi*, for example, Pietro is seriously shaken when, on seeing Ghìsola's rounded belly and realizing she is pregnant, he is confronted with her infidelity. The reader then learns that he has collapsed, as the novel concludes with the following lines: 'Quando si riebbe dalla vertigine violenta che l'aveva abbattuto ai piedi di Ghìsola, egli non l'amava più' (158) [When he came to from the violent vertigo that had thrown him down at Ghìsola's feet, he didn't love her anymore]. Similarly, when Leopoldo, in *Ricordi di un impiegato*, sees his fiancée Attilia's lifeless body, he experiences comparable sensations: 'Mi sento girare la testa ... Non piango più, ma quando mi pare che dentro gli occhi, simili a una colla intorbidita, sia restato lo stesso sguardo di una volta, mi si piegano le gambe e vengo meno' (446) [My head is spinning ... I've stopped crying, but when I think that her same look from before is still present in her eyes, which are like cloudy glue, my legs give way and I faint]. In these two instances it is quite evident that the protagonists' dizziness is sparked by a dramatic event, a watershed moment, a catalyst of crisis.

Other cases of vertigo, of which there are many, seem to be generated more directly by the impact of surroundings. The sensations of spinning, dizziness, or of falling (often into an abyss) occur regularly in many of Tozzi's texts. One of the prose passages of *Bestie*, for example, contains a description of Siena that follows the narrator's statement about having had the fixation, at the age of nineteen, that he would be dead within a few months. He explains his relationship to his surroundings in the context of these morbid thoughts: 'mi sentivo doventare amico di tutte le cose e mi preparavo a salutarle qualche sera, quando la luce del tramonto si stendeva sopra i tetti di quella parte della città che guardavo' (590) [I felt as though I was befriending all things and I was preparing to say goodbye to them some evening, when the light from the sunset spread out over the roofs of that part of the city that I was looking at]. The narrator then describes the sensation of falling that accompanies the view from his window: 'Ma i tetti erano là, cominciando dal mio davanzale, come un pendio che volesse precipitare la mia anima nell'oscurità silenziosa e diaccia della campagna' (590) [But the roofs were there, starting from my windowsill, like a slope that wanted to hurl my soul down into the silent, frozen darkness of the countryside]. Clearly, in this instance, the landscape symbolizes the narrator's own anguish.

Another Sienese panorama in *Bestie* elicits a similar response:

> Una strada scende: anche un'altra scende e le viene incontro: si fermano insieme. Dalla prima, a metà, se ne parte un'altra che scende per un altro verso e ne trova subito un'altra, più bassa, che fa lo stesso ... Altre strade le tagliano e scendono. Le case hanno paura a stare ritte tra questi precipizii e si toccano con i tetti pendenti. Ma anche i tetti, a pendere così, non potrebbero cadere tutti giù? ... E perché quel cadere perpetuo dei tetti insieme con le strade?
>
> Non si ha, al contrario, il senso che le strade salgano: si sente soltanto la discesa fatta in fretta, con ansia: e, dal punto più basso, anche il meriggio è così lontano che resta soltanto per gli altri rioni di Siena.
>
> Cominciano le strida dei porci scannati: ognuno basta ad empire di sangue due secchi. (611–12)

> [One road descends: another descends, too, and meets it: they stop together. From the first, halfway down, another begins which descends in a different direction and immediately finds another one, lower down, which does the same ... Other roads cut across them and descend. The houses are afraid to stand up straight amidst these precipices and touch each other with their sloping roofs. But the other roofs, that slope so much, couldn't they all fall down too? ... And why are the roofs perpetually falling, along with the roads?
>
> You don't have the sensation, on the other hand, that the roads are rising: all you can feel is their hasty, anxious descent: and, from the lowest point, even the midday sun is so far away that it stays only in the other Sienese neighbourhoods.
>
> The shrieks of the slaughtered pigs start up: each one bleeds enough to fill two buckets.]

In this cityscape the configuration of roads and buildings sparks off the impression that the geography could collapse. Another trait common to Tozzi's delineations is the personification of the inanimate, in this case, of architecture: the houses are characterized as being afraid of falling.[6] The entire scene is then punctuated by the closing lines, with the macabre imagery of the sound of butchered pigs screaming and the vision of their blood. The troubling image of an animal concluding the passage is a recurrent textual mechanism in *Bestie*, and while the emblematic function of the beasts may be opaque,[7] the ominous tone evoked by them is undeniable.

The above topographical sketch is quite typical of Tozzi's representations of Siena as provoking vertigo, a recurrent topos in his oeuvre. The implications of this kind of depiction are twofold. On the one hand, the Tozzian subject clearly relates to the outside world in such a way that his/her surroundings elicit sensations of unsteadiness that denote a psychological malaise. On the other, Siena's own architectural geography – a legacy of its medieval past – with its crooked buildings, narrow, curved streets, and steep hills, can be considered a setting that induces this sort of feeling to begin with, as many who have been there, myself included, might concur (see figure 2).

Nonetheless, it is not only within urban environments that the protagonists experience dizziness or a fear of falling; these symptoms can also display themselves in rural locales, where they might perhaps not seem so justified, given their configuration. Why is it, then, that Tozzi's characters undergo the sensation of vertigo so frequently? The word 'vertigine' stems from the Latin *vertigo* (m), derived from the verb *vertĕre*, meaning 'to turn.' We can therefore interpret Tozzi's protagonists as falling prey to this sensation when they feel the need to turn away – literally or symbolically – from whatever situation anguishes them. But the issue is still more complex. Indeed, there exist differing attempts to explicate its recurrence in Tozzi. Giorgio Melloni, in his article 'La scrittura come "Vertigine della dissoluzione"' (Writing as the 'Vertigo of Dissolution'), considers vertigo an existential condition for Tozzi's characters as well as for the author himself. Melloni links vertigo to a sense of verticality in Tozzi's oeuvre, in that it represents upwards and downwards movement, as well as the double bind of attraction-repulsion, a common Tozzian condition. While Melloni furnishes numerous examples of vertigo in Tozzi's texts and posits various intertextual influences, discussing the implications of the phenomenon in terms of Tozzi's own creative processes, the spatial aspect does not actually constitute the focus of his investigation.

Melosi, in her analysis of Tozzi's philosophical and psychological sources, also touches on the theme of vertigo, attributing a sexual connotation to its manifestation in his writings: 'Particolarmente indagato [da Tozzi] è proprio il motivo della vertigine che ricorre con frequenza nella narrativa tozziana ... Nella definizione, così come resa dagli appunti, la vertigine di solito si accompagna a stati d'animo alterati da

Figure 2 Siena, rooftops

una sensualità oltremodo eccitata, che produce appunto le singolari sensazioni di "deplacement del corpo riguardo agli oggetti intorno" e di "perdita d'equilibrio"' (161–2) [The topic of vertigo is one that is particularly well researched [by Tozzi], a motif that recurs frequently in Tozzi's fiction ... In the definition, given in his notes, vertigo usually accompanies states of mind that are altered by a sensuality that is overly excited, which produces precisely the singular sensations of 'displacement of the body with respect to the objects around it' and of a 'loss of equilibrium'].

This erotic aspect of a psychosomatic phenomenon should not be surprising; Stendhal, after all, experiences sensual delight in viewing the art and architecture of Santa Croce just before his collapse narrated in *Rome, Naples et Florence*. Lucy Honeychurch, too, is in the midst of a sexual awakening during her visit to Florence when she faints in the Piazza della Signoria. Argento's heroine, Anna Manni, is clearly sexualized for the male gaze in the film *La sindrome di Stendhal* when she succumbs to the syndrome. These examples drawn from Stendhal, Forster, and Argento (and analysed in greater detail in chapter 4) imply an encounter with the sublime and, ultimately, with (cultural or sexual) Otherness. Yet for Tozzi, the case is somewhat different. Tozzi's vertigo seems less connected to the sublime[8] and indicates an even more deeply conflictual relationship between Self and Other, between the subject and the object. Kirby, in *Indifferent Boundaries: Spatial Concepts of Human Subjectivity*, asks if vertigo could not signal a disruption between the subject and his/her surroundings: 'What if ... this dizziness comes from being stuck in a situation that is at odds, sometimes violently, with the subject? Could vertigo – even simple disorientation – be called the product of a certain antithesis between the subject, and her internal spaces, and the external, material and social, spaces that she occupies?' (98–9).[9] For Tozzi, vertigo reveals how characters continually attempt but repeatedly fail to establish a connection with the Other, be it human or inanimate, and the manner in which this manifests itself is particularly striking.

Legendary Psychasthenia

Ricordi di un impiegato provides several examples of vertigo as it affects Leopoldo Gradi, but what is notable about these episodes is how this dizziness can, in certain instances, appear in tandem with his compulsion to bond with the space around him:

Il cipresso dell'orto, a mezzogiorno, pare più leggero della sua ombra; la lucentezza abbarbaglia; e dovento pazzo fino al punto di chiedermi se anche le mie mani non sembrino verniciate di rosso, quasi come il cancello del campo ...

Che m'importa se i germogli sono già più grossi? Che m'importa se questi campi sono dolci, se la mia anima non è ancora più dolce di loro?

Dianzi, il meriggio m'aveva tutto chiuso entro i campi e gli alberi: io non avrei potuto escire.

E in quella luce pareva che non ci fosse più niente; all'infuori della mia anima ...

Per la mia anima non ci sono che bare e agonie, che passano l'una dopo l'altra; con qualche ghirlanda comprata per farle abbracciare il feretro; povera ghirlanda che ha paura di scivolare ai sobbalzi delle ruote.

E, s'apro la finestra, mi sento afferrare il cuore, e portare giù a capofitto nella strada. (423)

[The cypress in the garden, at midday, seems lighter than its shadow; the brightness is dazzling; and I become so crazy that I wonder if even my hands seem painted red, almost like the gate to the field ...

What do I care if the buds have already grown larger? What do I care if these fields are sweet, and if my soul is no sweeter than them?

Earlier, the midday sun had enclosed me within the fields and the trees: I couldn't have gotten out.

And in that light it seemed that there was nothing left, except for my soul ...

My soul has nothing but coffins and agony, which pass by, one after the next; with the odd wreath bought to embrace the bier; the poor wreath is afraid of sliding off with the wheels' bouncing.

And, if I open a window, I feel as though my heart is being grabbed, and I am being thrown headfirst into the street.]

This passage illustrates a number of distinctive features of the character-setting relationship in Tozzi. Leopoldo experiences a kind of osmosis with his surroundings: he imagines his hands coloured red, like the gate; he feels hemmed in by the meadows and trees. This desire to connect with the outside world is clearly linked to his own anguish, as he describes his soul's fixation on death. The portrayal of the anthropomorphized wreath as being afraid of sliding off the coffin elides into his own fears of falling headfirst out his window, in yet another instance of vertigo. Significant, too, is Leopoldo's own awareness of his mental instability ('dovento pazzo'), since clearly the subject's melding into background connotes a psychological disturbance.

This permeability of the boundaries between the body and the environment arises not infrequently in Tozzi's texts. Another example from *Ricordi di un impiegato* demonstrates subject–object interplay; in this instance, Leopoldo perceives an interconnection between his soul (the 'anima' constituting a recurrent theme in Tozzi) and the weather: 'Oggi piove. Baleni che sembrano umidi; e la pioggia chiara chiara sotto le nuvole grigie. Se piovesse anche dentro la mia anima! Sentirei, dopo, quella freschezza che resta nell'oliveta. Le foglie dei pioppi tremolano come in estate il canto delle cicale. Per i solchi lunghi cantano non so quali uccelli, e i miei pensieri sono umidi' (*Ricordi* 426) [Today it's raining. Lightning flashes which seem humid; and the pale rain beneath the grey clouds. If only it would rain within my soul! Afterwards, I'd feel that freshness that remains in the olive grove. The poplar leaves tremble like the cicadas' song in summer. In the long furrows birds – I don't know what kind – are singing, and my thoughts are humid]. Not only is Leopoldo's soul linked to the rain, but his thoughts, in a synesthetic trope, are wet as well.

In yet another manifestation of the subject's affinity for his surroundings, Leopoldo's soul is compared to the flowing water, and his body's movements are synchronized with those of the poplar trees:

> Alla fine, sono tornato tra i pioppi dell'Arno; perché sento che la mia anima si fa più leggiera; imitando forse l'acqua che corre e pare immobile, tanto è più limpida e silenziosa. Tremo anche io con i pioppi; e, se mi fermo, credo che la stesa dell'erba nata tra i gambàni mi si raduni intorno; perché mi sembra di fare amicizia anche con l'aria.
>
> Non sono diventato erba anch'io, per farmi falciare insieme con tutta quella del campo? (*Ricordi* 432–3)

> [In the end, I've come back to the poplar trees on the Arno; because I feel that my soul is becoming lighter; perhaps in imitation of the water which is running but looks immobile as it is so clear and silent. I tremble, too, with the poplars; and, if I stop, I think that the expanse of grass born amidst the tree trunks is gathering around me; because I feel as though I am becoming friends with the air. Haven't I turned into grass, too, so as to be cut, along with all the grass in the field?]

Leopoldo, therefore, relates to his environs to such an extent that he believes he has become grass and that he could be cut just like the grass growing in the meadow (a familiar biblical metaphor for mortality). The autobiographical narrator in *Bestie* also expresses a similar sentiment with regard to the green fields: 'Mi ricorderò sempre dei bei prati verdi che cominciavano dalla mia anima e da' miei piedi, e finivano quasi all'orizzonte' (*Bestie* 578–9) [I will always remember the beautiful green fields which began from my soul and from my feet, and ended almost at the horizon].

These last three examples might seem to point to an idealized empathy between the human and the floral in Tozzi, yet this interplay is actually indicative of a psychological disruption. The term adopted by Caillois for the process whereby a human endeavours to assimilate with nature is 'legendary psychasthenia.' In his 'Mimicry and Legendary Psychasthenia' (originally published in French in *Minotaure*, 1935), Caillois traces examples of faunal to floral mimesis and draws the conclusion that, contrary to widespread belief, animals' assimilation to the vegetable and mineral world around them does not constitute a viable defence mechanism,[10] but rather is a 'dangerous luxury' (25), and a result of an 'overwhelming tendency to imitate, combined with a belief in the efficacy of this imitation, a tendency still quite strong in 'civilized' man' (27). Caillois continues: 'the end would appear to be *assimilation to the surroundings* ... It is thus a real *temptation by space*' (27–8). In a startling swoop, Caillois thus shifts from his discussion of fauna to that of people, and he proceeds to delineate how mimicry affects the human subject. He posits that imitation is essentially a 'disturbance in the perception of space' (28) and that this affects personality:

> The feeling of personality, considered as the organism's feeling of distinction from its surroundings, of the connection between consciousness and a particular point in space, cannot fail under these conditions to be seriously undermined; one then enters into the psychology of psychasthenia, and more specifically of *legendary psychasthenia*, if we agree to use this name for the disturbance in the above relations between personality and space. (28)

Caillois proceeds to liken the characteristics of psychasthenia to schizophrenia (30): little wonder, then, that Tozzi's protagonists' manifestations of psychasthenia derive from a precarious psychological state.

Furthermore, vertigo in itself is linked to a sense of instability which problematizes the distinction between the human and the environmental. Kirby traces a direct connection between vertigo and the dissolution of boundaries between the internal and the external:

> 'Vertigo,' then, represents the experience of subjects out of step with the social order and the reality it sets up ... In a hostile environment, the self feels out of place, which leads to a dissociation of self from that place, and a sense of the wrongness of the self itself, in the first place ... 'Dissociation,' I am compelled to note, refers not only to a detachment of subject from the world, but also to the deterioration of the internal ordering of the world ... The internal–external relation breaks down, resulting in a degeneration of interior organization, and finally – one could imagine, in advanced stages – in a confusion of the external order too. Things begin to circulate, and no longer know their places. Foundations and frameworks crumble and things loop and circle and shift and spin: the inside flies to pieces and explodes outward, the outside melts and fragments, and elements from both sides drift freely across an indifferent boundary ... 'Vertigo' ... seems to refer to three things: a rift between subject and reality, the mobilization of the internal processes of the subject, and a new fluidity of the external realm. (101–2)

For Kirby, vertigo, as both a physical and metaphorical experience, resonates with implications for relations between the subject and the external world. Kirby then discusses the relevance of vertigo to postmodern theorists and in particular to Caillois's concept of psychasthenia as examined by Grosz. In fact, the one crucial aspect of psychasthenia that Caillois, Grosz, and Kirby underline is its indication of instability of the subject vis-à-vis external reality.

Grosz, in her *Space, Time, and Perversion*, elaborates on Caillois's notions of mimesis and legendary psychasthenia: 'Mimesis is particularly significant in outlining the ways in which the relations between an organism and its environment are blurred and confused – the way in which its environment is not clearly distinct from the organism but is an active component of its identity' (88). She then connects the concept of psychasthenia to the construction of identity and subjectivity:

> Caillois regards psychasthenia as a response to the lure posed by space for the subject's identity. For the subject to take up a position as a subject, he must be able to situate himself as a being located in the space occupied by his

body. This anchoring of subjectivity in *its* body is the condition of coherent identity, and, moreover, the condition under which the subject has a perspective on the world, becomes the point from which the vision emanates. (89)

Grosz proceeds to outline what occurs when subjectivity is not rooted fully in the body; the consequence being, namely, a state of psychosis:

In certain cases of psychosis, this meshing of self and body, this unification of the subject fails to occur. The psychotic is unable to locate himself where he should be; he may look at himself from outside himself, as another might ... He is captivated and replaced by space, blurred with the position of others ... Psychosis is the human analogue of mimicry in the insect world ...: both represent what Caillois describes as the 'depersonalization by assimilation to space' ... The representation of space is thus a correlate of one's ability to locate oneself as the point of origin or reference of space: the space represented is a complement of the kind of subject who occupies it. (89–90)

Following in Caillois's footsteps, Grosz maintains that the subject's relationship to space is crucial in identity formation; when the relationship between the body and space is unclear, when the usual points of reference are confused, psychosis results. We can therefore posit that in Tozzi's works the obfuscation of borders between the body and the outside world – characteristic of psychasthenia and indicative of psychosis – can be linked to his characters' own precarious psychological equilibrium, symptomatic of insanity in certain instances.

This last affirmation is not stretching a point: it is well known that Tozzi the writer had an avid interest in exploring mental disorders in his texts, a concern most likely linked to his own experience of mental illness.[11] While some critics choose to underplay or dismiss altogether Tozzi's period spent in seclusion, subsequent to an ocular ailment – the ramifications of which hold significance as a Tozzian topos, as is obvious from the mere title of *Con gli occhi chiusi* – Gioanola in particular views Tozzi's self-imposed isolation as symptomatic of psychological disturbance.[12] Moreover, Gioanola refers to Tozzi's characters exhibiting schizophrenic tendencies, in particular in their relationship to reality, that is, to their physical surroundings:

Siamo al tema diffusissimo in Tozzi della perdita dei confini tra l'io e la realtà, tra interno ed esterno, tra personaggio e paesaggio, nell'ambiguità dei toni e motivi, contesi tra abbandono estatico e angoscia. È ciò che Paul

Federn, che ha particolarmente approfondito il problema delle condizioni dell'io nella situazione di follia, ha chiamato 'stato dell'Ego-cosmico', sulla base del concetto di 'confini dell'io' secondo il quale si registra un'estrema labilità del senso della distinzione tra sé e il mondo esterno, fino alla confusione inestricabile di soggetto e oggetto. (136–7)

[Here we find the theme, widespread in Tozzi, of the loss of borders between the self and reality, between the internal and the external, between character and landscape, in the ambiguity of tones and motifs, which are divided between ecstatic abandon and anguish. This is what Paul Federn, who has given an especially thorough investigation of the problem of the condition of the self in situations of madness, has called 'the state of the cosmic-Ego,' on the basis of the concept of the 'borders of the I' according to which an extreme lability of the sense of the distinction between the self and the external world is noted, to the point of inextricable confusion between the subject and the object.]

Gioanola, too, notes the psychological precariousness of the lack of distinction between the subject and his/her surroundings, citing Federn's work in this area.

Caillois's theories on legendary psychasthenia derive not only from zoological and botanical studies, but also from psychology, in particular the work of Pierre Janet.[13] Obviously, Caillois's article emerged after Tozzi's death – some fifteen years later – but nonetheless the term psychasthenia holds significance for the Tuscan writer. We know that Tozzi had familiarity with Janet's work and, in his unfinished novel *Adele*, the narrator refers to Fabio's inertia in the following terms: 'Tale indolenza dolorosa è un fenomeno di psicastenia' (562) [Such painful indolence is a phenomenon of psychasthenia]. Critics have ascertained that Tozzi consulted and even owned writings by Janet and avidly studied pre-Freudian psychology (not only the work of Janet, but also that of William James, among others).[14] Caillois's definition and employment of the term are somewhat different from Janet's, but nonetheless the phenomenon resonates within Tozzi's fiction. In recent times, the term 'psychasthenia' has generated considerable interest in critical theory. Olalquiaga, for instance, associates the psychological state with the post-modern city,[15] and Soja also includes the concept (citing Olalquiaga) in his encyclopedic text *Postmetropolis*. Yet the term originates with psychologists familiar to Tozzi, and its application to a modernist writer thus to me seems warranted and, moreover, highly pertinent.

The psychological imbalance which plagues most of Tozzi's characters can in part be attributed to a negative father-son rapport, as mentioned earlier. Sons, in Tozzi, constantly seek to evade a domineering father, one who is not averse to implementing his will through physical force when a son disobeys. This clash between the abusive father and the disobedient son constitutes the essence of *Con gli occhi chiusi* and underlies some of Tozzi's short stories and other texts. Tozzi's own biographical case illustrates a similar kind of conflict, where after a row with his own father, he seeks refuge in a monastery. The imagery used in the following passage, quoted from a letter dated 15 September 1907 in which Tozzi revisits his past, again denotes a psychasthenic tendency:

> Una volta questionai con il padre, e andai la sera a bussare all'Osservanza. Più che bisogno del mangiare o del dormire, mi piaceva il significato che aveva per me un convento ... Mi davano una tenerezza infinita i cipressi e le valli. Io scorgevo da per tutto un significato ...
> Ero giunto a sopprimere qualsiasi contatto morale. Gli uomini erano sensazioni. Gli ultimi giorni che stetti a Siena, ero riuscito, pensando, a trasformare tutto un paesaggio d'intorno. Lo sentivo dentro di me ...
> Gli uomini mi sembravano affini alle bestie.... Io amavo le cose e, principalmente, le piante. Le trovavo uguali a me. E ho desiderato spesso di divenire uno stocco di granturco...
> (Anche di ciò, ora non ho maggiore chiarezza). (*Novale* 158)

> [One time I argued with my father, and that evening I went and knocked on the door of the Osservanza. What I liked more than the need to eat or sleep, was the meaning a monastery held for me ... The cypresses and the valleys gave me an infinite tenderness. I found meaning everywhere ...
> I had gone so far as to suppress any moral contact. People were sensations. The last days I stayed in Siena, I had managed, with my thoughts, to transform an entire landscape around me. I felt it inside me ...
> People seemed to me to be similar to beasts ... I loved things and, above all, plants. I felt they were the same as me. And often I desired to turn into a stalk of corn ...
> (Even now, I have no greater clarity about this).]

Tozzi narrates to Emma how he senses the landscape within himself, transforming it through his thoughts. His osmosis with the non-human world brings him to declare that he wishes he could become a stalk of corn. The writer's relating more easily to plants and things than to people clearly signals problematic subject–object interactions. Also significant is Tozzi's affirmation that, even in retrospect, he lacks understanding regarding his stance: his behaviour is mysterious even to himself.

Similarly, in the short story 'La capanna' [The Hut], the son, Alberto Dallati (a young man trapped in a familiar father-son impasse not unlike Pietro and Domenico's in the autobiographical *Con gli occhi chiusi*), believes he is turning into a tree. In one instance of violence, his father strikes him and he topples to the ground: 'Allora gli venne da piangere. Voleva chiudere gli occhi per non vedere più niente; perché non osava guardarsi né meno attorno. Aveva perfino paura che avrebbe potuto essere un albero e non un uomo; un albero come quello rasente alla casa' ('La capanna' 1029) [Then he felt like crying. He wanted to shut his eyes so as not to see anything; because he didn't even dare to look around. He was even afraid that he could turn into a tree and not a man; a tree like the one close to the house]. The story concludes with the father's death and the son seducing his father's lover, in a patent Oedipal vindication.[16]

In these last two examples of filial disobedience of paternal authority, the male subject both desires and fears a merging with the floral in an attempt to evade his father's control, impulses which are in keeping with the psychasthenic processes illustrated thus far. At the same time, this trope of human-vegetal grafting is obviously not one invented by Tozzi, for literary precedents are numerous.[17] Human-vegetal fusion is evidently a recurrent literary trope and, if one wishes to label the phenomenon, perhaps the term formulated by cultural geographer J. Douglas Porteous, relating to the human body's portrayal as topography or the plant world, is most apt: 'geomorphism.'[18]

While Tozzi's use of 'geomorphism' evidently appertains to a longstanding strand of literary leitmotivs, attempting to classify the examples of legendary psychasthenia present in his oeuvre as belonging to a specific modern or contemporary artistic movement or school proves a more arduous undertaking. Indeed, Tozzi's poetics defy categorization, despite efforts by scholars to relate him – and his visual delineations – to any one (or more) of the following: Impressionism, Expressionism, the Macchiaioli, Cubism, Fauvism, and Primitivism, among others. In her study of his descriptions, Fratnik finds parallels between Tozzi's visual aesthetics and a number of movements, preferring not to pigeonhole him as adhering to any individual one. In one section, entitled 'La dissolution du monde' [The Dissolution of the

World], Fratnik makes a case for Tozzi's being influenced by Impressionism in his depiction of the world as disintegrating, as witnessed in his later works that deal with Rome.[19] The French critic, however, does not enter into a discussion of subject–object intermingling at this juncture, yet obviously the portrayal of external surroundings as dissolving relates to a degree to psychasthenia.

I would suggest that a more relevant source for contemplating which visual aesthetics may have made an impact on Tozzi's depictions of people's intermingling with place perhaps lies in contemporary Italian artistic movements. The Futurists Boccioni, Carrà, Russolo, Balla, and Severini, inspired in their turn by Divisionism and Cubism, published 'La pittura futurista. Manifesto tecnico' on 11 April 1910, wherein they outline their credo regarding artistic representation:

> Lo spazio non esiste più; una strada bagnata dalla pioggia e illuminata da globi elettrici s'inabissa fino al centro della terra ... Chi può credere ancora all'opacità dei corpi, mentre la nostra acuìta e moltiplicata sensibilità ci fa intuire le oscure manifestazioni dei fenomeni medianici? Perché si deve continuare a creare senza tener conto della nostra potenza visiva che può dare risultati analoghi a quelli dei raggi X?
>
> Innumerevoli sono gli esempi che dànno una sanzione positiva alle nostre affermazioni.
>
> Le sedici persone che avete intorno a voi in un tram che corre sono una, dieci, quattro, tre: stanno ferme e si muovono; vanno e vengono, rimbalzano sulla strada, divorate da una zona di sole, indi tornano a sedersi ... E, talvolta sulla guancia della persona con cui parliamo nella via noi vediamo il cavallo che passa lontano. I nostri corpi entrano nei divani su cui ci sediamo, e i divani entrano in noi, così come il tram che passa entra nelle case, le quali alla loro volta si scaraventano sul tram e con esso si amalgamano. (De Maria 23–4)

> [Space no longer exists; a street wet with rain and lit up by electric globes hurls itself down to the centre of the earth ... Who can still believe in the opacity of bodies, when our sharpened and increased sensitivity allows us to understand the obscure manifestations of phenomena of the medium? Why should one continue to create without bearing in mind our visual potential, which can give results like those of the X-ray?
>
> There are countless examples which give positive reinforcement of our affirmations.
>
> The sixteen people you have around you on a moving tram are one, ten, four, three: they stay still and they move; they come and go, they bounce

on to the street, devoured by a sunny spot, and then return from it to sit down ... And, sometimes, on the cheek of the person we are talking to in the street, we can see the horse that is passing by in the distance. Our bodies enter the sofas on which we are sitting, and the sofas enter us, just as a passing tram enters houses, which in their turn throw themselves onto the tram and merge with it.]

The above passage illustrates Futurist notions regarding the interpenetration of planes and the permeability of forms. Some of the descriptions in their manifesto seem to share common ground with Tozzi's version of legendary psychasthenia, especially in the mingling and interchanging between figure and background. Obviously I am not claiming that Tozzi was a Futurist or even that he ascribed to their theories, especially as it is known that he was on less than congenial terms with the movement's Tuscan representative, Soffici. The Futurists' artistic conceptualization of space derived in part from their exposure to Cubism, but also from the impact of technological developments that altered previously held beliefs of space and time (hence the reference to X-rays in the manifesto). While Tozzi's agenda did not include the ideals – such as speed, mechanization, and dynamism, among others – promoted by the Futurists, he must have been exposed to them, given the public nature of their manifestos. In any case, I believe, it seems that Tozzi's characters' interactions with space resonate with certain concepts endorsed by the Futurists, although this by no means signifies classifying his work under a specific cultural movement.

Shifting from a discussion of the possible cultural influences on – or at least the intercultural echoes with – Tozzi's development of his characters' relationship to external space, the motivations behind their psychasthenic episodes also merit some consideration. As seen in several examples I mentioned earlier, often the figure-surroundings merging follows on from a dispute between father and son, and is connected to instances of vertigo. Another distinctive aspect of Tozzi's characters' experience of psychasthenia is its association with death. An example is found in *Il podere* when Remigio again relates to the physical aspect of his farm: 'Remigio si sentì pieno d'ombra come la campagna. Guardò il podere, giù lungo la Tressa; e dov'era già buio. E gli parve che la morte fosse lì; che poteva venire fino a lui, come il vento che faceva cigolare i cipressi. Istintivamente, si trasse a dietro' (*Il podere* 310) [Remigio felt full of shadow, like the countryside. He looked at the farm, down by the Tressa; and where it was already dark. He felt as though death were there; and that it could come up as far him, like the wind that made the cypresses creak. Instinctively, he drew back]. Remigio's perception of his internal shadows mimics those of the topography and he receives an ominous sense of death being located there, a feeling symbolized, too, by the cypress trees, traditionally known as symbols of mortality, despite their widespread presence in the Tuscan landscape.[20] Again the surroundings prefigure the protagonist's fate, as his murder at the hands of Berto takes place on the grounds of the *podere* itself.

The connotations of death appear also in the following example from *Bestie*, the same text from which the passage quoted earlier, in which the narrator describes his obsession at the age of nineteen that he was about to die, was taken:

> Una mattina mi alzai con la voglia di uccidermi: dalla finestra pareva che anche il mio campo si travolgesse come me, nel vento; come mi volesse portar via tutti gli olivi. I muri della camera si facevano sempre più stretti, accostandosi insieme, e il mio respiro si mescolava con il loro: sentivo il sapore della calcina. Sono certo che piangevo! Mi pareva di cadere con la testa in giù, senza aver niente a cui sorreggermi. (*Bestie* 589)

> [One morning I woke up with the desire to kill myself: from the window it looked like my field was being swept away, like me, by the wind; as if it wanted to take away all my olive trees. The walls of my room closed in, drawing near to each other, and my breath mingled with theirs: I could taste the lime plaster. I'm certain I was crying! I felt as though I was falling headfirst, with nothing to support me.]

This particular passage provides an illustration not only of vertigo and psychasthenia, but in its claustrophobic connotations, paints an especially anguished portrait of the narratorial subject and his surroundings. Clearly the narrator's relationship to the world reflects that within himself, while highlighting his death drive. Caillois points out, in fact, that psychasthenia is linked to an impulse towards mortality: 'This assimilation to space is necessarily accompanied by a decline on the feeling of personality and life. It should be noted in any case that in mimetic species the phenomenon is never carried out except *in a single direction*: the animal mimics the plant, leaf, flower, or thorn, and dissembles or ceases to perform its functions in relation to others. *Life takes a step backwards.*' (30) He concludes: 'alongside the instinct of self-preservation, which in some way orients the creature toward life, there is generally speaking a sort of *instinct of renunciation* that orients it towards a mode of reduced existence, which in the end would no longer know either consciousness or feeling—the *inertia of the élan vital*, so to speak' (32).[21]

Tozzi's protagonists do indeed seem to renounce normal contact with those around them. Their ineptitude and incapacity to relate to the human community prohibit fruitful interpersonal relationships. Equally, their attempts to mimetize with the inanimate sphere invariably fail, and indicate their psychological fragility. Ultimately, for Tozzi, everything constitutes the Other, from people, to animals, to objects, to vegetation, to geography, but bonding with this external reality proves impossible: his characters' efforts 'di colmare la differenza, di costituire, o ricostituire, l'accordo' (Saccone *Allegoria* 9) [to overcome difference, to establish, or reestablish, agreement] are destined to fail. Yet in the end, it is precisely his spatial perceptions, characterized by vertigo and psychasthenia, that render Tozzi's vision of urban and rural Tuscany disquieting in their illustrating his individualistic sense of alienation, and at the same time testify to his modernity. Furthermore, the inexplicable, indeed mysterious, quality of so many of his characters' spatial and interpersonal interactions in all likelihood accounts, at least in part, for the fascination that his fiction exerts on readers and critics even today.

2 Palazzeschi's Spaces of Difference: The Materassi Sisters at the Window

Textual space for Palazzeschi, as for Tozzi, is intrinsically linked to questions of difference, yet the Florentine writer's sense of alterity is connected above all with sexuality. Much of his poetry and prose is set in his native city, and the modes of portraying the Tuscan capital vary widely throughout his oeuvre, from his earlier abstract text *La Piramide* (The Pyramid, 1926), to his 'realist' narratives such as *Stampe dell'800* (Nineteenth-Century Prints, 1932) and *Sorelle Materassi* (The Sisters Materassi, 1934) or his post–Second World War pieces 'Il paesaggio' ('Landscape,' 1947) and 'Ho sognato Firenze' ('I dreamt of Florence,' 1948), which feature explicit toponyms and greater mimetic detail, to his surreal novel, *Stefanino* (1969), published late in his career, where geographical setting is referred to only obliquely.[1]

The central concerns of *Sorelle Materassi*, Palazzeschi's commercially most successful novel and the one on which my analysis focuses, revolve around difference and the performance of sexuality. For Palazzeschi gender is a labile concept; his characters rarely conform to normative heterosexist paradigms and display a wide range of sexual behaviours, breaking down culturally constructed parameters of femininity and masculinity. Space, be it internal or external, is illustrative of the writer's commitment to articulating difference and staging sexuality, and the locales portrayed encapsulate a sense of liminality. *Sorelle Materassi* insists, for example, on spaces representing the in-between: a Florentine periphery that straddles the boundaries between country and city, or the architectural iconography of the window, a zone that is neither interior nor exterior.

Palazzeschi's *buffi*: Difference and Sexuality

On a superficial reading, *Sorelle Materassi* might not appear overly preoccupied with the erotic, given that its protagonists are two middle-aged virginal seamstresses, Teresa and Carolina Materassi, who lead uneventful existences. Yet despite their apparently unremarkable lives, the sisters (as well as other characters in the novel) constitute the embodiment of alterity, a hallmark of Palazzeschian poetics, and behave in such a manner as to trouble conventional notions of sexuality.

The two women, furthermore, clearly represent the writer himself, as scholars of Palazzeschi have demonstrated. Marchi, states, in fact, that the characters in *Sorelle Materassi* 'inscenano una sorta di sua autobiografia truccata' (Marchi, *Palazzeschi* 65) [stage a kind of disguised autobiography of his] and the critic then proceeds to draw, in my view, convincing parallels between Teresa and Carolina's defining traits and activities and the author's own biography: for example, the sisters are just either side of fifty, the same age as Palazzeschi was when he wrote the text. Moreover, their embroidery, executed in seclusion in their workroom, can be juxtaposed, Marchi maintains, with Palazzeschi's work with words in his study during this reclusive period in his life. Over and above Marchi's persuasive comparison between the writer and his characters, it is through their spatial and corporeal practices, I would argue, that the Materassi sisters enact Palazzeschi's sublimation of his sexuality. Through their bodies, Teresa and Carolina perform a parody of femininity and inhabit spaces that become symbolic of Palazzeschi's interrogation of bourgeois heterosexist norms.

Teresa and Carolina can be classified as *buffe* ('funny people' or 'misfits'), a category of characters who are in some manner marginalized and exemplify the author's obsessive interest in Otherness.[2] Palazzeschi outlines what he means by 'buffi' in his preface to the 1957 collection of his short stories, some of which had been published earlier in a volume entitled *Il palio dei buffi*, or *A Tournament of Misfits* (1937):

> Buffi sono tutti coloro che per qualche caratteristica, naturale divergenza e di varia natura, si dibattono in un disagio fra la generale comunità umana; disagio che assume ad un tempo aspetti di accesa comicità e di cupa tristezza; ragione per cui questo libro forma una commedia tragicomica nella quale i 'buffi' vengono portati alla sbarra.

[*Buffi* are all those persons who, because of some (peculiar) trait or natural divergence of various kinds, writhe in discomfort amidst the general community of humans. This discomfort assumes at one and the same time tones of heightened comedy and deep gloom. That is why this volume forms a tragicomic drama in which the 'buffi' are brought to the dock.]³

The Materassi sisters, two women who have shunned men in favour of devoting themselves entirely to embroidering for their exclusive clientele, exist outside middle-class, heterosexist norms of comportment and have all but renounced the outside world, thus epitomizing – via their self-imposed exile, as well as other idiosyncratic modes of behaviour – the Palazzeschian *buffi*.

Through these female figures and their patent 'difference' Palazzeschi is able to play with the boundaries of sexuality and verbalize, indirectly, his own homoerotic desire.⁴ Generally speaking, in Palazzeschi's literary production, difference, according to Gnerre (as well as others), stands as a metaphor for the writer's homosexuality:

Il tema dell'omosessualità, di chiara derivazione autobiografica, è presente in modo evidente solo nel primo romanzo, :*riflessi* del 1908; ma a volte più esplicito, spesso abilmente dissimulato o sublimato, non tanto però da impedirne la decifrazione, è presente in vari modi in tutta la produzione dello scrittore. Il modo più evidente in cui si manifesta è l'insistenza del tema della diversità, perlopiù legata proprio alla sessualità. (Gnerre 61)

[The theme of homosexuality, clearly of autobiographical origin, is overtly present only in his first novel, :*riflessi*, of 1908; but it is present in all of the writer's production in various ways; it is at times explicit, or often ably concealed or sublimated, but not to such a degree that it cannot be deciphered. The most evident way in which it manifests itself is in the insistence on the theme of difference, usually connected precisely to sexuality itself.]

Difference is thus the conduit through which Palazzeschi is able to reveal (albeit obliquely) his closeted self, and the Materassi sisters incarnate this core aspect of his poetics through their spatial and corporeal practices.⁵

Difference and sexuality are, moreover, concepts played out on/by the body in space, as Knopp explains:

> Social relations ... would appear always to be organised around some kinds of difference. And while difference is a fundamental feature of human experience, it has no fixed form or essence. What constitutes it, ultimately, is different *experiences*. To make these mutually intelligible and socially productive (as well as destructive!), we associate our different experiences with particular markers and construct *these* as the essences of our difference. These markers may be practices, they may be objects (such as features of our bodies), or they may be abstract symbols and language. Because human beings exist in space, these differences and the social relations which they constitute (and through which they are also reconstituted) are also inherently spatial. The relations of sexuality are no exception. (Knopp 159)

It stands to reason, then, that Teresa and Carolina's difference should be acted out upon the body (for instance, through their mode of dress, their behaviour), within spatially significant spheres (such as the house they live in and the rooms within it). Thus, this chapter will investigate the spatial constructions of Palazzeschi's textual representation of a flexibly conceived sexuality.[6]

Florentine Places

Before introducing the novel's two female protagonists, *Sorelle Materassi* opens with a panoramic description of Florence's skyline and the surrounding hills, a portrait that could in fact risk seeming relatively standard since, despite the writer's providing toponyms, little attention is paid to specific monuments or landmarks, with Palazzeschi choosing to pay tribute to the landscape's proverbial beauty. In fact, his depiction of Florence is centred more on literary antecedents (Dante and, even more importantly, Boccaccio)[7] than on the architectural configuration itself.

Of greater significance, however, is the writer's singling out of a dynamic between the low plain on which the city rests and the adjacent hills:

> se in questa terra la collina vi tiene il posto della signora, e quasi sempre signora vera, principessa, la pianura vi tiene quello della serva, della cameriera o ancella ... Della signora sono tutti gli onori e i meriti, le libertà e molte licenze ... Dominando a questo modo compresa, insolente ed altèra, neppure le frulla in testa di guardare la sottoposta o le dà una sbirciatina dall'alto e di traverso, uno sguardo di degnazione al solo scopo

d'indispettirla, e dal quale emerge soltanto la sua incontrastata, intangibile superiorità.

La povera serva invece, la guarda dal basso socchiudendo gli occhi, fingendo di neppure accorgersi del trattamento poco rispettoso, e rimane a testa bassa. (*Romanzi I* 506, 507)

[If in this countryside the hills occupy the position of the lady – and almost always she is the true lady, the princess – the plain takes the place of the servant, the chambermaid or handmaid ... To the lady, the princess, belong all honours and favours, all liberties and many licenses ... Insolent, proud, her sway accepted, she never takes it into her head to look at her subordinate; or gives her, at most, a quick close inspection askance and from above, a look of condescension intended merely to irritate and to display her own unquestioned superiority.

The poor servant, on the other hand, looks up at her from below with half-closed eyes, pretending not even to notice the disrespectful way in which she is treated; she keeps her head bowed.][8]

Critics have remarked on a number of features found in this opening description which remains, nonetheless, rather enigmatic, given that the rest of the novel is set in a suburban zone and Florence's city centre is practically absent for the rest of the novel. Yet certain aspects of the dynamic between the *collina-signora* and the *pianura-serva* resonate for the themes elaborated in *Sorelle Materassi*. Clearly the haughtiness of the *signora* is emphasized and implicitly critiqued by the author, much as the Materassi sisters' pride and disdain towards their rural and working-class neighbours is shown up in the end, after their financial downfall.

With this initial delineation of the Florentine milieu Palazzeschi is therefore highlighting issues of class which resurface throughout the text, and his characterization of the hill and plain as female evidently connects the geography to the women protagonists of the novel[9] and institutes a paradigm of class difference that operates on the axis of high-low, or top-bottom, emphasizing verticality, an important aspect of textual space as identified by Lotman.[10] Yet qualities attributed to the servant ('si stringe alle proprie virtù mostrandosi paziente, laboriosa, sottomessa' [508] [she clings to her own virtues, proving herself patient, industrious, submissive]) are also applicable to the Materassi sisters, in that they, too, are hardworking and patient in their embroidery, and acquiesce to the will of their nephew, Remo. Thus, their social class is associated both with the low-lying mount and the flat Florentine terrain.

In fact, the two sisters are associated directly with the plain once the focus of the initial wide-scale panorama of Florence's hills shifts to the modest neighbourhood in the valley, Santa Maria a Coverciano, in which they reside.[11] Coverciano represents an area that is neither urban nor rural. The small grouping of houses and church, north-east of the city below the hill-town of Settignano, does not form part of the city itself, nor is it strictly countryside, but rather is a 'larva di paese' (*Romanzi I* 509) [ghost of a village]. Marchi fittingly defines the area as one that ambiguously presents itself (79) as 'un paese non paese, un anomalo agglomerato di case in cerca di definizione terminologica' (79) [a non-village village, an anomalous group of houses in search of a terminological definition]. Thus, the neighbourhood lacks a classifiable geographical, economic, and social status, and its amorphous quality, I would argue, represents the fluidity of the sisters' social class and gender, as well as that of many of the other characters portrayed in the text.[12] Even Remo and Peggy's wedding in the church of Santa Maria a Coverciano is characterized as a hodge-podge of urban and rural elements, a 'matrimonio fiorentino e campestre' (777) [a wedding both Florentine and countrified], as a 'spietata parodia di Strapaese e Stracittà' (Febbraro 386) [pitiless parody of Strapaese and Stracittà].[13]

The Materassi sisters are essentially 'nouveau riche,' a status evoked by the very architectural features of their house. Their bailiff grandfather made his fortune by buying property, and his son (their father) subsequently dissipated all the family wealth, leaving his wife and daughters penniless on his death. As a result, since adolescence, Carolina and Teresa have worked unstintingly to provide for themselves and their remaining family members. Their business is remarkably successful and their clientele belong to the Florentine elite, yet it must be remembered that the sisters function as the providers of luxury goods for the upper classes, and while their craftsmanship is of the highest standard, they are primarily supplying undergarments to the well-heeled, an activity that signals Palazzeschi's humorous undermining of the sisters' inflated self-importance, as well as the irony in the virginal spinsters' role of furnishing the trappings of seduction to brides-to-be and, in some cases, even to mistresses. So while the sisters clearly believe that their affluence entitles them to a superior social ranking, the precariousness of this illusion is borne out by their bankruptcy at the end of the narrative, and their concession to produce serviceable articles of clothing for local working-class women.

The manner in which the Materassis' four walls epitomize the ups and downs of their own and their family's financial history is rendered explicit by its layout:

Il lato di fondo di questa fabbrica è composto da una casa di tre piani che ha un po' dell'alveare come tutte le case della povera gente, e i bracci che raggiungono il muro sulla via, stretti e lunghi, di due piani solamente. Salta subito agli occhi che tale costruzione venne eseguita in più riprese, e che il braccio sud è più antico assai e di diversa intonazione, più signorile di architettura e con accenno di ornamenti, non solo, ma che le sue finestre, anziché guardare nel cortile come le altre, guardano tutte sul campo, a mezzodì, e che esso al cortile volta sdegnosamente le spalle lasciandovi un'unica finestra, quella di un corridoio, che si direbbe aperta soltanto per guardarvi a discrezione. Tale parte privilegiata possiede un suo ingresso speciale sulla via, un cancello bianco, sempre aperto a metà, e assai mangiato dalla ruggine. (*Romanzi* I 509–10)

[The farthest side of this building is composed of a three-storeyed house which has something of a beehive look about it, like all poor people's dwellings; and the wings which join on to the wall beside the road are long and narrow and have only two floors. It is immediately obvious that this structure must have been built at various periods, and that the south wing is much more ancient and different in type from the rest, for it is not only of a more gentlemanly architectural style, with some remains of ornamental dignity, but has all its windows facing, not, like the others, on to the courtyard, but over the fields, southwards towards Florence; and it turns its back disdainfully on the courtyard, with only one single window opening upon it, and that from a corridor at the back, so that you would think it had been put there merely in order to peep out into it at its own convenience. The privileged part of the building – the first part you come to – possesses its own private entrance from the road, a white iron gate of which one half is always open and which is much eaten away by rust.]

The sisters' eclectic house therefore supplies a spatial representation of the economic and social status of its inhabitants. On the one hand, it would seem to typify an abode of 'povera gente,' but its construction has clearly taken place over various phases, some richer, some poorer. This contradiction incarnated by the house echoes the sisters' journey from financial ruin to wealth and their eventual return to impoverishment.[14] Moreover, the nobler south wing of their residence stands in juxtaposition to the adjoining courtyard, and its windows overlook the fields, thus ignoring the more modest residences next door. This arrangement mirrors Teresa and Carolina's aloofness towards their neighbours. Their detachment from their working-class tenants is made manifest also through their separate entrance, with its shabby-genteel, rusty white gate, a feature regularly mentioned by the narrator, its image emblematic of the virginal yet aging sisters themselves.

The domestic interiors centre around Teresa and Carolina's workspace – where they spend the bulk of their time – and to an extent their bedroom, as well as the kitchen (along with its cellar), which figures prominently in one dramatic incident of conflict between Remo and his aunts. Palazzeschi is at pains to delineate the sisters' self-imposed relegation to their dwelling; their house, rather than being a home, forms the centre of their working lives to such an extent that they rarely leave it, except to attend Sunday mass, or the fair in Fiesole, just once a year.

Gender Performances at the Window

The house's exterior denotes its piecemeal nature: it is neither fish nor fowl, reflecting the fluctuations of the Materassis' fortune and social standing. At the same time, its description quoted above stresses the position of the windows, an equally polyvalent architectural icon that assumes great significance since it is where, up until the arrival of their nephew, the sisters regularly spend their Sunday afternoons. A quintessential liminal space, the window for Palazzeschi represents the labile quality of categorizations such as internal/external; private/public; reality/fantasy; male/female; country/city; containment/escape. In her study of the Dutch window, cultural anthropologist Irene Cieraad concentrates on the concept of the borderline and its relationship to windows: 'Borderlines of any sort, physical or symbolic, are manifestations of cognitive classifications. The nature of these borderlines, be they solid or permeable, and the way they are transgressed or maintained ... are indications of the importance of the classifications involved' (32). Cieraad considers borderlines a cardinal component of fenestration: 'The special character of the window as a borderline has not only to do with its fragility in contrast to the solidity of the walls, but also with its relationship to the other opening in the façade: the door' (32). It seems fitting, then, that the window, with its (often permeable) borderline, should constitute such a pivotal function for Palazzeschi's oeuvre, since its symbolic potential facilitates the elaboration of key thematics for the author.

In Palazzeschi's earlier autobiographical *Stampe dell'800*, for instance, the iconography of the window assumes a key role: from the author's childhood 'finestra/minestra' (window/soup) episode, it represents freedom, or evasion of parental control and of repressive nineteenth-century bourgeois values. The window also stands for the writer's creativity, when, as a child, he lights a row of matches that burn the sill, a mischievous deed he keeps hidden from his father. The writer later evokes the black burn marks on the window frame as he compares them to the letters used to write poetry, the pyromaniacal drive thus being equated with fantasy, impulses that, like his sexuality, he desires to conceal from his father.[15]

The window's liminality for the Materassi sisters, too, physically illustrates the problematics of gender, sexuality, and space that Palazzeschi teases out in the text.[16] For Cieraad, the window has patent sexual associations (she comments, for instance, on the correlation between the window and prostitution, or the visual iconography of the windowpane as hymen), and she judges it (rightly or wrongly) part of the feminine realm. It seems fitting, then, that the two women should choose the window as the locus where, every Sunday afternoon, they resurrect their femininity ('destinavano, senza accorgersene, tutto il pomeriggio a riesumare la loro femminilità' (542) [though they were no longer aware of it – they devoted the entire afternoon to the re-exhumation of their femininity]), in a series of rituals whereby they paint their faces and adorn themselves in antiquated garb and outdated ornaments before standing at their bedroom window to observe the passers-by:

> Dopo essersi addobbate la vita e il collo di fiocchi, il petto con qualche altra calìa, la testa con forcine e pettini luccicanti, incominciavano a incipriarsi la faccia facendo a picca, quasi se lo facessero per dispetto, a chi se la imbiancava meglio e di più; e una volta infarinate come pesci da friggere, e dopo aver fatto mille smorfie e piroette davanti allo specchio, osservando in tutti i sensi la loro persona che rivedevano dopo sette giorni, si mettevano alla finestra l'una attaccata all'altra, a gomito, con le braccia bene composte sul davanzale. (Palazzeschi, *Romanzi I* 544–5)

> [After they had decorated their waists and necks with bows, their bosoms with hairpins and gleaming combs, they started to powder their faces, quarrelling as they did so, as though they did it out of spite towards anyone who whitened her face better and more thoroughly; and once they were well floured, like fish ready for frying, after making a thousand grimaces and pirouettes in front of the looking glass and inspecting, from every angle, the faces and figures which they had not seen for a week, they took up their positions at the window with elbows touching and arms carefully arranged on the sill.]

The bizarreness of the sisters' appearance is ridiculed not only by passers-by, but is reinforced in textual analogies as well, through the architectural composition of the area of the house proximate to the window where they stand:

> La cosa più originale si è che, sopra la finestra alla quale stavano affacciate, il muro non finiva col tetto come in tutte le case di queste terre, dove i tetti danno il carattere ai paesi e alle città, ma nella linea orizzontale di un muretto liscio e bianco come quello di una casetta araba di Tripoli o di Bengasi, cosa insolita veramente, e su cui erano due vasettini con due agavi indistruttibili e incapaci di crescere, decrepite e bambine, ciò che aumentando il ridicolo dava un colore equivoco al quadro domenicale. (551)

> [The oddest thing was that, above the window at which they sat, the wall did not end in a roof, as it does in all the houses in that neighbourhood, where the roofs give their character to the villages and towns, but in the horizontal line of a smooth, white parapet like that of the pretty little Arab houses of Tripoli or Benghazi – a most unusual thing indeed; and on this parapet stood two terra-cotta urns with agave plants in them – plants indestructible yet incapable of growing, decrepit yet immature – which made this Sunday-afternoon picture even more ridiculous and gave it a somewhat equivocal flavour.]

Thus, the eclectic house is portrayed spatially in such as way as to underscore Teresa and Carolina's own unconventionality, with its singular features connoting a kind of exoticism, the pseudo 'foreignness' of the house reiterating the Materassis' own difference. The two plants, furthermore, obviously symbolize the aging yet infantile sisters, caught in the oddness of their behaviour, mature yet simultaneously childlike.

During their day-to-day working lives, however, the sisters pay no attention to their appearance as women, and the narrator informs us that only outside the confines of their *laboratorio* is their femininity played out: '[p]er vederle femmine bisognava sorprenderle lontane dal lavoro, fuori da quella stanza che le aveva atrofizzate' (542) [To see them as real women, you had to come upon them by surprise away from their work and from that room which had withered them up]. In fact, the sisters' gender goes practically unnoticed by those around them, since 'erano combinate in modo che a nessuno era balenato il pensiero di sposarle, come non fossero state donne' (546) [they were decked out in such a way that the thought of marrying them had never crossed anyone's mind, just as though they were not women at all].[17] Yet Teresa and Carolina enact a quasi-parody of their femininity over and over again, displaying a complete ignorance of fashion, despite their profession as up-market seamstresses.

This indeterminacy of gender embodied by Teresa and Carolina and figured in the window image, I would argue, is a means through which the author can indirectly represent his own sexuality and, moreover, convey just to what extent sexuality is a construct. In another text, *I Fratelli Cuccoli*, written in the same decade as *Sorelle Materassi* but published in 1948, Palazzeschi, through the pronouncements of Celestino (the character most closely aligned with the writer himself), promotes a conception of gender that privileges variety, difference, non-conformity. In one of the scenes at the Ball at Villa Letizia, the uncompromising Donna Maria voices her disapproval of Fofo and Mac, two androgynous characters: 'La confusione dei sessi mi irrita, detesto la confusione dei sessi. In questa materia amo la chiarezza: da una parte ci sono le donne coi loro caratteri precisati bene e riconosciuti universalmente, e la loro femminilità; dall'altra gli uomini coi loro, ben definiti e definitivi, e la loro virilità' (*Romanzi II* 222) [Confusing the sexes irritates me, I hate confusing the sexes. I love clarity in this matter: on one side you have women with their well-defined and universally recognized characteristics, along with their femininity; on the other you have men with their characteristics which are well-defined and definitive, along with their virility]. Celestino responds, advocating a more open-minded conceptualization of sexuality: 'Non c'è nulla di definito e di definitivo, di assoluto nell'opera della natura e nella vita umana che è parte di essa. Codeste divisioni fatte con l'ascia, rappresentano una violenza, una tirannia' (ibid.) [There is nothing definite, definitive, absolute in nature's work and in human life which is part of it. These divisions made with a hatchet represent violence, tyranny].

Palazzeschi thus demonstrates – for his time, at least – remarkable latitude concerning sexuality, both in *I fratelli Cuccoli* as well as in *Sorelle Materassi* (not to mention other texts), in his subversion of heteronormative paradigms. It could be argued, in fact, that the writer is prefiguring more recent developments in theories of gender and identity. Butler, for example, explains that the concept of gender is not innate or fixed: 'Gender ought not to be construed as a stable identity or locus of agency from which various acts follow; rather, gender is an identity tenuously constituted in time, instituted in an exterior space through a *stylized repetition of acts*' (Butler 179, emphasis in original). According to Butler, we shape our gender via the body through repeated rituals:

> The effect of gender is produced through the stylization of the body and, hence, must be understood as the mundane way in which bodily gestures, movements, and styles of various kinds constitute the illusion of an abiding gendered self. This formulation moves the conception of gender off the ground of a substantial model of identity to one that requires a conception of gender as a constituted *social temporality*. Significantly, if gender is instituted through acts which are internally discontinuous, then the *appearance of substance* is precisely that, a constructed identity, a performative accomplishment which the mundane social audience, including the actors themselves, come to believe and to perform in the mode of belief. (Butler 179, emphasis in original)

Gender, therefore, is an act which is performed by and on the body, in both the spatial and the temporal realms. These notions resonate with behaviour manifested by the Materassi sisters, since through their bodies in space, Teresa and Carolina perform (and also undermine) their gender through repeated actions.

While Butler insists on the ritualistic, public, and performative nature of gender, she chooses not to elaborate on the concept of theatricality. Yet the performative, indeed histrionic, dimension is precisely that which seems to characterize the Materassi sisters' identity, as they stage their femininity regularly. The novel in fact highlights the notion of enactment as related to their appearance:

> All'alba del lunedì ... tutti gli svaghi e le delizie del giorno festivo erano dimenticati nella maniera più completa, erano due altre donne: non un fronzolo né un ornamento sulle persone, né il ricordo della cipria sopra le faccie, era come se avessero recitato una commedia.
> La vita era quella, interamente, a essa s'erano date tutte, allontanandosi dall'altra, dalla vita vera, che non era oramai se non una commedia per esse, e non aveva nulla di reale. (551–2)

> [At dawn on Monday ... all the amusements and delights of the day of rest utterly forgotten, they were two different women: not a ribbon nor an ornament upon them, nor even a memory of powder on their faces; it was as though they had been acting in a play.
> That was their life, completely and absolutely, and to it they had given themselves wholly, cutting themselves off from the other, the real life; and it was that which had now become, for them, a play, with nothing real about it.]

The narrator insists on the staged quality of the sisters' performance of femininity, and the dramatic-arts metaphor in this context also elicits the reality/fantasy opposition, a dualism explored in Palazzeschi's oeuvre more generally, and one that is applicable to Teresa and Carolina as they fantasize about their (non-existent) past love affairs while observing couples passing by, on their way up to the hills for sexual trysts. This vicarious visual pleasure sparks their own foray into imagination that contrasts starkly with their sexual abstinence and the 'reality' of the quotidian work routine that consumes them.

Critics have in fact commented on the Materassis' staging of their sexuality, and Marchi, drawing on textual references, builds on the theatrical imagery that characterizes their Sunday afternoons:

> Il domenicale giorno di riposo di Teresa e Carolina ... coglie le due donne fuori dalla loro 'fucina', agghindate e loquacissime, partecipi di un'altra commedia recitata, facendo di loro 'due dame in un palchetto all'opera o alla commedia' e nel contempo personaggi recitanti, carnevalesche 'maschere' di 'fanciulle impietrite': 'due vecchie grulle che pretendevano di fare le graziose e le bambine' che irradiano anche sulla nuova scenografia che le accoglie i caratteri del loro dramma: una finestra aperta su un muro bianco di sapore arabo.[18] (Marchi 78)

> [Sunday, Teresa and Carolina's day of rest ... captures the two women away from their 'forge,' adorned and extremely loquacious, participants in another comedy performance, making of them 'two grand ladies in a box at the opera or the theatre' and at the same time characters who perform, carnivalesque 'masks' of 'frozen girls': 'a couple of old sillies pretending to be pretty and girlish' who project the signs of their drama also on to the new set in which they act: an open window in a white wall with an Arabic flavour.]

Marchi rightly asserts that the Materassi sisters encompass the role not only of actors, but also of audience in this pantomime at the window.[19] Furthermore, while emphasizing the theatricality of the sisters' Sunday performances, the critic also cites a related image employed by the author (552), that of the mask.[20]

Certainly it seems fairly evident that Teresa and Carolina operate as masks for the writer's own sexual identity, a suitable metaphor when confronting questions of homosexuality in the novel. Indeed, Duncan – citing an article by the author of *L'eroe negato* – comments on the concept of 'masking' in gay authorship:

Gnerre points out that gay Italian authors have characteristically written using the 'techniques of masking' rather than outright revelation or confession to broach their homosexuality ... This suggests both the author's wish to reveal something about his sexuality to a perhaps knowing reader, and the feeling that such a revelation had to be tempered. There is the sense though that a gay man can be found somehow, somewhere in the text. (Duncan 6)

In Palazzeschi's case, the sisters' staged femininity, their loose 'masking' of the writer himself, expose the complexities of gender, all the while disguising yet simultaneously disclosing his sexuality. In her analysis of gender Butler explores, furthermore, the notion of drag as a parody of gender identity, and the Materassi sisters can – and, I believe, should – in fact plausibly be interpreted as a form of authorial transvestism, as critics such as Marchi and Gnerre have indeed noted. These metaphorical maskings or veilings of sexuality reach their apex in the scenes depicting the Materassis performing their gender at the emblematic space of the window; thus, the sisters divert their own sexual impulses through a kind of safety-valve mechanism that is staged one afternoon per week, and the writer sublimates his own sexuality via the double female figures and their spatial practices. The Materassis' regular Sunday afternoon enactments cease, however, with the arrival of a flesh-and-blood object of desire within their home: their fourteen-year-old orphaned nephew, Remo.

Remo and the Space of the Closet

Incapable of escaping their domestic confines and of living out in the world, Teresa and Carolina are content with standing at the liminal space of the window, performing their own femininity while admiring the men who pass by, a clear example of vicarious pleasure. The eruption of the adolescent Remo into their lives provides the presence of an attractive male in their very own milieu. Remo is portrayed as the indifferent yet consensual recipient of his aunts' affections, as illustrated by the descriptions of Carolina's lingering kisses which he accepts, much to Teresa's irritation (and envy):

Carolina, forse per giustificare a se medesima la forza del proprio impulso, o per sciogliersi da un groviglio di sensazioni che le stringevano il cuore, a quel sorriso che si ripeté non fu capace di resistere: abbracciò il ragazzo e lo baciò sulla bocca. E quegli, a sua volta, più che renderle il bacio abbandonò la bocca alla bocca della donna, né facendo atto di ritrarla ma disposto ad elargirla a piacere. Fu essa che, avvertendo un ignoto turbamento a quel contatto che si protraeva, si ritrasse smarrita seguitando a guardare la bocca di lui rimasta impassibile, imperturbabile, quasi che il colpo di tenerezza avesse rappresentato per lui un atto meccanico, senza la più piccola profondità e senza lasciare la minima traccia. (580)

[Carolina, perhaps in order to justify to herself the strength of her own impulse, or to free herself from the tangle of sensations that oppressed her heart, was quite incapable of resisting that twice-repeated smile: she threw her arms round the boy and kissed him on the mouth. And he, on his side, did not exactly return her kiss but abandoned his mouth to hers, making no attempt to withdraw it, prepared to surrender it as freely as she wished. It was she who, becoming aware of an unknown agitation at this protracted contact, drew back in bewilderment, still continuing to gaze at the mouth of the boy, who remained impassive and imperturbable, as though the sudden access of tenderness had been, for him, a purely mechanical act, with no depth of feeling in it, and leaving not the slightest trace.][21]

Thus, Remo neither declines nor reciprocates his aunt's physical attentions, remaining an impassive, mysterious figure. The adolescent's masculinity conjures up unacknowledged erotic longings in his aunts and the gaze of the middle-aged women clearly stands for the male author's same-sex desire, in this way highlighting yet again the Materassis' function as masks for Palazzeschi himself. At the same time, Remo's presence titillates his aunts' repressed sexuality, and alludes to another taboo: that of incest, a risqué topic couched within the seemingly innocent narrative of *Sorelle Materassi*.

The spatial mappings of the text from Remo's arrival onwards basically see the Materassis, consumed by their rigid regime of work, still relegated to the domestic sphere while Remo progressively moves further and further away from the home, wandering around the city and its environs, his whereabouts unknown. The young man does not engage in study or work, and, in adulthood, his freedom of movement is facilitated (as well as represented) first by his motorcycle, and subsequently by his car. Remo has managed to extort funds for these vehicles from the women around him (including Niobe, servant to the sisters) and this trend of demanding money from his aunts continues until the coffers are completely depleted. Remo eventually succeeds in convincing his aunts to start going out on the town with him, and gradually the renowned seamstresses begin to take on less challenging work in order to execute it more rapidly so as to earn fast cash to meet their nephew's profligate spending.

Remo's classic good looks and sensual appeal continue into adulthood, and his hold over Teresa and Carolina remains intact, if not stronger. His grip on the women in the Materassi household (all except the third sister, Giselda) comes to its dramatic head when he forces Teresa and Carolina to sign a *cambiale*, or promissory note, once they have become utterly bankrupt. The sisters initially refuse, but their nephew locks them in the cupboard under the stairs in the kitchen (with Niobe standing by ineptly) and holds them prisoner until they agree to sign. Remo thus exerts his despotic control over the sisters, incarcerating them in their own home. Teresa and Carolina finally emerge, defeated and resigned, having consented to the will of their nephew.

The spatial dynamics in this scene illustrate the power relationships in the novel, and the home's innermost room – the very same one they had hidden in years before in an attempt to observe Remo's morning routine of jumping down from his bedroom to the kitchen window – becomes a prison for the two sisters ('Quando capirono di che si trattava, non reagirono più. Venivano rinchiuse in quel tugurio ripugnante: si era giunti a tanto' (735) [When they realized what was happening, they ceased to struggle. There they were, shut up in this repulsive kennel; it had come to that]). Yet this spatial figure of the closet is also an evocative one in a novel so concerned with questions of sexuality and gender. By this I do not intend to foist the English idiom of 'coming out of the closet' onto the Italian, yet the move from secrecy to openness is a relevant one in a text so concerned with sexuality. Once the two sisters resurface from the pantry closet, the extent of their subjugation to Remo's control is rendered patent and, at the same time, they are compelled to confront their dire financial situation.

Sedgwick has expertly interpreted the intricacies of the closet image, and Duncan reflects on the theorist's contribution in interpreting this highly charged symbolic space:

> Her understanding of the closet as a potent, metaphorical space constructed round the figure of the homosexual where uncertainties and ambiguities over what is known, acknowledged, and confessed effectively produce the homosexual subject addresses the issue of how configurations and articulations of space are themselves expressive of how we are

mapped in the social landscape, and of how we make sense of it through a presumption of knowledge, and of ignorance. (Duncan 89)

Thus, it is significant that Palazzeschi's alter-egos, Teresa and Carolina, are forcibly contained in the space of the closet, only to exit from it once they have acknowledged their economic debts as well as their capitulation at the hands of Remo. From this temporary incarceration, the sisters then go up to their bedroom and dress up in their outdated finery, having agreed to go out for the evening with Remo shortly after their stand-off. A spatial shift is thus enacted, where there is a movement from an inner, private space to the public sphere, as if the sisters finally recognize the complete relinquishment of their desire to their nephew: their love for him is so self-abnegating, so consuming, that it reduces them to bankruptcy and total submission. At the same time, they have not admitted, not even to themselves, that their nephew has become a tyrant who uses violence against them in order to obtain what he wants; thus, the egress from the closet does not, ultimately, lead to a true revelation but alludes to the author's unveiling of his own sexuality.

Furthermore, Remo as an object of (homoerotic) desire is a problematic one. A paragon of classic physical attractiveness (he is likened to ancient Greek or Renaissance statuary, 652), his characteristics render him ambiguous, to say the least. Passive recipient of his aunts' attentions, he nonetheless has the upper hand, essentially forcing them to carry out his bidding. Even though Remo represents a welcome and seductive explosion of vitality for the Materassi sisters (reiterating the youth–old age dualism common to Palazzeschi's poetics), this does not overshadow the fact that he exploits them as long as it suits him, only to abandon them once the money has run out. Furthermore, for all his physical appeal, he nevertheless incarnates aspects that characterize him as cold, inaccessible, and manipulative.

Critics have interpreted Remo in various ways: some have seen him as uncalculating (Pullini 105), others have drawn parallels between him and the Fascist male, referring to him as a 'squadrista *in pectore*' (Febbraro 389) [an undeclared *squadrista*]. In fact, many of his traits correlate to the ideals of Fascist masculinity: he is athletic, a man of action, a seducer (for example, he gets Laurina, the daughter of a vegetable gardener, pregnant, a matter conveniently resolved by Niobe and the sisters), he is fascinated with machines and speed. Remo is, in essence, a kind of beautiful bully whose principal aim is parasitic, and in some ways can be read as a precursor of Fellini's *vitelloni*. At the end of the novel, once Remo has left for America, Niobe shows the sisters a photograph of him wearing only a bathing suit. Enthralled, Teresa and Carolina have it enlarged and hang it on the wall in their sewing room. Remo's apotheosis via his semi-naked image serves as a reminder of his sexual attractiveness, yet it is also reminiscent of Fascist iconography depicting Mussolini half-naked, used for propagandistic purposes to emphasize his strength and physical prowess.[22]

While possessing traits that link him to Fascist virility, Remo's own sexuality is no clear-cut matter, reiterating Palazzeschi's poetics of gender slippage. Despite his seduction of Laurina and his marriage to Peggy, Remo appears most often with a male companion, Palle, who in the end joins him and his bride in their move to the United States. Remo and Palle are depicted as another double in the text (parallel to the sisters Teresa and Carolina) and their inseparability is stressed to such an extent that the author seems to be hinting at a friendship that has potential to go beyond the platonic:

> Remo, in fondo, non amava che Palle, quello che passava per il suo garzone rappresentava la parte migliore di sé.... La gioia reciproca più grande era di dormire insieme.... Si comprendevano a gesti, a monosillabi, a occhiate; e tutti e due stavano bene fra i maschi per parlare dei loro argomenti.... Per Remo il tempo che dedicava alle donne era pesato con le bilancine d'oro, le guardava freddo e indifferente come un campo da conquistare nel minor tempo possibile. (681–3)

> [Remo, really and truly, loved no one except Palle, and the boy who passed as his henchman represented the best part of himself ... The greatest joy, for both of them, was to sleep together in the same bed ... They understood each other by gestures, by monosyllables, by glances; and both of them were perfectly at ease in talking of their own subjects with other men ... With Remo, the time that he dedicated to women was weighed out as carefully as gold: he looked upon them with coolness and indifference, as a field to be conquered in the shortest possible time.]

And while the narrator states that the young men are neither sentimental nor sensual (683), clearly a symbiotic relationship or acute mutual understanding exists between the two.

Chronological references are all but absent in *Sorelle Materassi*: there is no mention of politics, let alone the Fascist regime and its ramifications for Italian citizens. Yet Remo's complex and enigmatic figure has certain valences that can be read as an implicit critique of Fascism, a stance that, in 1934, could not have been voiced openly: he is fascinating but turns out to be a freeloading thug, as if he were an embodiment of Fascism's charismatic drawing power and the violent reality of its hegemony. In his later essays published in *Tre imperi ... mancati. Cronaca (1922–45)* (1945) Palazzeschi's loathing of the regime is clearly stated, but in his earlier fictional works this sentiment had to be couched in other terms. The same is true of sexuality under Fascist rule; it would have been too hazardous for Palazzeschi to depict openly gay characters in his texts of the period, hence the masking of homoerotic desire via the female figures of the Materassi sisters.[23] The author's closeted self is only revealed to the attuned reader via the text's interstices.

The Wedding Performance

The Materassi sisters' performance of femininity reaches its absurd yet tragicomic heights on the occasion of Remo and Peggy's wedding, where Teresa and Carolina present themselves as aging brides, dressed in parodic wedding gowns.

> Le Materassi indossavano l'abito di raso bianco rituale, tutte coperte da un lungo velo appuntato sopra la testa, e con una coda lunghissima ... Avevano nei capelli dei mazzettini di fiori d'arancio, e fiori di arancio portavano alla vita, sul petto, in fondo alle sottane. (776)

> [The Materassis were wearing the ritual garment of white satin and were completely covered with long veils fastened on their heads; they also wore very long trains ... They had little bunches of orange blossom in their hair, and wore orange blossom at their waists, at their breasts, and at the edges of their skirts.]

The mock brides, however, are repeatedly described as corpse-like objects of ridicule; for them, Remo's marriage is not a celebration of life, it signals instead their own death-like state ('Le loro faccie erano di un pallore funebre, gli occhi fissi, le bocche contratte' (787) [Their faces were of a deathly pallor, their eyes stared fixedly, their mouths were pinched]), a trope developed further in the latter part of the text, as witnessed in the last section's title: 'Sepolte vive' [Buried Alive].

The sisters' performance forms part of the general spectacle that is Remo and Peggy's nuptials. The locals congregate along the via Settignanese early that morning to witness the scene; thus, the wedding party has an audience. Throughout the event, Teresa and Carolina console themselves by repeating to each other that Remo does not actually love Peggy, that it is a marriage of convenience. But their comments, says the narrator, would only make Peggy laugh if she understood them: 'Quello che per esse era il dramma in cui erano impegnate fino all'ultima goccia di sangue, sarebbe stato per lei una nuova ragione di allegria' (785) [What, for them, was a drama in which they were concerned to the last drop of their blood, for her would have been merely another cause for laughter]. The wedding, therefore, is a drama for Teresa and Carolina in which they, too, are actors. Remo and Peggy, moreover, are mistaken for film stars when they arrive at the wedding, with Peggy being compared to Greta Garbo ('È Greta Garbo! È Greta Garbo – ripetevano le ragazze affascinate ... E rivolte allo sposo sussurravano a bassa voce i nomi di tutti i divi che popolavano i loro sogni' (780) [the girls kept repeating: 'Greta Garbo! Greta Garbo!' ... And turning their attention to the bridegroom, they whispered the names of all the male stars that thronged their dreams]). In another instance Remo is likened to Valentino (as well as other Hollywood leading men, 765–6), an icon whose sexuality can be considered ambiguous, as is true of Garbo.

In fact, virtually none of the characters presented in *Sorelle Materassi* exhibit a cut-and-dried version of heterosexist normativity; Palazzeschi is intent on presenting an alternative vision of sexuality. As I have already discussed at length, Teresa and Carolina are female stand-ins for the author, and while they openly admire young men, they themselves have no sexual experience and reminisce about a non-existent romantic past during their performances at the window. Niobe, their domestic help, was seduced by two separate men in different periods of her life, gave up the two children she gave birth to as a result of these affairs, but nonetheless continues to display an unabashed (yet unrequited) admiration for men – in particular Remo – and disdain for women. The youngest Materassi sister, Giselda, in contrast, despises all men after her unsuccessful marriage to a philanderer who has squandered all his money; defeated and embittered, she resents Teresa and Carolina's fixation on their nephew. Remo's sexuality, as described above, has connotations both of Fascist virility as well as homosexuality, and even effeminacy in some instances. His side-kick Palle seeks no other companionship except Remo's and has an almost religious adoration for his mother. These, and even other, minor characters (such as the local priest or the Russian countess) display, or at the very least hint at, sexual alterity.

The House as Prison

The closing sequences of the novel depict the sisters' changed circumstances spatially. After the wedding the sisters return to the house, increasingly portrayed as closing in on them (hence the section title 'Buried Alive'). The new owners of their former farm and residences next door (in earlier times rented out by Teresa and Carolina) have erected a wall alongside the Materassis' house:

> Sulla linea dov'era il muretto basso, coi vasi poco rigogliosi davanti alla casa, avevano alzato un muro alto due metri e cinquanta, che partendo dal cancello andava lungh'essa incassandola, formandole davanti un cortiletto a andito, togliendo respiro e luce a tutto il pianterreno che ora, con le sue inferriate, sembrava un convento, per non dire una prigione.
> Era stato murato anche l'usciolino della cucina che dava sul campo. (797)
>
> [On the line where the low wall had been, with its not very imposing vases, in front of the house, there was now a wall nearly ten feet high which, starting from the iron gate and running right along, formed a narrow passage in front of the house, shutting it in completely and taking away all light and air from the ground floor, which now, with its rusty gratings, really looked like a convent, not to say a prison.
> The little door leading from the kitchen into the fields at the back had also been walled up.]

The house's confines have shrunk so much as to encroach on the sister's territory and obstruct their view, graphically illustrating the oppressiveness of their penury. The domestic walls have thus become associated – as is commonly done – with female imprisonment within the confines of the home.

In these final scenes Teresa and Carolina return to the same routine as before Remo's arrival, that of staying within the house and emerging only to go to Sunday mass. Yet in this instance their domestic confinement is not a result of a strict work regimen; they go out as little as possible because, now that they are financially disgraced, they are embarrassed to be seen by their former tenants. They no longer stand at the window which, in earlier days, had provided them with a vantage point, allowing them to look down at people beneath them, thus underscoring their sense of superiority. Instead, subsequent to their financial ruin, they are forced to keep it closed because of disparaging comments that filter in from those standing below it, or because of the off-putting smell of manure used by Fellino, the new owner of the property next door, on the vegetable beds that have replaced the linden trees he chopped down. And after the final showdown with their embittered sister Giselda, Teresa and Carolina see her off, hurling insults, gripping the gate which will not stay shut, and shouting at the crowd that has gathered. The bystanders 'le stavano a guardare tenendosi a distanza, impauriti e annichiliti, quasi fossero state due belve che tentavano di squassare la gabbia per divorarli furiosamente' (817) [motionless and breathless, stood watching them, keeping at a distance, frightened, humiliated, just as though they were two wild beasts trying to break out of their cage and devour them]. Thus, the Materassi sisters have been metaphorically reduced to animals in a cage, and Niobe arrives with chains that she wraps around the front gate and padlocks shut.

It is at this stage that the Materassi sisters have reached rock bottom and Niobe suggests the solution of their sewing for local women. The doors of the Materassis' house therefore open again, only now to working-class and rural clientele, the novel's conclusion thus indicating that they will most likely overcome their economic hardship. The enlarged portrait of the semi-nude Remo stands over their workroom, a reminder of the cause of their ruin but also of their self-deluded happiness. The novel's closure is typical of Palazzeschi's melancholic humour, as are the Materassi sisters themselves, these pathetic yet comic figures. Teresa and Carolina are no doubt a veil for Palazzeschi's own identity, yet, one could argue, their portrayal as ridiculous, infantilized old women is essentially misogynistic and it is perhaps surprising that he should choose to depict himself via such figures. Indeed, Palazzeschi's apparent sexism in this novel, as well as in many other texts (for example, *Interrogatorio della Contessa Maria*) renders his prose, at least in my experience as reader, deeply problematic at times, in his resorting to stereotypically disparaging images of women. On the other hand, E.M. Forster's use of an intelligent, attractive, and, by-and-large, likeable young woman as a filter to embody a sexual awakening (quite likely associated with his own experience in Italy), that of Lucy Honeychurch in *A Room with a View* (a text examined in greater detail in chapter 4), provides an interesting contrast for such a textual strategy. The Forsterian heroine may be shown to possess flaws and some amusing aspects, but she is never presented as having such negative associations as those of the Palazzeschian sisters, despite embodying an analogous function, that of stand-in for the author's masked homosexuality.

However, notwithstanding the undignified and almost derogatory portrayal of the Materassi sisters, the two women – emblems of Palazzeschi's poetics of difference – easily garner the reader's sympathy, possibly precisely because their marginalization, their fey alterity, are something to which we can relate, in our own individuated sense of difference. Furthermore, the fact that the Materassi sisters are willing victims of their nephew's exploitation, and that Remo himself is a manipulator, complicates the situation further, making us wonder if their representation might not reflect a certain authorial ambivalence about his own sexuality in presenting such an ambiguous object of desire. Palazzeschi does not leave the reader with clear-cut solutions, just as he plays with rigidly defined dichotomies such as hetero/homosexual, old/young, male/female, reality/fantasy, upper/lower class, stretching and blurring the boundaries between them, teasing them out in his textual spaces.

3 Vasco Pratolini's Florentine Spaces of Exclusion

Like his fellow Florentine, Palazzeschi, Vasco Pratolini is fascinated with portraying spaces of marginalization and alterity, locating them primarily in the periphery in his novel *La costanza della ragione* (The Constancy of Reason, 1963). Pratolini's in-between zones represent not so much the author's own sense of alienation as his interest in accentuating the Other, an Other predicated on ethnic, sexual, or gender difference. For Pratolini, Florentine neighbourhoods – be they central or suburban – are imbued with these concerns.

Indeed, Pratolini's fiction obsessively returns to his native city. In fact, the majority of his works are set in streets of which he had firsthand knowledge, having actually resided there in his youth. Thus, Florence has played a key role in nearly all of Pratolini's oeuvre, from one of his first prose works, *Via de' Magazzini* (1942, later appearing in *Diario sentimentale* [Sentimental Diary, 1956]), named after the street (just off the Piazza della Signoria) where he once lived as a child, to his best-known and most successful novel, *Cronache di poveri amanti* (A Tale of Poor Lovers, 1947), to his later literary production.[1] This intimate familiarity with place is displayed, moreover, in the author's meticulous toponymical mapping in many of his Florentine texts, a symptom of his Neo-Realist formation that privileges mimetic detail, a technique especially discernible in his early fiction.[2]

Il Quartiere (The Neighbourhood, 1944), for instance, takes place in the mid-1930s in the neighbourhood near Santa Croce that was destroyed under the Fascist regime's plan of 'risanamento' or supposed modernization. The novel's action revolves around the modest neighbourhood that reflects the residents' working-class condition, while simultaneously symbolizing a sense of solidarity against Fascist hegemony. From the novel's opening ('Noi eravamo contenti del nostro Quartiere' [*Romanzi I* 299] [We were happy about our Neighbourhood]) to its conclusion, the primacy of place is made explicit:

> Andavamo, tacendo, alta la testa, per le strade del Quartiere popolato della sua gente ... E Marisa disse:
> 'Hai trovato diverso il Quartiere. Ma la gente c'è ancora tutta, lo sai. Si è ammassata nelle case rimaste in piedi come se si fosse voluta barricare. Quei pochi che sono andati ad abitare alla periferia, dove c'è l'aria aperta e il sole, nel Quartiere li considerano quasi dei disertori.'
> 'Infatti' le risposi. 'Anche l'aria e il sole sono cose da conquistare dietro le barricate.' (*Romanzi I* 471)

> [We walked, without speaking, our heads held high, through the streets of the Neighbourhood, populated by its inhabitants ... And Marisa said:
> 'You've found the Neighbourhood changed. But you know, everyone is still here. They've gathered in the houses that are still standing as if barricading themselves in. The few who have gone to live in the outskirts, where there's fresh air and sunshine, are practically considered deserters by people in the Neighbourhood.'
> 'That's true,' I replied. 'Even the air and sunshine are things that need to be won behind the barricades.']

In these, the protagonist's (and the novel's) final words, Valerio, having returned to Florence after his military service, voices the communal sense of opposition to Fascism and locates it within the confines of his neighbourhood. The novel concludes before the onset of the Second World War, hence his allusion to the local struggle that will be necessary in order to overthrow the regime and regain basic civil rights.

The same esprit de corps animates Pratolini's subsequent novel, *Cronache di poveri amanti* (1947), which features a little-known but centrally located street, via del Corno, situated behind the Palazzo Vecchio.[3] Despite its proximity to the seat of local government, via del Corno constitutes a space of marginalization for its inhabitants in which debris and signs of abjection are figured, as if to stress the people's humble condition.[4] Descriptions of via del Corno often focus on its rubbish and the bad smells that emanate from it:

> Nel vicolo dietro Palazzo Vecchio i gatti disfanno i fagotti dell'immondizia ... È maggio, e nell'aria notturna, senza alito di vento, affiorano i cattivi odori. Davanti alla mascalcia è accumulato lo sterco dei cavalli ferrati

durante la giornata. Il monumentino, all'angolo di via dei Leoni, è colmo e straripa ormai da mesi. I fagotti e le biche della spazzatura domestica sono stati seminati fuori delle porte come di consueto. (*Romanzi I* 591)

[In the narrow street behind the Palazzo Vecchio the cats tear up the bundles of rubbish ... It is May, and in the nocturnal air, without a breath of wind, bad odours come out. The excrement of the horses that have been shod that day is piled up in front of the blacksmith's. The urinal, at the corner of via dei Leoni, is full and has been overflowing for months. Bundles and heaps of domestic waste have been strewn outside the doorways, as usual.]

This emphasis on the physical detritus of via del Corno also calls into play the degeneracy of certain residents, such as the local prostitutes at the Albergo Cervia, or the debauched Nesi and the corrupt Signora, doyenne of the street.[5]

This chapter concentrates on a text that has received somewhat less critical attention than other works by Pratolini, perhaps in part because of its chronological setting (post–Second World War rather than at the time of the Fascist regime) and its protagonist, Bruno, who in some respects can be considered a morally indistinct character. Yet, *La costanza della ragione*, written in 1962, published the following year, and winner of the Premio Marzotto, inscribes a peculiar Florentine space that merits investigation.[6] Rather than focusing on such central and historic neighbourhoods as Santa Croce, depicted in *Il Quartiere*, or the via del Corno of *Cronache di poveri amanti*, the Florence it presents is quite unlike that which readers familiar with Pratolini's other works might expect, since the narrative action of *La costanza della ragione* takes place in the years leading up to and during Italy's *miracolo economico*,[7] in Rifredi, the heart of the city's industrial quarter, as Parronchi has noted:

La zona di Firenze che interessa il romanzo è nuova rispetto ai libri precedenti. La realtà del 'quartiere' è sempre stata l'unità di misura topo-somatica dei personaggi di Pratolini ... La *Costanza della ragione*, nuova cronaca di vita popolare, si svolge nella zona industriale fiorentina, una zona industriale ridotta rispetto a quella delle grandi città, ma pure piccola metropoli, universo per chi ci vive. (XIII)

[The area of Florence which interests this novel is new with respect to his previous books. The reality of the 'neighbourhood' has always been the toposomatic unit of measurement of Pratolini's characters ... *La Costanza della ragione*, a new chronicle of working-class life, takes place in the industrial zone of Florence, a limited industrial zone when compared to large cities, but nonetheless a small metropolis, a universe, for those who live there.]

Finocchiaro Chimirri also mentions the importance of Florence and, more specifically, industrial Florence, in the novel:

> Firenze è quasi la condizione ispirativa di Pratolini: da viverci lontano e rivivere nella memoria il suo egoismo, i suoi tratti generosi, le fervide stagioni, l'eterna vicenda della città moderna e operaia: come egli torna a raffigurarla attraverso il giovane protagonista della *Costanza*, coi suoi slanci e rivolte, con le sue amicizie e i suoi amori di ragazzo di quartiere ... Sono, in questo libro, freschissime pagine dedicate alla Firenze suburbana, a certe aperture di paesaggio tra urbano e campestre, a certi notturni di strade cittadine, a certi interni squallidi e dignitosi. (138–9)

> [Florence is almost an inspirational condition for Pratolini: to be lived from a distance, and to relive in memory its egotism, its generous aspects, its lively seasons, the eternal narrative of the modern, working-class city: that is how he goes back to representing it through the young protagonist of *La costanza*, with his sudden impulses and rebellions, with his friendships and his loves typical of the local boy ... In this book you will find the freshest of pages dedicated to suburban Florence, to certain stretches of landscape between the urban and the rural, to certain interiors which are squalid yet dignified.]

Finocchiaro Chimirri does well to point out the novelty of the spatial configurations of *La costanza della ragione*, especially since critics for the most part have tended to direct their attention primarily to Florence's traditional neighbourhoods when interpreting Pratolini's texts, as is the case with Carlo Cresti's 'Vasco Pratolini e l'architettura: La città, il quartiere, la strada, la casa' (Vasco Pratolini and Architecture: The City, the Neighbourhood, the Street, the House),[8] and Alessandra Gabelli's 'Un luogo di Firenze: Via del Corno nella vita e nell'opera di Vasco Pratolini' (A Florentine Place: Via del Corno in the Life and Works of Vasco Pratolini), or of Anthony Costantini who, in his 'Il paesaggio nella narrativa del primo Pratolini' (Landscape in Pratolini's Early Fiction), focuses on the writer's earlier works that explore the city centre and its ties to the past, or the more bucolic surroundings of the outlying hills.

La costanza della ragione presents a contrasting vision of Florence in its concentration on the outskirts, on suburban zones heretofore ignored by Pratolini, making a contextualization and analysis of Rifredi's importance to the novel worth undertaking. Moreover, the industrial Florence Pratolini delineates in *La costanza della ragione* is significant precisely because it explores spaces that most literature on the quintessential Renaissance *polis* generally ignores: spaces of the factory, of the periphery, and of marginalization. Furthermore, Pratolini's industrial Florence reveals a concern with the economic, political, and social context in which it is set and themes of socio-geographical exclusion common to Pratolini's work resurface more acutely still in this novel, along with an even greater engagement with questions of alterity.

La costanza della ragione reveals a fixation on the Other, be it in terms of gender, race, or sexual orientation, and even regarding age. The interpersonal relationships revolve around an ethically ambiguous protagonist who in certain instances could be categorized as sexist, racist, or homophobic, and at other moments might seem to hold a moral high ground, one seemingly aligned with authorial point of view. The spaces certain characters are found in or inhabit often reflect their marginalization, especially from the male protagonist's perspective, and are frequently signalled by elements denoting abjection, as I endeavour to illustrate in my analysis. Indeed, the discourse of alterity is marked by an insistence on a lexicon relating to notions of purity/cleanliness/health/youth versus defilement/dirt/disease/old age, indicative of the opposition between 'us' and 'them' endorsed by the novel's hero in particular.

The story is narrated by nineteen-year-old Bruno Santini, who lives with his mother Ivana in a relatively new building in the recently developed industrial quarter of Rifredi. Through a complicated series of flashbacks, Bruno traces his life from infancy to the fictional present (1960), when he and his mother engage in a sustained dialogue, comparable to psychoanalytic sessions (Bertoncini 195).[9] For years, the somewhat unstable Ivana has deluded herself that her husband, Bruno's father – long since dead – could still return from Africa, where he fought as a soldier during the Second World War. His 'surrogate' father and ideological mentor, Millo(schi), exerts a pivotal role in Bruno's development, until one day the fifteen-year-old boy confronts him, reproaching him for having an affair with his mother and hypocritically refusing to admit it (an unfounded accusation, as it later turns out), thus distancing himself from the man who has introduced him to Marxist ideas and imbued him with a strong work ethic and aspirations for a job in the local optics factory, 'le Officine Galileo' or 'la Gali,'[10] where Millo himself works (see figure 3).

Figure 3 Workers leaving the Officine Galileo, Viale Morgagni, 1963

The adolescent Bruno has a series of relationships, starting with a brief affair with a Greek immigrant, Elettra,[11] and later with another young woman from the same community, Rosaria. All this takes place alongside his friendships with Armando (son of a restaurant owner), Dino (who we learn later is gay), Gioe (the son of an African-American GI and a Neapolitan prostitute), and Benito (a young neo-fascist). Bruno's most significant relationship, however, is with Lori, a young woman from his neighbourhood, who dies of tuberculosis and, he learns (when she is on her deathbed), has been sexually involved with her brother-in-law, despite her love for Bruno. The story concludes roughly a year after Lori's death, with Bruno's imminent employment at la Gali, a lifelong ambition about to be fulfilled, and his mother fully 'healed' of her delusion that her deceased husband will return.

The novel encompasses themes typical of Pratolini's oeuvre: his fascination with memory, youth, illness (stemming from his own experience of tuberculosis), death, and sexuality, for instance, is evident in this and in many of his other works. Also, other standard Pratolinian ideological concerns are revealed in the post-war fascist/anti-fascist debate, as Bruno befriends Benito, the troubled son of a *squadrista*, and the two spend much time in dialogue, in an effort to figure out their political allegiances. Benito dies, however, serving in the Foreign Legion, and the novel concludes with Bruno joining the Communist party, in part to atone for his allowing the local priest who runs an orphanage (Don Bonifazi, modelled on the actual Don Facibeni of the Opera della Madonnina del Grappa) to put in a good word for him at the Officine Galileo.[12]

The 'Officine Galileo': Socio-economic Context and the Space of the Factory

The 'Officine Galileo' has a central function in the text, for it is where Bruno's father was employed before leaving for Africa, it is where Millo works for many years, and it is where Bruno hopes to work, too, since, he believes, his place should be guaranteed not only because of his skill and good performance, but also because he considers it his father's legacy. Founded in 1860, and later located in Rifredi (until 1980), la Galileo assumes paternal connotations for Bruno, as he associates it with Milloschi's voice, after their rift and before their eventual rapprochement:

> E come sono mescolati a quell'età sentimenti e ragioni, ogni sera, mentre suonavano le sirene, pensavo a Millo. Un tuffo al cuore che il mio orgoglio fronteggiava fino a soffocarlo in un angolo buio della coscienza, nella parte più nera di noi, dove a noi stessi spaventa guardare. Era così, come se l'ululo della Gali fosse la sua voce che mi chiamava, la sua mano che mi colpiva la nuca, il puzzo del suo sigaro che mi saliva alle nari. (125)

> [And as emotions and reasons at that age are mixed, every night, when the sirens wailed, I would think of Millo. My heart would miss a beat, and my pride would confront it to the point of suffocating it in a dark corner of my conscience, in the blackest part within ourselves, where we ourselves are frightened to look. That's how it was, as if the Gali's howl was his voice calling me, his hand hitting the back of my neck, the stench of his cigar rising to my nostrils.]

The factory siren thus becomes the voice of Bruno's conscience, as he cannot help but equate Milloschi with la Gali and regrets their falling out.

Yet Milloschi's own relationship with the factory is in reality conflicted, since he loses his job there as a consequence of his directing protests against the massive layoffs announced by the administration. In fact, Bruno's association with Milloschi subsequently leads to the young man not being hired, since he, too, is considered a potential agitator. The narrator of *La costanza della ragione* describes the managerial mentality of the Galileo and the firing of those workers deemed a threat, Millo included: 'ora che il lavoro c'era, ora che i licenziamenti erano sospesi, si procede alla 'disinfestazione.' Non ci si assicura la normalità della vita aziendale finché sussistono nel suo seno gli agitatori ... Perciò, fuori i militanti più accesi ... Così per Millo, una vampata di paglia, nonostante l'affetto e il prestigio di cui godeva' (185). [Now that there was work, now that the sackings had been suspended, there was a move towards 'disinfestation.' The normality of company life is not assured so long as agitators are in its midst ... Therefore, out with the most fervent militants ... And that's how it went up in smoke for Millo, despite the affection and prestige that he enjoyed.]

This kind of action typifies the general attitude of private industry towards trade unions during the *miracolo economico*, as Sassoon clarifies:

> The only long-term trade-union policy private industry adopted was that of trying to deepen the divisions within the labour movement: it sought to strengthen the Catholic trade union (the CISL) and the social-democratic one (the UIL) against the CGIL (socialist and communist) by sacking communist shop stewards and trade unionists or shifting them to the most demanding jobs or to self-enclosed sections of the plants. (Sassoon 43)

Milloschi's circumstances indeed reflect the actual events of the late 1950s: on 15 November 1958 the Officine Galileo announced that 980 workers would lose their jobs. After several months of protests and strikes, supported also by many citizens of Florence, the majority were rehired or relocated, and the final number of layoffs became 64.[13] Labour protests such as these were not of course confined to the Officine Galileo; other Florentine companies such as Nuova Pignone underwent similar labour disputes during those years, as did industries throughout the country.[14]

The impact of the Officine Galileo on the local area cannot be underestimated; Bruno's mother and Milloschi demonstrate an awareness of the symbolic importance of the factory when discussing Bruno's career choices with him early on in the novel. Ivana says: 'Tu vuoi entrare alla Gali, sissignore, per chi nasce a Rifredi è un destino ... Non c'è altro di più grande per un rifredino, la Gali è l'universo, la Gali è la mecca, la Gali è tutta la vita' (69). ['You want to go to the Gali, yessir, for those born in Rifredi it's destiny ... There's nothing greater for people from Rifredi, the Gali is the universe, the Gali is Mecca, the Gali is all of life.'] Milloschi agrees:

> 'Pressappoco' Millo aggiunse. 'È un simbolo, oltre che il pane. Questi ragazzi ci arrivano con l'istinto alla verità delle cose. Se non vogliamo contare che è una delle industrie più perfezionate. Ora magari è un po' invecchiata, avrebbe bisogno di una nuova strutturazione.'

> ['More or less,' added Millo. 'It's a symbol, as well as our daily bread. These kids reach the truth of things through instinct. And we could add that it's one of the most specialized industries. Now perhaps it has aged a bit, it could use being renovated.']

The above dialogue precedes a watershed moment for Bruno, for in this exchange he manages to convince his mother and Millo that his studies are less important than being hired at la Gali, and so Ivana agrees to rule out his furthering his education beyond secondary school, regardless of his evident aptitude for learning, and thus his fate is sealed.

While it may be the much-desired goal for the youth of Rifredi, the Gali constitutes a problematic presence. It can be both protective and discriminatory (as Finocchiaro Chimirri points out [148]), a stance confirmed by the initial rejection of Bruno as an employee, despite his evident qualifications. In effect, the Galileo, in its simultaneous presence and absence (we never actually enter the factory as readers nor do we witness Bruno working there), can be seen to stand for the paternal, inasmuch as Bruno's father worked there before disappearing in Africa, and his surrogate father Milloschi is eventually laid off after many years there. The Gali therefore constitutes an authoritarian and conflicted emblem for Bruno, despite his evident idealization of it.[15]

Urban Peripheries

Even though, in some respects, it represents an absence, the Galileo (as well as other Florentine industries) leaves an imprint on the urban topography. The novel's landscapes are dominated by images of the periphery and its factories: 'C'è sempre un cielo grigio e celeste al di sopra del davanzale, gli alberi sono sempre verdi, le ciminiere rosse, i capannoni di lamiera, il canneto luccica e il vento lo scuote' (27) [The sky above the window ledge is always grey and blue, the trees are always green, the smokestacks red, the factory sheds made of sheet-metal, the canebrake sparkles and the wind shakes it]. Many descriptions also involve aural elements, such as the sound of factory sirens, or crowds, with scenes of workers on their way to the plant on their bicycles. Furthermore, Bruno and his friends prefer their own area and its industries to the historic monuments of Florence, such as the Duomo of Santa Maria del Fiore, mentioned only once, when Bruno and Lori stop to look at the panorama from the hill of Fiesole:

> Sotto di noi, la distesa dei tetti, con le cime dei campanili, delle torri, e il grande uovo della cupola, non faceva nessuna impressione, colpiva invece il giro delle colline dove il verde e il nero della vegetazione superstite, spiccava in quella luce azzurrina, contro un cielo laminato che teneva nascosto il sole.
> 'Bello' lei disse 'ma è tutto fermo, pare ci manchi qualcosa.'
> 'Le ciminiere e i capannoni di Rifredi.'
> 'Vista così, una città rassomiglia a un camposanto, sembra che la gente ci viva sotterrata.' (158)
>
> [Below us, the expanse of roofs, with the spires of belfries and towers, and the large egg of the cupola, made no impression. What was striking instead was the ring of hills, where the green and the black of the surviving vegetation stuck out in that bluish light against a laminated sky which kept the sun hidden.
> 'Beautiful,' she said, 'but everything is still, it's like something is missing.'
> 'The smokestacks and factory floors of Rifredi.'
> 'Seen from up here, a city resembles a graveyard, it's as if people live buried beneath it.']

Bruno and Lori perceive the distinctive medieval-Renaissance features of the Florentine skyline as static, dead, and yet it is these landmarks that guarantee the city's legibility, as Kevin Lynch has pointed out:

> The Duomo of Florence is a prime example of a distant landmark: visible from near and far, by day or night; unmistakable; dominant by size and contour; closely related to the city's traditions; coincident with the religious and transit center; paired with its campanile in such a way that the direction of view can be gauged from a distance. It is difficult to conceive of the city without having this great edifice come to mind. (Lynch 82)

In a rejection of the typically aestheticized gaze, Brunelleschi's dome, the object of so much admiration by tourists and scholars alike, is disparagingly compared to an egg by the narrator/protagonist, and Florence's city centre is likened to a cemetery, Lori's morbid statement essentially prefiguring her own demise. Just as the youth of Rifredi idealize their local factories, the young Bruno and Lori evidently favour Florence's modern, industrialized periphery with its recent constructions over the city's historic past.

Another example of this attitude occurs during their visit to Pisa's Campo dei Miracoli (again a sightseer's paradise), which leads them to reflect on their own native city:

'Secondo te' ella mi chiede 'è più bella questa torre come il campanile di Giotto, o un grattacielo?'

'Non c'è paragone.' Questa è roba, rifletto, che si lascia solo guardare. Forse a chi è istruito gli dà una vera emozione, il segno di un'epoca, li chiamano stili. Come il nostro campanile, le chiese, i palazzi di Firenze, infatti, dei quali siamo fieri. Si ammirano, e poi? È un fatto di cultura, io credo, e almeno per ora, non ci posso arrivare. M'interesserebbe semmai sapere quanta gente ci lavorò, quanto buscava e quanta ne morì nel corso dei lavori. Oggi a cosa serve? Per salirvi in cima e godere il panorama, non ha altra funzione. Mentre in un grattacielo! Lì c'è formicolio di persone tutte con degli incarichi precisi. Sono costruzioni fatte perché gli uomini di oggi li animino coi loro traffici e le loro beghe, la luce entra da tutte le parti, ci sono mobili moderni, i cervelli elettronici, gli indici di produzione. (224)

['Which do you think is more beautiful,' she asks me, 'this tower, like Giotto's bell-tower, or a skyscraper?'

'There's no comparison.' This stuff, I reflected, is only for looking at. Perhaps to a cultured person it gives true emotion, the sign of an epoch, styles, they call them. Like our bell-tower, the churches, the palaces of Florence, in fact, of which we are proud. We admire them, and then what? It's a question of culture, I think, and at least for now, I can't get there. I'd rather know how many people worked on it, how much they earned and how many died while building it. What use is it now? For climbing up to the top and enjoying the view, it has no other function. But a skyscraper, that's another story! It's crawling with people, all with specific responsibilities. They are constructions made so that men of today will animate them with their commerce and their troubles, light enters from everywhere, there is modern furniture, computers, indicators of production.]

Bruno and Lori continuously associate the urban past and its monuments with the superfluous, and the new with vitality, usefulness, and functionality, in a characteristic Pratolinian analogy between the old (associated with death) and the young (representative of life). Paradoxically, however, Bruno's words illustrate the ambiguity of his position; despite his Marxist tendencies – illustrated by his thoughts on the labour that has gone into the construction of the old monuments – he forgets the oppression of workers involved in building modern structures, and ignores the fact that the skyscrapers he prefers are most likely destined to be inhabited or worked in primarily by those more affluent than himself. Bruno's reflections seem to echo mantras of modernity and productivity typical of the *miracolo economico*, a growth period that, however, as is commonly known, did not benefit the average worker.

In-between Zones: Spaces of Marginalization and Difference

Certain sections of the suburban, industrial quarters of Florence in *La costanza della ragione* can also be considered in-between zones, areas not wholly associated with the country or the city, such as the grass under the nearby railway bridge, or outlying fields, or the banks of the small Mugnone and Terzolle rivers, frequented by ambiguous Others (for example, a fisherman with a pirate-like eye-patch), places where Bruno plays as a child, supervised by the mentally ill Signora Cappugi:

> Staccavo la corsa dando calci ai barattoli di cui era cosparso il prato; mi fermavo per sorprendere i ramarri, ma come le nostre ombre la sera, non si lasciavano schiacciare. Uno stecco dietro l'altro, ostacolavo il via vai delle formiche; facevo casematte di sassi; e coi barattoli, dei torrioni che franavano al quinto o sesto piano. Oppure seguivo il fumo delle ciminiere senza mai riuscire a cogliere il momento in cui la coda veniva inghiottita dal cielo. Gli aeroplani – i trimotori, i caccia, gli Hurricane, come zio Millo mi aveva insegnato – passavano altissimi, avanti di scavalcare Monte Morello, mentre le rondini, a stormi, calavano più basse e io indovinavo la direzione verso la quale avrebbero virato. Quindi raccoglievo margherite e fili d'erba, i papaveri, gli asfodeli, li strappavo con fatica e messo insieme un mazzetto, tornavo correndo dalla vecchia sedutasi dignitosamente su un fusto arrugginito. (30)

> [I would burst into a run, kicking cans that were strewn across the field; I would stop to take lizards by surprise, but like our shadows in the evening,

they would not let themselves be squashed. With one twig behind another, I would block the ants' comings and goings; I would make casemates of stones; and with the cans, I made towers which would collapse at the fifth or sixth floor. Or I would follow the smoke from the smokestacks without ever capturing the moment in which the tail was swallowed up by the sky. The aeroplanes – triple engines, fighter planes, Hurricanes, as Uncle Millo had taught me – passed, high above, before going over Monte Morello, while the swallows in flocks would dip lower and lower and I would guess the direction in which they would turn. Then I would pick daisies, blades of grass, poppies, asphodels, I would tear them out with some difficulty and after putting together a little bunch, I would run back to the old lady who was sitting decorously on a rusty barrel.]

These areas, neither wholly urban nor purely bucolic, are mixtures of signs of industry (smokestacks, waste) and technological innovation (planes overhead), on the one hand, and indices of nature (daisies, grass, poppies, asphodels, lizards, ants, swallows), on the other, therefore defying categorization as strictly country or city.

Yet Florence's suburbs can also lead to disorientation, as is the case when Signora Cappugi becomes lost with Bruno:

La sera viene all'improvviso siccome si sono accesi i lampioni; e verso casa c'è un velo di nebbia, ma non ci s'entra mai dentro, come fossimo noi a scostarlo e a farlo allontanare ... Si cammina e cammina, io tremo e vorrei soffiarmi il naso; la signora Elvira è ammutolita: va diritta e biascica la sua pasticca ... Si avanza sullo sterrato, completamente al buio, ogni tanto passano dei ciclisti col lumicino. Ci sono delle ombre e dei bisbigli; i buoi mugghiano e i cani abbaiano, ma di lontano. Finché ci troviamo in mezzo a un prato, coi piedi nel fango e davanti a noi un fossato ... Non ci sono più case, la nebbia è sempre più vicina, si sale per un viottolo, casco e mi riprendo, ho le mani piene di mota. Nemmeno la vecchia si regge, slitta e agitando le braccia, fa all'indietro il sentiero, sparisce mentre la sento che grida: 'Dio, Dio, Dio!' (39)

[The evening comes on suddenly since the streetlights have gone on; and on the way home there is a veil of fog, but we never enter it, as if we were pushing it aside and making it go away ... We walk, and we walk, I'm trembling and I wish I could blow my nose; Signora Elvira has gone quiet: she keeps walking straight ahead and sucks away on her pastille ... We move on to the dirt road, in complete darkness, and every now and then cyclists go by with their little lights on. There are shadows and whispers; the cattle moo and the dogs bark, but from afar. Until finally we end up in the middle of a field, with our feet in mud and a ditch before us ... There are no more houses, the fog gets closer and closer, we go up along a path, I fall down and pick myself up again, my hands covered in mud. Not even the old lady manages to stand, she slips and, waving her arms, goes backwards down the path, and disappears while I hear her shouting: 'Oh God! Oh God! Oh God!']

In this particular episode, Florence's periphery assumes menacing connotations, its geography becoming unrecognizable in the misty darkness. Landmarks are indistinguishable, and neither signs of city life (such as streetlights) nor of the countryside (fields, animal noises) suffice for the distraught Signora Cappugi to gain her bearings. She and Bruno become utterly lost, and slip down a bank, where they remain until they are found just before dawn, covered in mud. Thus, the landscape mirrors the mental fog into which Signora Cappugi has descended. During their wanderings, the elderly woman mistakes Bruno for her deceased son, and as a consequence of this delusional episode she ends up in the local mental hospital, where she eventually dies.

Thus, during his childhood and adolescence, Bruno (often along with his friends) is recurrently depicted in a kind of no-man's-land, as he and his chums create spaces of their own, separate from their own houses or families. This hinterland, a kind of urban-rural amalgam that represents the degradation of industry, sharply contrasts with the more rigidly defined areas found in Pratolini's earlier novels, such as *Il quartiere* or *Cronache di poveri amanti*, where urban neighbourhoods are characterized by a sense of rootedness, and are quite distinct from the outlying countryside, which, when mentioned, is described often in Arcadian terms.[16]

Certain Florentine zones in *La costanza della ragione* are even more marginalized and removed than these in-between spaces; they epitomize, I contend, Foucauldian heterotopias, locations inhabited by Others (such as refugees) or places frequented by foreign soldiers and associated with prostitution, such as the Fortezza da Basso, where Signora Cappugi takes Bruno when he is a child and where she engages in black-market dealings as well as palmistry. Signora Cappugi functions as Bruno's guide in this area, and she is in fact labelled in terms that characterize her as an outsider; her fortune-telling leads to comparisons with a gypsy (Bruno remarks that he had 'la funzione del canarino nella gabbia delle zingare'

[35] [the function of the canary in the gypsy-women's cage]), the pirate-like fisherman refers to her as 'la solita Befana' (29) [the usual witch], and one American GI calls her an '*old witch*' (37). Signora Cappugi herself becomes emblematic of the marginalized spaces she frequents (with Bruno in tow), in her representation as hag, excluded because of both her age and her psychological disorder.

Another 'heterotopia' is the area where the Greek immigrants reside, perceived by their Florentine neighbours as a zone of illicit activity. In the comments of the locals, reported in this telling passage, Pratolini elicits the reader's sympathy for the refugees, who are victims of discrimination:

> Durante questo periodo, in una zona isolata, tra gli ultimi prati e il villaggio ospedaliero, erano state portate a termine e consegnate 'le case dei greci.' Sindaco prefetto musiche bandiere, di cui c'era appena giunta l'eco. Come se i profughi che da tanti anni vivevano accasermati, fossero arrivati nottetempo col loro carico di miserie; e i loro traffici: sigarette, scatolame, accendini, dei quali tutta Firenze era al corrente e che rappresentavano la fonte di guadagno di 'codesti pidocchiosi.' Ora avevano trasportato la loro corea in abitazioni civili, nuove, belle, complete di servizi e colorate di marrone, 'quasi una zona residenziale,' ma presto, si prevedeva, come una stalla modello dove gli animali non hanno custodi, sarebbero diventate un sudiciume. 'Gli uomini equivoci, ladri, e le donne puttane.' Qualche centinaio di persone, che si trovarono davanti una specie di cordone sanitario, la diffidenza e il disprezzo della gente di Rifredi. La quale, essi, a loro volta 'chiusi in tribù come gli zingari,' altrettanto immediatamente dimostrarono di ignorare. Il loro mercato lo svolgevano nell'interno della città, in zone ed angoli di strade obbligati; e i vecchi le donne e i ragazzi, stavano come in un fortino dentro il quadrato delle palazzine percorso da vialetti e da aiuole subito appassite e recinto da un basso muro su cui si alzava un'inferriata. Ai tre ingressi c'erano sempre poliziotti in perlustrazione. Come un lebbrosario. (100–1)

> [During this time, in an isolated zone, between the last fields and the hospital complex, 'the Greeks' houses' had been completed and handed over. Mayor, prefect, music, flags, of which we barely heard an echo. As if the refugees who had been living in barracks for many years had just arrived the night before with their burden of miseries; and their trade: cigarettes, boxes, lighters, which all of Florence was aware of and represented the source of income for 'those louses.' Now they had transferred their slum to lovely new civilized houses, complete with modern conveniences and

painted brown, 'almost a residential area,' but soon, it was predicted, much like a model stable where the animals have no caretakers, they would become filthy. 'The men are shady, thieves, and the women are whores.' A few hundred people, who found a kind of sanitary cordoning-off before them: the diffidence and disdain of the people of Rifredi whom the immigrants, 'closed off in tribes like gypsies,' immediately ignored in turn. Their trade took place in the city, in restricted zones and street corners; and the elderly, the women, and the children, lived as if in a fort within the square of buildings crossed by little avenues and flowerbeds which immediately withered, and fenced in by a low wall topped off with iron bars. At the three entrances there were always policemen on patrol. Like a leper colony.]

The Greek community, like most spaces of exclusion, is relegated to the edge of the city and the disparaging observations of the neighbouring Florentine residents exemplify the kinds of opinions commonly held about immigrant populations, and bring to mind similar such attitudes prevalent in Italy today; take, for example, the disparaging remarks about the Greeks being like a 'tribe of gypsies,' or the use of 'corea,' a word meaning slum that developed in the period when Pratolini was writing the text, and clearly indicative as a signifier of ethnic difference.[17] Due to this perception of the immigrants as Others, they are consigned to the bordered areas, literally and metaphorically sectioned off from the rest of the city. While the Greek refugees are now residing in an estate that is considered sanitary and up-to-date, stigmas of immigrants as dirty, animal-like, and sexually uninhibited prevail nonetheless, sentencing them to the realm of the abject. As David Sibley observes: 'Material improvements in housing, water supply and sewage disposal have literally cleaned up the city, but ... places associated with ethnic and racial minorities ... are still tainted and perceived as polluting in racist discourse, and place-related phobias are similarly evident in response to other minorities, like gays and the homeless' (59).

Not surprisingly, then, the Greek community is defined by vocabulary that focuses on questions of hygiene ('cordone sanitario'), and comparisons to a leper colony connote their utter segregation via a metaphor of disease. While the narrator-protagonist's sympathy for the Greek colony can be intuited in the above comments, Bruno's behaviour with respect to Others is, like his perceptions of the family and the factory, ethically ambiguous. Although superficially he might seem not to share these racist categorizations of the Greek community, he nevertheless is guilty of a certain degree of prejudice himself, specifically against gays and prostitutes, but also in his shoddy treatment of the two young Greek women he becomes involved with.

Pratolini's hero's homophobia, moreover, echoes Fascist rhetoric against difference, as evidenced by a further example of his bigotry. Bruno's meeting up by chance with his old friend Dino and his ex-lover, Rosaria, in another space of exclusion, the Cascine (a vast park just outside the city centre and notorious location of the sex trade) brings him to the full realization that Dino is gay and that both he and Rosaria are professional prostitutes. On the evening when Bruno learns that Lori's condition is worsening, he and his old friend Armando go out on the town. While Armando is cruising, their car is approached by Rosaria and Dino, offering their services, unaware of the passengers' identity. Bruno is incensed at what he judges to be moral corruption: 'Adesso non c'è altro al mondo che mi riguarda, al di fuori di Dino e della sua abiezione' (275) [At this moment there is nothing else in the world that concerns me, apart from Dino and his abjection], and he immediately attacks Dino, punching him violently. Here, too, the Other is portrayed in terms of physical and ethical revulsion, with Bruno defining his former friend's homosexuality as 'abject.' Repeatedly Bruno labels threatening otherness in similar terms, for, as David Sibley remarks, 'the urge to make separations, between clean and dirty, ordered and disordered, "us" and "them," that is, to expel the abject, is encouraged in western cultures, creating feelings of anxiety because such separations can never be finally achieved' (Sibley 8).

(Body)spaces of Abjection: Sexuality and Otherness

Bruno's discriminatory stance is evidenced also in his opportunistic use of two young Greek women's bodies. His relationships with Elettra and Rosaria are purely physical; both young women are portrayed as sexually predatory (and even ill, in the case of Elettra's alleged nymphomania) and meet a tragic fate (Elettra's suicide and Rosaria's prostitution). Descriptions of Rosaria (defined as Greek, even though she is Italian-born) are particularly revealing, in that they rely heavily on a lexicon of abjection. In certain instances, Bruno refers repeatedly to her unappealing smell ('il suo forte odore di carne mi ripugnava' [103] [her strong smell of flesh revolted me]. On another occasion, he describes her body as repugnant yet fascinating: 'Il suo contatto, le sue labbra umide, la sua pelle sudata, mi ripugnavano, nondimeno l'ascoltavo, con un compiacimento e un odio che non riuscivo a districare' [121] [Her touch, her moist lips, her sweaty skin, revolted me, and yet I listened to her, with a satisfaction and a hatred that I couldn't disentangle]). Bruno continues to frequent her, despite his mixed feelings of attraction and repulsion: 'ancora oggi sussiste dentro di me lo stesso sentimento odioso e vigliacco di allora, come d'un marciume, a cui di tempo in tempo tornavo, richiamato dal suo lezzo e dalla sua fresca risata' (122) [even today the same odious, cowardly feeling lingers inside me, like a kind of rottenness, to which I returned from time to time, drawn by her stench and her fresh laughter]. Bruno's desire for Rosaria elicits in him a sense of decay (presumably moral, due to his guilty conscience for using her solely for sex), but he breaks off contact with her only once Dino informs him that Rosaria is prostituting herself. The relationship with Rosaria is thus defined through parameters of defilement, and the young woman represents Bruno's phobias regarding female sexuality and ethnic alterity.

This vision of women as sexually corrupt applies also to Lori, Bruno's primary love interest, who keeps hidden from him the truth about her sexual relationship with her brother-in-law. Initially, when the romance between Bruno and Lori is blossoming, a vocabulary of purity underscores her image and the budding relationship itself. In one instance, Lori's cleanliness is contrasted with Elettra and Rosaria: 'Fu dolce, tenera, risentita, come Elettra e come Rosaria insieme, in quel bacio; e tuttavia pulita, naturale' (157) [With that kiss she was sweet, tender, cross, like Elettra and Rosaria rolled into one; and yet clean, natural]. However, from early on Lori fears illness, and orders Bruno not to see her should she ever become sick: 'Noi ci amiamo perché siamo perfetti, mentre la malattia sciupa. Se perdiamo la bellezza e la forza, si appassisce anche nello spirito, è finita ... Io non sopporto l'idea che tu mi possa amare perché ti faccio pena' [We love each other because we're perfect, whereas illness ruins you. If we lose our beauty and our strength, then our spirit will also wither, and we're finished ... I can't stand the thought that you could love me because you feel sorry for me], to which Bruno replies, 'Lori, cos'è questo rancidume?' (181–2) [Lori, why such rancidity?], his use of the word 'rancidity' linking Lori's premonitory fears of illness to the abject. Indeed, by the end of the novel, Lori believes her supposed 'badness' has manifested itself as a virulent disease, and ultimately she dies of tuberculosis.

Lori and the other young female characters of *La costanza della ragione* typify Pratolini's depiction of women, whereby they are often associated with death, as Bertoncini explains:

La fanciulla (ma oltre a lei ogni personaggio femminile di qualche rilievo nella storia sentimentale di Bruno: si pensi ad Elettra) si profila secondo il modello ormai noto delle donne pratoliniane: quello di un segreto, di una prevaricazione subìta, se non di una vera e propria violenza o ... di un segno di morte alle origini della propria vita sentimentale; la circonda un contesto (familiare e/o sociale) sfavorevole o degradato; infine, le è destinato un'insufficienza del compagno nella comprensione e nella compartecipazione. (200–1)

[The young woman (but along with her every female character of importance in Bruno's romantic history: one need think only of Elettra) is portrayed along the lines of the well-known model of Pratolinian women: the model of the secret, of having undergone some offense, if not an actual act of violence, or... of a sign of death at the beginning of her romantic life; she is surrounded by an unfavourable or degraded context (familial and/or social); and, finally, she is destined to have a companion who is deficient in terms of empathy and involvement.]

Clearly, in Lori's case her sickness and demise reflect her moral 'fall,' for initially she is depicted as youthful, fair, and full of life, but by the end of the novel she is reduced to being a diseased body.

While Bruno's and Lori's early sexual encounters take place in the flat he and his friends have rented, tellingly nicknamed 'la tana' ('the cave': an obvious allusion to female sexual organs), she and Bruno are also figured outside. In their last liaison before her illness, they go for a day trip to the seaside and the idealized Lori is described as 'l'emblema della gioventù e della salute' (221) [the symbol of youth and health], and the couple make love in a secluded wooded area. When Lori's condition becomes serious, merely a few days later, she is relegated to internal spaces: first to her own bedroom, then to Careggi, the hospital, an environment that, perceived from Bruno's point of view, prefigures Lori's corporeal deterioration and imminent death: 'C'era un odore freddo, di disinfettante di cibo di orina e di sangue mescolati, così mi sembrava, trattenni il fiato per non ingoiarlo' (281) [There was a cold smell, of disinfectant, food, urine, and blood all mixed together, or at least that's how it seemed to me, and I held my breath so as not to swallow it].

But it is not only the clinical environment that Bruno finds repellent, Lori's body, too, elicits similar feelings, as it has metamorphosed into a grotesque parody of her former beauty. In the semi-darkness of her hospital room, Bruno is shaken at the sight of her; despite this, he says, 'la pietà ... fu più forte dell'orrore' (283) [pity ... was stronger than horror], yet her description does instil horror, as it bears signs of putrefaction. Lori's skin has taken on a bluish tone, her lips are chapped and broken, and in the corner of her eyes 'un umore giallastro, simile a delle lacrime rapprese, come cispa marcita' [a yellowish liquid, like clotted tears, like rotten eye-rheum] has formed (284). Bruno feels revulsion also when touching her: '[l]e toccai la mano, bruciava più dell'ultima volta che l'avevo accarezzata, ma era un fuoco che mi dava dei brividi ora, come se ne provassi repulsione' (284) [I touched her hand, it was burning up even more than the last time I had caressed it, but it was a fire that gave me shivers now, as if she revolted me]. In a rather predictable analogy, Lori's ethical 'male' [badness] has become 'malattia' [illness]. The moribund woman's physically repugnant appearance symbolizes her moral abjection and it immediately precedes Bruno's shocking realization that throughout their four-month relationship she had continued her sexual involvement with her brother-in-law: 'Ella ci amava entrambi, un estremo candore e una cupa dissolutezza coesistevano nella sua anima, il male era dentro di lei, per cui trovavo spaventosamente giusto che lei ora morisse, stravolta in ciò che aveva di più caro: la perfezione e la bellezza del suo corpo' (287) [She loved both of us, an utter purity and a dark dissoluteness coexisted in her soul, the badness was inside her, and for this reason I found it frighteningly just that she should be dying now, so contorted within that which she held most dear: the perfection and beauty of her body]. Lori's image by the end of the novel is the antithesis of the youthful, healthy girl she initially seemed to be, now that Bruno's romanticized vision of her is shattered to such an extent that he views her corporeal demise as deserved.

Yet Rosaria's and Lori's bodies are not the only ones to induce the sensation of disgust: Bruno's mother, Ivana, is repeatedly painted as an aging woman, a mask of her former good looks, on the verge of decrepitude, at the venerable age of thirty-seven:

> Forse non avevo mai visto la sua faccia 'al naturale,' senza creme, ciprie, rimmel e segni di matita: era stranamente diversa, le labbra esangui e la pelle lattiginosa, tirata sulle narici, sulla fronte, sul collo, gli occhi sembravano acquistare una maggiore intensità, nonostante li cerchiassero i calamari, profondi come nere ferite o lividure. Tutto il suo volto appariva più vecchio e più giovane nello stesso tempo, marcato da un'enorme stanchezza che la finezza dei lineamenti stemperava in una grazia quasi infantile. (196)

[Perhaps I had never seen her face 'au naturel,' without creams, face powder, mascara, and cosmetic pencil marks: she was strangely different, with her pale lips and her milky skin, drawn at the nostrils, on her forehead, on her neck; her eyes seemed to acquire greater intensity, despite their being encircled by dark rings, as deep as black wounds or bruises. Her entire face looked older and younger at the same time, marked by terrible fatigue that the fineness of her features softened with an almost child-like grace.]

On another occasion, Bruno notes his mother appearing with 'il solito velo d'untume che le copriva il viso come un sudore artificiale' (215) [the usual veil of grease that covered her face like artificial perspiration], referring to her habit of covering her face in cream.

If, as Kristeva posits, the abject is an essential component of the male's attempt to separate himself from maternal Otherness, namely, from the body of the (m)other,[18] then perhaps this serves to explain Bruno's obsession with impurity, and his linking of the bodies of his mother, and his lovers, to the realm of the abject. Kelly Oliver elucidates: 'The abject is on the borderline, and as such it is both fascinating and terrifying. Ultimately, the abject is identified with the maternal body since the uncertain boundary between maternal body and infant provides the primary experience of both horror and fascination' (Oliver 225).

Once the separation from his mother has been effected, in an explosive confrontation where he obliges her to admit that Moreno (her husband and Bruno's father) has been dead for years, Bruno and Ivana can finally communicate as adults ('Sei diventato un uomo a furia di patire' [233] [you have become a man through suffering], she tells him). Bruno is now able to sanction her potential relationship with Millo, declaring that, as he is about to begin working at the Officine Galileo, he could soon move into a flat on his own. Significantly, a few months after Lori's death, the reader learns, Bruno has started seeing a fifteen-year-old girl named Maria, a name that readily evokes the idea of virginity, in what is obviously a rejection of the threatening sexuality of his former lovers. In effect, Bruno's relationships reflect the Madonna/whore dichotomy so prevalent in Pratolini's prose, with women being classified above all in these two categories. And while Pratolini the author's ideology is manifestly anti-Fascist, his vision of women often reiterates Fascist norms of womanhood, whereby they are classified either as sexually uninhibited, corrupt, and diseased or, in contrast, as virginal, naive, healthy.

The character of Bruno Santini is, therefore, fundamentally ambivalent and, unlike his last name, not particularly saint-like. Along with his condemnation of those friends and lovers he views as 'fallen,' his (supposed) concession in allowing the priest to vouch for his reputation with the employers at the Officine Galileo at the end of the novel could be considered ideologically, even morally, weak (indeed, it has been by several critics), despite the fact that his ability to use his reason, 'ragione,' in order to reach a compromise could in fact be interpreted as a sign of maturity, of coming of age.[19] Bruno's ambiguity is reiterated not only in his relationship with la Galileo itself, but also in his disparate vision of the local surroundings, from the revered factories to the marginal wastelands.

These conceptions of cityscapes stand in stark contrast to the attitudes found in Pratolini's earlier works located in Florence's centre. Characters in *Il Quartiere* or *Cronache di poveri amanti* are firmly rooted in their area, not only out of a sense of solidarity but also because of their impression of being connected with the neighbourhood's history. They, too, like the characters living in Rifredi, belong to the proletariat, but they are engaged essentially in pre-industrial activity; for the most part they are artisans, craftsmen, or vendors, skills that are linked to Florence's past. Bruno, on the other hand, idealizes the Galileo, as well as industry, technological advancement, and modernity in general, yet the area of Rifredi in which he lives and works, with its smokestacks and waste, simultaneously embodies both the socio-economic benefits as well as the environmental degradation resulting from Florence's industrial development during the *miracolo economico*. Moreover, Bruno's espousal of modernity and progress and his idealization and partiality towards the role of industry itself, and what it means to Florence's urban space, seem to be shared by the author:

> Firenze, per me che ne seguo le vicende come ogni altro italiano di una città d'Italia, è là dove si pone la sua cultura progressiva, là dove è laica, nelle università e nelle case editrici grandi e soprattutto nelle piccine perché nuove, è dalle parti di Rifredi e del suo universo operaio, si capisce; dove non c'è più fiorentinismo: tutto quello che con i miei mezzi ho tentato di storicizzare narrandolo perché lo si rifiuti anche. (Marabini 109)

> [Florence, for me who follows its events like any other Italian from an Italian city, is to be found in those places where its progressive culture is located, where it is secular, in the universities and in the major presses and above all in the small ones because they are new, it's in the area of Rifredi and the universe of its labourers, obviously; where there is no

longer 'Florentinism': everything that I – with the means at my disposal – have attempted to consign to history by narrating it so that it can be rejected even.]

Pratolini evidently believes that the most 'genuine' Florence is to be found in its advanced lay culture, but in particular in the working-class, industrial area of Rifredi that dominates his text, an attitude that seems to align his sympathies, and possibly even his ideology, then, with those of his protagonist.

Throughout the novel Bruno presumably develops his personalized notion of Communism, yet his ideas on women, homosexuals, and difference are, by contrast, decidedly retrograde for the most part, and would seem to be legacies of Italy's Fascist past. Pratolini's sub-textual Fascism is not particularly surprising, as much of his anti-Fascist fiction ends up reiterating certain values of the regime, of which he was of course a product, a tendency that has been noted by various critics.[20]

In comparison, Palazzeschi's portrait of another ambivalent male figure – Remo in the *Sorelle Materassi* – alludes to the young man's proto-Fascist tendencies as well, but on careful reading it becomes quite clear that the author is undermining the young man's seductive appeal by depicting him as an undeterred manipulator. Readers of Palazzeschi's novel would tend to identify more closely with the eccentric Materassi sisters, and can comprehend, while at the same time acknowledging the dangers of, Teresa and Carolina's attraction to Remo. Bruno, however, is the nearest stand-in for Pratolini's own voice, yet his redeeming qualities are few and far between, and thus his ideological stance is ambiguous; for this reason the reader has difficulty sharing his attitudes.

Pratolini's willingness to confront issues such as adolescent sexuality, homoeroticism, and ethnic otherness might indicate an open-mindedness somewhat ground-breaking for his time, yet close textual analysis of spatial configurations and the characters within them in *La costanza della ragione* reveals, in the end, a not particularly evolved stance towards alterity. Pratolini's portrayals of Florentine industrial suburbs as 'heterotopias' are innovative and provide a vivid and thought-provoking contrast to standard visions of the historic centre. Yet these spaces of exclusion are undermined by the development of a male protagonist who, while espousing progress, displays antiquated prejudices towards the Other.

4 The Stendhal Syndrome, or The Horror of Being Foreign in Florence

While Florentine marginal or suburban zones constitute the spatial referents for Palazzeschi and Pratolini's expressions of alterity, the city's historic quarter is the epicentre of a phenomenon that signifies a head-on encounter with Otherness for writers such as Stendhal or E.M. Forster or for the filmmakers Merchant and Ivory or Dario Argento. The expression 'Stendhal Syndrome' – coined by the psychologist Graziella Magherini and derived from Stendhal's own account of his visit to the Tuscan capital – is used to describe a psychosomatic reaction to the city's profusion of art and history, whereby the subject, generally a foreign tourist, experiences symptoms ranging from unease to faintness to panic, when she or he is exposed to Florentine architecture or museums. If there exists any city that can be said to overload tourists with art, Florence is surely such a place; some contend that it is home to one-fifth of the world's artistic patrimony. The city's unique landmarks and its artistic wealth, moreover, qualify it as a most notable example of an urban 'sublime.'

The emotional and physical reactions of the unwitting visitors to Florence who suffer from the Syndrome are actually not that surprising perhaps, since responses of distress or fear are considered common characteristics of an encounter with the sublime. Edmund Burke, in his core text *A Philosophical Enquiry into the Origin of our Ideas of the Sublime and the Beautiful*, explains: 'Indeed terror is in all cases whatsoever, either more openly or latently the ruling principle of the sublime' (58). Furthermore, Burke, although discussing instances of the sublime in nature (as opposed to those found in man-made environments) also points out the horrific aspect of the sublime, saying: 'The passion caused by the great and sublime ... when those causes operate most powerfully, is

Astonishment; and astonishment is that state of the soul, in which all its motions are suspended, with some degree of horror' (57).

While in earlier epochs (for example, up to and even during the Romantic period) the sublime was conceived as relating to natural phenomena (such as a mountain landscape the vastness of which could inspire awe), later the sublime came to be viewed as a possible response to products of human creativity, namely, art, architecture, or even literature. Crowther, for instance, interprets Kant's theories on the sublime as being applicable to works of art:

> One can glean from a book that such and such a building, or dam, or monument, or whatever, is an impressive feat of engineering, but it is only in the perceptually overwhelming presence of the object itself that we feel an authentic astonishment at what human creativity can achieve. This harmonious tension between what is perceptually overwhelming and what is nevertheless known to be artifice provides, I would suggest, the basis for one aspect of a specifically artistic sense of the sublime (construing 'artistic' here in the broadest possible sense). (153–4)

Others have studied how the sublime occurs in artificial environments, and Nye, in his examination of the concept of the technological sublime as a manifestation of principles similar to those found in the sublime of the natural world, emphasizes how the sublime is by no means restricted to nature: 'In art history the concept of the sublime is often applied to paintings that are unreal, monstrous, nightmarish, or imaginary. In architecture a sublime building usually is vast and includes striking contrasts of light and darkness, designed to fill the observer with foreboding and fear' (1). Thus, a city's sublime buildings and artistic works can evoke a sense of horror in the observer, something that occurs in all four works, both literary and filmic, examined in this chapter in relation to the Florentine syndrome.[1]

My analysis focuses first of all on the malady's origin in Stendhal's *Rome, Naples et Florence* (1826), then traces its occurrence in E.M. Forster's *A Room with a View* (first published in 1908), as well as touching briefly on its appearance in the eponymous cinematic adaptation of 1985 by Merchant and Ivory, and finally in Dario Argento's 1996 horror movie *La sindrome di Stendhal*. These instances of the Stendhal Syndrome all reflect the effects of the sublime, and at the same time can be considered a response to some form of perceived Otherness, be it cultural or sexual.

The expression 'Stendhal Syndrome' has in recent years become more widespread, leading to its adoption by the media. The 9 May 1994 issue of the American *People Magazine* provides an example of a reduction of significance of the illness. Its article on 'The 50 Most Beautiful People in the World' opens with the following words:

> Warning: This issue of PEOPLE may be hazardous to your health. Ever hear of a psychological disorder called the Stendhal syndrome? We kid you not. It's a kind of psychic overload which occurs when someone is exposed too quickly to a surplus of – that's right – beauty! It was first diagnosed among tourists who swooned in the picture galleries of Italy. As we prepared our fifth annual survey of the 50 Most Beautiful People in the World, those travelers were never far from our minds. (54)

This quote evidently oversimplifies somewhat the implications of the 'Stendhal Syndrome,' since the disease can in fact generate reactions that span the range from the relatively mild to the extremely severe.

Stendhal in Florence

Before examining in detail how the Stendhal Syndrome comes into play in Forster's novel and in the two films, it is important to consider the origin of the 'disease' in Stendhal's text. In his account of his Italian sojourn, Stendhal describes his first glimpse of the city: his excitement mounts as he considers Florence's past, its historical, artistic, and literary figures, its buildings, art, sculpture, and citizens. This emotional upheaval is equated by the author himself with the kind of sensual turmoil encountered in an amorous relationship:

> Florence, *22 janvier 1817* – Avant-hier, en descendant l'Apennin pour arriver à Florence, mon coeur battait avec force. Quel enfantillage! Enfin, à un détour de la route, mon oeil a plongé dans la plaine, et j'ai aperçu de loin, comme une masse sombre, *Santa Maria del Fiore* et sa fameuse coupole, chef-d'oeuvre de Brunelleschi. 'C'est là qu'ont vécu le Dante, Michel-Ange, Léonard de Vinci!['] me disais-je ... Enfin, les souvenirs se pressaient dans mon coeur, je me sentais hors d'état de raisonner, et me livrais à ma folie comme auprès d'une femme qu'on aime. En approchant de la porte *San Gallo* et de son mauvais arc de triomphe, j'aurais volontiers embrassé le premier habitant de Florence que j'ai rencontré. (Stendhal 270–1)

[Florence, 22 January 1817 – Yesterday, while descending the Apennines on the way to Florence, my heart was beating fast. What a childish thing! Finally, at a curve in the road, my gaze fell on the plain, and from afar I saw a dark mass: *Santa Maria del Fiore* and its famous dome, Brunelleschi's masterpiece. 'This is where Dante, Michelangelo, Leonardo da Vinci lived!['] I said to myself ... And then the memories swarmed in my heart, I felt unable to reason, and I abandoned myself to my madness, just as one does in the presence of the woman one loves. While approaching the gate of San Gallo and its ugly arch, I would happily have embraced the first inhabitant of Florence I met.]

Shortly thereafter, Stendhal visits Santa Croce, where he is overpowered not only by Florence's immense cultural history, but also by the sight of the illustrious church and its contents:

Là, à droite de la porte, est la tombe de Michel-Ange ... J'aperçois ensuite le tombeau de Machiavel; et, vis-à-vis de Michel-Ange, repose Galilée. Quels hommes! Et la Toscane pourrait y joindre le Dante, Boccace et Pétrarque. Quelle étonnante réunion! Mon émotion est si profonde, qu'elle va presque jusqu'à la piété. Le sombre religieux de cette église, son toit en simple charpente, sa façade non terminée, tout cela parle vivement à mon âme. Ah! si je pouvais oublier! ... J'étais arrivé à ce point d'émotion où se rencontrent les *sensations célestes* données par les beaux-arts et les sentiments passionnés. En sortant de *Santa Croce*, j'avais un battement de coeur, ce qu'on appelle des nerfs à Berlin; la vie était épuisée chez moi, je marchais avec la crainte de tomber. (Stendhal 271, 272)

[Michelangelo's tomb is to the right of the door ... Then I saw Machiavelli's tomb; and, across from Michelangelo, rests Galileo. What men! And Tuscany can add Dante, Petrarch and Boccaccio to these names. What an incredible gathering! My emotion is so great that it almost becomes religious devotion. The pious darkness of this church, its simply constructed roof, its unfinished façade, all these things speak vividly to my soul. Oh, could I but forget! ... I had reached that stage of emotion where *celestial sensations* given by art and passionate feeling meet each other. Upon leaving *Santa Croce* I had heart palpitations, which in Berlin are called nerves; I was totally exhausted, I was afraid of falling as I walked.]

Stendhal's condition of overstimulation is induced above all by *visual* means; his *seeing* the imposing church and its famous tombs results in his feeling ill, as his heart palpitations force him to sit down on one of the benches in Piazza Santa Croce, away from the bewildering art and artefacts housed within the church.

Santa Croce is not the only Florentine landmark to evoke strong feelings in Stendhal. In his journal entry for the following day, he tells how he is beset by melancholy, an 'émotion muette et profonde' [deep, mute emotion], as he wanders aimlessly, 'les yeux très ouverts et ne pouvant parler' [wide-eyed and speechless], exploring the city's medieval palaces, which make him feel as though he is living in the same epoch as Dante (Stendhal 274). Both the city's history as well as its architecture (which, for Stendhal, is the embodiment of its past) repeatedly elicit a sense of intense despondency as well as admiration in him.[2] In his essay 'On échoue toujours à parler de ce qu'on aime' [One always fails to talk about that which one loves], Barthes points out just how excessive Stendhal's attachment to Italy is, saying that the French writer's adoptive 'motherland' constitutes 'l'objet d'un veritable transfert' [the object of a genuine transference]. Barthes goes on to say: 'On reconnaît dans cette promotion amoureuse ... un élément constitutive du transfert (ou de la passion): la partialité. Il y a dans l'amour d'un pays étranger une sorte de racisme à l'envers: on s'enchante de la différence, on s'ennuie du Même, on exalte l'Autre' (Barthes 333, 334) [One recognizes in this loving promotion ... the constitutional element of transference (or of passion): partiality. In the love for a foreign country there is a sort of reverse racism: one becomes enchanted with difference, one is bored with the Same, one exalts the Other]. Barthes views Stendhal's adoration of Italy, therefore, as symptomatic of a kind of reverse discrimination, a privileging and promotion of the Other.

Stendhal is certainly not unique in his passionate but also psychosomatic response to the 'alien' or 'different' Florence, to its physical presence and to what he perceives as its cultural 'baggage.' In *La sindrome di Stendhal* (1989), Graziella Magherini, a psychologist at the hospital of Santa Maria Nuova in central Florence, supplies case studies of patients who suffer from what she terms the 'Stendhal Syndrome.' Magherini maintains that the Stendhal Syndrome is not an exclusively literary phenomenon, but that it has affected real visitors to Florence, many of whom are not able to cope in as positive a manner as Stendhal himself. *La sindrome di Stendhal* outlines how a visit to Florence, and an exposure to its proverbial profusion of art, culture, and history, can elicit a variety of reactions in tourists, ranging from a temporary mental and/or physical state of distress to a more serious psychological crisis that necessitates hospitalization. Certain patients' inner conflicts bear a striking resemblance to Stendhal's Florentine experience as well as to that of *A Room with a View*'s heroine, Lucy Honeychurch, and even to Anna Manni's response in Argento's *Sindrome di Stendhal*.

Forster's Florence

Lucy Honeychurch, a first-time British visitor to Florence, is not only engaged in a journey of the discovery of Italy, but in one of self-discovery as well. The focus of the novel is on the achievement of self-awareness and the process involved in attaining it.[3] *Insight* is what many of Forster's characters strive for and the term is not used loosely here, for it is precisely through *seeing* that Lucy is able to gain greater self-knowledge.[4] Indeed, the novel's emphasis on sight is exemplified not only in explicit textual references, but also in the characters' names themselves. Lucy, whose name derives from the Latin *lux*, meaning light, is also frequently addressed with her Italian equivalent, *Lucia*, by her cousin Charlotte Bartlett. The most notable Lucia in the Italian hagiographic tradition – and one of the most celebrated Italian saints – is the Sicilian Lucia of Syracuse, patron of the eyes, guardian of those who suffer from ocular ailments. Legend has it that 'her eyes were put out by [a] tyrant, or that she herself tore them out to present them to an unwelcome suitor who was smitten by their beauty. In either case they were miraculously restored to her, more beautiful than before.'[5] Lucy's eyes are frequently emphasized in *A Room with a View*, as witnessed, for example, in the narrator's comment after her return to England, when the transformation of her mental outlook (or rebirth), which occurred in Florence, the so-called cradle of the Renaissance, is described: 'Her senses expanded ... She returned with new eyes' (130).

Lucy's fiancé, or *fiasco* as her family calls him, is of an entirely different nature. He, unlike Lucy, is anything but open-minded. His name, Cecil, derived from the Latin *caecus*, meaning blind (Dunkling and Gosling 44–5), is most appropriate: he is by no means concerned with gaining insight into himself or others.[6] Cecil, synonymous with a lack of vision, is equated with the Middle Ages, a period that Forster represents as antiquated and oppressive and diametrically opposed to the Renaissance, which instead stands (not surprisingly) for rebirth and self-discovery:

> He was medieval. Like a Gothic statue ... with ... a head that *was tilted a little higher than the usual level of vision*, he resembled those fastidious saints

who guard the portals of a French cathedral ... He remained in the grip of a certain devil whom the modern world knows as self-consciousness, and whom the medieval, *with dimmer vision*, worshipped as asceticism. (Forster, *Room* 106, emphasis mine)

The match between the blind Cecil and the visionary Lucy cannot help but be ill-fated from its outset.[7]

Lucy's unconscious search for the attainment of insight and autonomy does not proceed without impediment. Society's dictates constantly impose themselves on her, primarily through the oppressive figure of her chaperon, Charlotte Bartlett, among others. The conflict Lucy has to contend with is that between the rigid constraints of British protocol – doing what she 'ought' to do – and her desire to explore her surroundings (in particular Florence) on her own. This division is evidenced above all in Piazza Santa Croce, precisely the same square where Stendhal's attack occurs. Lucy, abandoned by her escort, Miss Eleanor Lavish, waits anxiously for her return and begins to worry: 'She remembered that a young girl *ought* not to loiter in public places.' She then realizes Miss Lavish has left her:

> Tears of indignation came to Lucy's eyes – partly because Miss Lavish had jilted her, partly because she had taken her Baedeker. How could she find her way home? How could she find her way about in Santa Croce? Her first morning was ruined, and she might never be in Florence again. A few minutes ago she had been all high spirits, talking as a woman of culture, and half persuading herself that she was full of originality. Now she entered the church depressed and humiliated, not even able to remember whether it was built by the Franciscans or the Dominicans. (40)

Worse than Miss Lavish's desertion is Lucy's loss of the Baedeker, not merely a guidebook but rather the emblematic manual of cultural correctness and social restriction. Lucy, puzzled by the massive church of Santa Croce, is unsure how to approach it, since she has been deprived of the 'intellectual' apparatus she believes she needs:

> Of course, it must be a wonderful building. But how like a barn! And how very cold! Of course, it contained frescoes by Giotto, in the presence of whose tactile values she was capable of feeling what was proper. But who was to tell her which they were? She walked about disdainfully, unwilling to be enthusiastic over monuments of uncertain authorship or date. There

was no one even to tell her which, of all the sepulchral slabs that paved the nave and transepts, was the one that was really beautiful, the one that had been most praised by Mr. Ruskin. (*Room* 40–1)

The Baedeker's absence results in creative innovation for Lucy. Instead of regurgitating prefabricated material on the subject (e.g., the references to Giotto's 'tactile values' and Ruskin),[8] she is forced to investigate the city and its monuments for herself, using her own judgment. While she is taken aback by this unforeseen autonomy, Stendhal, by contrast, seeks it out and is eager to find his way without a guidebook:

J'ai si souvent regardé des vues de Florence, que je la connaissais d'avance; j'ai pu y marcher sans guide. J'ai tourné à gauche, j'ai passé devant un libraire qui m'a vendu deux descriptions de la ville (*guide*). Deux fois seulement j'ai demandé mon chemin à des passants ... Enfin, je suis arrivé à *Santa Croce*. (Stendhal 271)

[I have looked so often at views of Florence that I knew it ahead of time; I was able to walk around there without a guide. I turned left, I went past a bookshop owner who sold me two descriptions of the city (guide). Only twice did I ask passers-by for directions ... Finally I reached *Santa Croce*.]

So although Stendhal, unlike Lucy, prides himself on his ability to orient himself with little or no help from guidebooks, what is common to both their experiences is that the guidebook becomes an issue immediately before reaching the same specific destination: *Santa Croce*, a Mecca of Florentine culture and art. Jeffrey Meyers, in *Painting and the Novel*, acutely analyses the role of the Baedeker in *A Room with a View*:

In order to prepare herself for the expedition to Santa Croce Lucy took up 'Baedeker's *Handbook to Northern Italy*, and committed to memory the most important dates of Florentine history. For she was determined to enjoy herself on the morrow.' This *non sequitur* exposes the contrasts between facts and pleasure, between looking at art with the serious spectacles of Baedeker (or even of Ruskin) or with a direct and intuitive vision. Like the views and the violets and the kisses, Baedeker, the Bible of tourism, carries its own (negative) values, and identifies the travellers who carry the coupons of Cook and who see Italy as a museum of dead things. Late in the novel, when Lucy tries to run away from George, abandons her quest for self-knowledge and joins the 'vast armies of the benighted,' she prepares for Greece by borrowing a dictionary of mythology and by buying a Baedeker. (Meyers 39)

The Baedeker, therefore, has an important symbolic function in the novel: it stands for the values of oppressive British culture and (if one is to categorize it according to Forsterian parameters), for blindness or even 'muddle.' Without it Lucy is able to act freely: 'Then the pernicious charm of Italy worked on her, and, instead of acquiring information, she began to be happy' (*Room* 41).[9]

The Baedeker surfaces also in Magherini's assessment of the psychological mechanism that takes hold of present-day visitors to foreign lands. She shows how the omnipresent guidebook, a token of social acceptance for tourists, is symbolic of the educational values imposed on people in their home environment. Magherini, like Meyers, sees the Baedeker as representative of a split in the tourist's character. She posits that people develop a false self during their childhood, a self that lives in function of others and forces tourists to fulfil the expectations of their familial milieu so as to gain approval:

> Un viaggio intrapreso da una persona tipo falso Sé è, si può dire, intrapreso da due personalità: una ligia e zelante che viaggia per «istruirsi», con il famoso Baedeker o qualsiasi suo sostituto (apprestandosi quindi a fare secondo il suo solito: coltivare la sua maschera dignitosa emotivamente frigida, che lavora per potere al ritorno compiacere e ottenere nuove benemerenze tramite la «cultura» che si sarà fatta). (145)

> [A trip taken by a 'false self' personality type is taken, one can say, by two personalities. The first is loyal and zealous and travels 'to educate itself,' with the famous Baedeker or any other substitute (preparing to act in its usual way: cultivating a dignified and emotionally frigid mask, labouring in order to be able to please upon return and to obtain new merit through the 'culture' that it has acquired).]

Magherini then describes a second, more spontaneous and sensitive, personality type that emerges while travelling:

> Una seconda personalità, silenziosa ma sempre vitale, più autentica ... potrà all'improvviso venire alla ribalta, ad esempio *se dallo scenario del mondo le balzeranno agli occhi oggetti d'arte, come risvegliandola, riportandola alla vita.* Nelle persone di questo tipo, se sono dotate, di fondo, di una spiccata sensibilità estetica, di un potenziale sesto senso che tenda a metterle – tolta

la maschera – in contatto creativo con l'ambiente circostante, trovandovi risonanze con le parti del proprio mondo interno, l'esperienza estetica del viaggio può costituire un evento che innesca una 'catastrofe' ... che ha in sé importanti potenzialità evolutive, ma anche rischi di esplosioni psicopatologiche. (145, emphasis mine)

[The second personality, silent but always alive, more authentic ... can suddenly come into the limelight, if, for example, art objects from the world stage *hit its eyes, as if awakening it, bringing it back to life*. If people of this type are endowed, deep down, with a sharp aesthetic sensitivity, with a potential sixth sense that tends to put them – after having removed the mask – in creative contact with their surrounding environment, finding echoes there of their own internal world, then the aesthetic experience of the trip can constitute an event that sparks off a 'catastrophe' ... which in itself has important evolutionary potential, but also has risks of psycho-pathological explosions.]

This dynamic strikes a familiar chord when compared to Lucy Honeychurch's thought process in piazza Santa Croce, as well as in the rest of the novel. Magherini effectively points out what results the clash between these two 'personalities' (or opposing forces) can have on tourists. And indeed, *A Room with a View* can be seen as the perfect literary exemplification of this behavioural paradigm. Furthermore, another key factor in this formative yet hazardous procedure described by Magherini involves sight yet again: art objects must first 'hit' the tourists' 'eyes' in order for this mechanism to be set off, precisely the same sensory prerequisite necessary in Stendhal and Forster.

While Lucy Honeychurch does not experience emotive responses as radical as some of the more extreme cases that Magherini studies, many of her reactions to Florence coincide with those of the Florentine psychologist's subjects. There is one crucial scene in the novel where the heroine sustains a particularly intense psychosomatic reaction to her environment. It begins with Lucy venturing out on her own one evening at twilight and purchasing some photographs of Italian art, most notably Botticelli's *Birth of Venus*, the Renaissance painting par excellence, which Charlotte had previously impeded her from buying since it contains a naked figure. Restless and somewhat dissatisfied, Lucy thinks to herself, 'The world ... is certainly full of beautiful things, if only I could come across them' (61), thus expressing, in essence, a longing for the sublime, unaware that she is about to experience it first-hand in Florence's main square:

'Nothing ever happens to me,' she reflected, as she entered the Piazza Signoria ... The Loggia showed as the triple entrance of a cave, wherein dwelt many a deity, shadowy, but immortal, looking forth upon the arrivals and departures of mankind. It was the hour of unreality – the hour, that is, when unfamiliar things are real. An older person at such an hour and in such a place might think that sufficient was happening to him, and rest content. Lucy desired more.

She fixed her eyes wistfully on the tower of the palace, which rose out of the lower darkness like a pillar of roughened gold. It seemed no longer a tower, no longer supported by earth, but some unobtainable treasure throbbing in the tranquil sky. Its brightness mesmerized her, still dancing before her eyes when she bent them to the ground and started towards home.

Then something did happen. (61–2)

Forster depicts the square as if it were under a spell: it has acquired a quality of otherworldliness. The architecture is described in highly representative images, the tower of the Palazzo Vecchio acting as the quintessential phallic symbol, as both June Perry Levine, in *Two Rooms with a View: An Inquiry into Film Adaptation* (73), and Michael Ross, in his *Storied Cities* (80), have observed. A more explicit reference to such Freudian analogies between monument and phallus occurs in Forster's short story 'The Obelisk,' written much later (1939) but which is indicative nonetheless of the author's awareness and adoption of such associations. In this particular story, a sailor named Tiny makes some revealing lewd remarks on the obelisk: '"You said it, obblepiss ... Anyone ever seed a bigger one?" he inquired. No one replied, and how should they to so foolish a question? "Stands up don't it?" he continued. No one spoke. "No wonder they call that a needle, for wouldn't that just prick"' (Forster, *Life to Come* 159).

To follow along these interpretive lines, the 'shadowy' Loggia, pictured as the 'entrance to a cave,' can be viewed as standing in turn for the female genitalia. For, as Stone notes in his comments on feminine signs in Forster's opus, the cave is an important Forsterian figure: 'Circles, containers, hollows, and swellings are, with Forster, basic symbols. His fiction is thick with dells, grottoes, hollow trees, rings, pools, rooms, houses, and ... with caves ... Throughout his work, these feminine images operate in double roles ... They are obviously basic to Forster's fictive imagination' (298). Lucy's experience in the Piazza della Signoria (with its symbolic phallus and womb) can be considered a kind of troubling but ultimately productive rebirth (as prefigured in the photograph of *The Birth of Venus*) that imposes a lasting change on her. These evocative sexual images that appear in the Piazza della Signoria scene are, in any case, quite telling, since Lucy's voyage of self-discovery is primarily sensual (as well as intellectual), as she travels towards awareness of her attraction to the young George Emerson and eventual love for him.

That eroticized language should be used in connection with Lucy's Florentine epiphany is all the less surprising when her encounter with the city's art and culture is compared to Stendhal's narration of his own feelings in coming face to face with the same city. In the paragraph from *Rome, Naples et Florence* cited earlier, Stendhal equates his excitement at seeing Florence with the 'madness' one feels in the presence of a lover. Stendhal's descriptions of Santa Croce's interior are also charged with mystical-sexual connotations.

> Là, assis sur le marche-pied d'un prie-Dieu, la tête renversée et appuyée sur le pupitre, pour pouvoir regarder au plafond, les *Sibylles* du Volterrano m'ont donné peut-être le plus vif plaisir que la peinture m'ait jamais fait. J'étais déjà dans une sorte d'extase, par l'idée d'être à Florence, et le voisinage des grands hommes dont je venais de voir les tombeaux. Absorbé par la contemplation de la beauté sublime, je la voyais de près, je la touchais pour ainsi dire. (Stendhal 271–2)

> [There, seated on the footrest of a prie-dieu, with my head thrown back and resting on the lectern in order to be able to see the ceiling, Volterrano's *Sibyls* gave me perhaps the most vivid pleasure that painting has ever given me. I was already in a sort of ecstasy from the idea of being in Florence and from the proximity of the great men whose tombs I had just seen. Absorbed in the contemplation of this sublime beauty, I saw it up close, I touched it, so to speak.]

In this narration of his viewing of the Volterrano frescoes, Stendhal's body position – head bent back, gaze turned heavenward – brings to mind the sort of pose generally associated with saints lost in the contemplation of the divine, and is not unlike the mystical swoon exemplified by Bernini's well-known sculpture, the *Ecstasy of Saint Teresa*. The saint's semi-reclining body and rapturous expression reflect her not-entirely-chaste joy in encountering divine love and have led art historians to liken her spiritual ecstasy to orgasmic pleasure. Not only his stance but also the vocabulary Stendhal employs is a *mélange* of the saintly and the sensual: he speaks of 'pleasure,' 'sublime beauty,' 'ecstasy,' and, as cited earlier, of 'celestial sensations.' Immediately after this quasi-spritual experience in the face of art, Stendhal exits the church and undergoes his attack of 'nerves,' as he puts it in the paragraph quoted above.[10]

Both the Stendhalian and the Forsterian Florence, therefore, elicit powerful emotional responses laden with sexual implications. This is further exemplified in the denouement of the Piazza della Signoria scene in *A Room with a View*. Just when Lucy wishes that something would happen to her, one of the most significant events in the text takes place as she witnesses a gruesome display of aggression:

> Two Italians by the Loggia had been bickering about a debt. 'Cinque lire,' they had cried, 'cinque lire!' They sparred at each other, and one of them was hit lightly upon the chest. He frowned; he bent towards Lucy with a look of interest, as if he had an important message for her. He opened his lips to deliver it, and a stream of red came out between them and trickled down his unshaven chin.
>
> That was all. A crowd rose out of the dusk. It hid this extraordinary man from her, and bore him away to the fountain. Mr. George Emerson happened to be a few paces away, looking at her across the spot where the man had been ... Even as she caught sight of him he grew dim; the palace itself grew dim, swayed above her, fell on to her softly, noiselessly, and the sky fell with it. (62)

As Lucy faints, she drops the art photographs, representative of the weight of Italian art and culture. The last images she sees are of George Emerson and the medieval palace with its phallic tower (the Torre di Arnolfo), which collapses onto her; as Michael Ross puts it, 'When Lucy swoons, Florence itself falls erotically on top of her' (88).

Lucy's fall is in fact prefigured metaphorically in Santa Croce, where she is on the verge of feeling uplifted about her visit to the church and the emotions elicited by her conversation with Mr. Emerson, only to be interrupted by Charlotte's appearance: '[George] approached, his face in the shadow. He said "Miss Bartlett." "Oh, good gracious me!" said Lucy, *suddenly collapsing and seeing the whole of life in a new perspective.* "Where? Where?"' (48, emphasis mine). Lucy's figurative collapse – yet again described with the lexicon of *vision* – is equated here too with a transition and constitutes a revelational moment for her. Further echoes of Lucy's fall are also found in the hills overlooking Florence, just before George kisses her:

At the same moment the ground gave way, and with a cry she *fell* out of the wood. Light and beauty enveloped her. *She had fallen* on to a little open terrace, which was covered with violets from end to end ... George had turned at the sound of her arrival. For a moment he contemplated her, *as one who had fallen out of heaven*. (88–9, emphasis mine)

Lucy's fainting in Florence's main square thus resonates throughout the text. It is foreshadowed in Santa Croce and it prefigures another epiphanic moment in the novel: George and Lucy's first kiss. Moreover, her collapse in Piazza della Signoria recalls Stendhal's ecstatic pose below the Volterrano frescoes in Santa Croce, quoted earlier. Stendhal, too, while not actually falling, fears doing so when leaving Santa Croce ('je marchais avec la crainte de tomber'). Both Lucy Honeychurch and Stendhal fall prey to Florence's seductive power, as their physical stances and psychosomatic reactions testify. In their succumbing to Florence's charms there is an underlying erotic-spiritual current, as evidenced even in the language of this last passage, where Lucy herself is likened to the celestial, just when she is about to come into physical contact with George.[11]

Not only Lucy's collapse but the gory scene she witnesses in Piazza della Signoria could find its antecedent in Stendhal, in his reference to Florence's history of conflict:

Ce soir, assis sur une chaise de paille, en avant du café, au milieu de la grande place et vis-à-vis le *Palazzo Vecchio*, la foule et le froid, fort peu considérables l'un et l'autre, ne m'empêchaient point de voir tout ce qui s'était passé sur cette place. C'est là que vingt fois Florence essaya d'être libre, et que le sang coula pour une constitution impossible à faire marcher. Insensiblement la lune, qui se levait, est venue marquer sur cette place si propre la grande ombre du *Palazzo Vecchio*, et donner le charme du mystère aux colonnades de la galerie, par-dessous lesquelles on aperçoit les maisons éclairées au delà de l'Arno. Sept heures ont sonné au beffroi de la tour; la crainte de ne pas trouver de place au théâtre m'a forcé à quitter ce spectacle terrible: j'assistais, pour ainsi dire, à la tragédie de l'histoire. (Stendhal 276–7)

[This evening, seated on a straw chair in front of the café in the middle of the large square and facing the *Palazzo Vecchio*, neither the crowd nor the cold (neither of the two being all that considerable) were able to prevent me at all from seeing everything that had happened in this square. It was there that Florence attempted to be free twenty times and that blood was shed for a constitution that was unworkable. Imperceptibly the moon, which was rising, marked the large shadow of the *Palazzo Vecchio* on this square which is so clean, and it gave a mysterious charm to the colonnades of the gallery, below which one can see the lighted houses on the other side of the Arno. The tower belfry chimed seven – the fear of not finding a seat at the theatre forced me to leave that terrible spectacle; I witnessed, as it were, the tragedy of history.]

Stendhal's observations on the Piazza della Signoria have several elements in common with the scene set in the same square in *A Room with a View*. Stendhal, like Lucy, is facing the Palazzo Vecchio; there is a crowd in both scenes, the square is seen in shadows and is enshrouded in an air of mystery. But, most importantly, Stendhal mentions blood, thus associating the *piazza* with the city's history of violence and factionalism.

This same conflictual past is alluded to obliquely also by Forster, both in the stabbing itself as well as in the Reverend Eager's tasteless comment: 'This very square – so I am told – witnessed yesterday the most sordid of tragedies. To one who loves the Florence of Dante and Savonarola there is something portentous in such a desecration – portentous and humiliating' (*Room* 71–2). In a classic example of Forsterian irony, Reverend Eager states precisely the opposite of what is true: Florence's most notorious scenes of violence did in fact take place during Dante's lifetime and later during Savonarola's, and in fact the latter was burned at the stake in that very same location.[12] Reverend Eager's words prompt Lucy to notice 'the ghoulish fashion in which respectable people will nibble after blood' (72), her thoughts returning to this haematic image, a recurring topos in the novel and a trope mentioned also in Stendhal's travelogue, an image highlighted all the more in the filmic adaptation of the novel, and a theme that – not unexpectedly, given the genre – dominates Argento's horror film as well.

After Lucy faints upon witnessing the stabbing (the re-enactment of Florence's history of bloodshed), she is caught by George. She recovers and waits for him to retrieve her (bloodstained) photographs; the disorienting square is meanwhile restored to its original state:

> The palace tower had lost the reflection of the declining day, and joined itself to earth. How should she talk to Mr. Emerson when he returned from the shadowy square? Again the thought occurred to her, 'Oh, what have I done?' – the thought that she, as well as the dying man, had crossed some spiritual boundary. (63–4)

Indeed they have, and George has too, for he says to Lucy: 'Something tremendous has happened; I must face it without getting muddled. It isn't exactly that a man has died' (64). This episode in the piazza affects Lucy and George more deeply than either of them would expect: it is not only the beginning of their future relationship, it is a breakthrough for them – for Lucy in particular – in achieving greater intellectual independence and emotional self-awareness. Lucy's experience, like that of some of Magherini's patients, is ultimately productive, and fortunately does not cause her to suffer any more physical anguish than a momentary loss of consciousness. For Lucy, the sublime has begun to bring about a breakthrough, in a manner consonant with that described by Nye in his interpretation of Burke, for whom 'the encounter with the sublime was a healthy shock, a temporary dislocation of sensibilities that forced the observer into mental action. To seek out the sublime was not to seek the irrational but rather to seek the awakening of sensibilities to an inner power' (6).

Unlike the novel, the filmic adaptation of *A Room with a View* – considered by many critics as typifying the British 'heritage film' industry of the period[13] – emphasizes the sculptures found in Piazza della Signoria, and their dramatic poses disturb Lucy, as well as prefiguring the violent scene she is about to witness. Hutchings observes that the murder scene constitutes 'Lucy's violent introduction to male physicality and intimacy,' and that 'Director Ivory renders her sightseeing experience through a menacing montage of statues in aggressive and martial postures preceding the brawl and murder' (223).[14] A great deal of attention, certainly more than in the written text, is devoted to the horrific aspect of the sublime, that is, the grisly death of the young man. The motif of blood appears graphically on screen, as the stabbed man, like the Forsterian figure, seems to be about to speak to Lucy, his mouth dripping red. Interestingly, Goldman comments that 'the visual, visceral language of the body is communicated by the dying man,' and that 'this graphic image imposes a figure of menstruating female genitalia on to the man's face' (126).

The phallic tower, on the other hand, appears at the closing of the episode, this time between George and Lucy as they are talking by the river wall (see figure 4). The couple are framed by the architecture, and their identity of position, as Perry Levine has pointed out (72), refers to their future mutual sympathy, an aspect mentioned also by Forster.[15] The film, like the text, problematizes the Italian Other, in that Lucy makes trite observations on Italian identity, verbalizing remarks

Figure 4 Ivory, *A Room with a View*; Lucy and George near the Arno River, the Torre di Arnolfo in the background

Forster alludes to in the novel; her comments on the episode re-evoke the themes of blood and horror: 'She spoke of the Italian character; she became almost garrulous over the incident that had made her faint five minutes before. Being strong physically, she soon overcame the horror of blood' (49–50).

Both the literary and the cinematic fainting spell of Lucy can be attributed only partly to her distress at witnessing a brutal act. She is in fact overwhelmed by the whole environment that surrounds her, and the stabbing is both the cataclysmic and catalytic event that, within the context of her Florentine experiences, is partially responsible for triggering her psycho-physical response. In the novel, the imposing Florentine edifice overpowers Lucy to the extent that she perceives it as toppling onto her. Similar sensations of vertigo in the face of architecture affect Tozzi's protagonists, but in the Tuscan writer's case the context is not quite the same as that of Stendhal or Forster, since he is not negotiating cultural alterity but rather his own marked sense of alienation from society more generally. Furthermore, Tozzi's protagonists seem to experience this dizziness in environments that are not necessarily linked quite so blatantly to the sublime.

The sensation of architecture as being oppressive is, in any case, not uncommon to victims of the Stendhal Syndrome, as Magherini relates in her case studies. The story of Ilse, a young European patient who begins to feel ill after two days of touring the city, echoes Lucy's. Ilse, more capable of self-analysis than the fictional Lucy, is also more attuned to the city's dramatic effect on her, and in fact she seeks it out deliberately, as is illustrated by her response to the Duomo of Santa Maria del Fiore:

> improvvisamente mi trovai di fronte ad una mole enorme, una immensità colorata ed enigmatica, che è stata per me uno shock ... E dentro di me l'effetto scatenante altri effetti della grandiosità, la mole, i blocchi, i colori, quei tetti! ... Questa prima esperienza è stata tanto forte ma l'ho voluta così e l'ho subita. Mi sono accorta di non poter decidere da me le sensazioni da provare, che ci sono forze che ti possono abbattere se solo le guardi. Di solito quando vai in una qualche città, ti armi di una cartina e studi e leggi. Invece, per una volta la mia esperienza voleva essere semplice e ingenua ... Firenze mi si è imposta senza che nessuno mi dicesse che sarebbe stato così o così ... il nuovo mi dava un senso di precarietà perché era più forte delle mie possibilità di ricezione, c'era da sentirsi male, da smarrirsi. (Magherini 97)

> [Suddenly I found myself in front of an enormous mass, a colourful and enigmatic immensity, which for me was a shock ... And inside of me, the effect that triggered other effects of grandeur, massiveness, blocks, colours, those roofs! ... This first experience was very strong, but that is how I wanted it to be and I underwent it. I realized that I couldn't decide on my own what sensations I should feel, that there are forces that can knock you over just by your looking at them. Usually, when you go to a city, you arm yourself with a map and you study and you read. Instead, my experience wanted to be simple and naive for once ... Florence imposed itself on me without anyone telling me that it would be this way or that way ... This newness gave me a sense of precariousness because it was greater than my capacity for reception; I felt ill, lost.]

I myself, as well as countless others who have looked up at Florence's Duomo, can relate to Ilse's perception of the structure's massive dimensions as overwhelming, to the extent that they become almost impossible to comprehend, an impression that recalls Kant's description of the mathematical sublime as related to St Peter's in Rome (1790).[16] But in Ilse's case, her personal experience of Florence's imposing architecture constitutes such an acute emotional overload that she cannot cope with it on her own: she is in fact admitted to hospital. Yet Ilse has purposefully set out to let Florence work its effect on her, renouncing all guides, maps, books that could potentially 'contaminate' her perceptions: 'Non ero venuta a Firenze studiando prima la città; sono partita senza una particolare preparazione, perché volevo vivere. Volevo essere diversa e fare cose nuove che non avevo fatte mai' (97). [I arrived in Florence not having studied the city beforehand; I left home without any particular preparation because I wanted to live. I wanted to be different and do things I had never done before.] In this way she differs from Forster's Lucy, who is not so premeditated in her search for experience and is a long way from predicting that Florence's visual impact will be so potent. However, Ilse's internal conflict, like Lucy's, fits into the scheme Magherini delineates where the 'false self' and the 'authentic self' clash; in Ilse's case, she is determined to have the 'authentic self' prevail, a state of being that Lucy takes longer to achieve.

Both the real Ilse and the fictional and filmic Lucy fall into the standard patient profile drawn up by Magherini. Most of the tourists Magherini diagnoses as suffering from the Stendhal Syndrome are young, unmarried adults, usually from western/northern Europe. Often, she says, they are women who are on an individual tour of the city (as opposed to an organzied, group trip) and are not following a preset itinerary. According to Magherini, these women generally possess a 'sensibilità spiccata' [marked sensitivity]; they have great expectations for their trip, and are 'in tensione all'esperienza e alla vita' (Magherini 104) [poised for experience and for life]. These characteristics are applicable to Lucy Honeychurch's circumstances, even though clearly she cannot be typecast as mentally ill (although in the later stages of the novel, during her 'lying' phase, her behaviour is certainly erratic). Her reactions to Florence, however, are strikingly similar to those seen in Stendhal and in Magherini's patients, since they derive from the same cultural phenomenon that affects the other two writers' subjects, that is, an encounter with an unfamiliar, 'different' culture within an environment perceived as sublime.

But does the Stendhal Syndrome, while finding the origin of its definition in Florence, exist solely there? Even though Florence's cultural, artistic, and architectural patrimony may elicit extreme emotional responses in tourists, surely then other cities could affect their visitors in a similar fashion? Indeed, another famous site of singular historical and, in this case, particular religious importance has acquired a similar malady of its own: the Jerusalem Syndrome, whereby disoriented tourists assume the personality of biblical characters or prophets and wander around the city preaching repentance (Smith, B1, B4).[17]

It stands to reason, then, that other Forsterian subjects in *non-Florentine* environments as well should fall prey to cultural clashes; however, in these other instances, the cultural clashes often have a more detrimental outcome than in Lucy's experience. Much of Forster's work explores the Britisher's reaction when she or he is in contact with a foreign culture; this Otherness often evokes extreme behaviour. In *A Passage to India*, Adela Quested, for example, responds violently to what she perceives as an 'alien' culture, and imagines herself to have been sexually assaulted by Doctor Aziz during the infamous expedition to the Marabar caves (again, Forsterian sexual topographical imagery plays a pivotal role in another text centred on cultural alterity and sexuality). But the most remarkable instance of this kind of behaviour can be found in Forster's short story, written in the same period as the composition of *A Room with a View*, 'Albergo Empedocle' (1903). Here it is Sicily, not Florence, that unleashes a disastrous response in a young visitor named Harold, who travels with his fiancée and her family (as well as the omnipresent Baedeker). On visiting ancient Greek ruins in Girgenti, Harold is so overcome by the environment that he believes himself to have lived a previous life there as a king.[18] Like Lucy in *A Room with a View*, Harold has a fainting spell, only his results in disaster: his travelling companions become convinced that he has lost his mind and Harold suffers a nervous breakdown. He ends up in an asylum, unable to communicate in English, using instead a gibberish that he seems to think is Greek. The perception of Italy as Other and the ensuing cultural clash ultimately cost Harold his sanity, rather than leading to the kind of evolution experienced by Lucy Honeychurch.

In her study, Magherini points out that the Stendhal Syndrome constitutes a type of watershed in a person's mental make-up: it can bring about a psychological renewal but can also provoke a complete breakdown. She focuses above all on the clinical aspects of this mental affliction and, since her patients are not local, she is unable to conduct a follow-up for each individual. With Stendhal and Forster's characters, by contrast, we as readers can find out the final outcome of their Florentine experience; in *Rome, Naples et Florence* and *A Room with a View* the after-effects are essentially beneficial rather than detrimental. Forster's decision to have Lucy undergo a regenerative process reinforces the novel's aim; in a discourse that critiques the pretention and uptightness of post-Victorian (i.e., Edwardian) English values, Lucy's encounter with Florence serves to jolt her out of that stifling era. Only by rejecting the old world – her 'false self,' her Baedeker, and British society – and letting in the new – Florence and all that it evokes – does Lucy attain the independence needed to achieve insight. Paradoxically, it is the *old*, the historical Florence – the Renaissance city – that elicits this renewal in Lucy. The rebirth trope becomes fundamental to other foreigners writing about Tuscany in recent times as well, specifically Frances Mayes and David Leavitt and Mark Mitchell, whose re-settlement in the same region is examined in the following chapter. In Lucy Honeychurch's case, at any rate, while the impact of Florence may be temporarily disturbing, the end result is constructive: her room with a view has afforded her clear vision, both of the outside world and of her inner self.

Argento's Syndrome

A far more severe case of the Stendhal Syndrome than that found in Forster's novel or in its cinematic adaptation, or in Stendhal's own travelogue, is depicted in Dario Argento's *La sindrome di Stendhal*. Argento's horror movie tells the story of a young police detective, Anna Manni (played by the director's own daughter, Asia Argento, frequently featured as protagonist in his films), who is on the trail of a serial rapist and murderer, known as Alfredo. The film begins in Florence, where Anna is on a special assignment to exchange information on the killer with her Florentine colleagues, since three of his victims were raped in the Renaissance city. While in Florence, Anna falls prey to the Stendhal Syndrome, and suffers an attack in the Uffizi art gallery, which lies just around the corner of the Piazza della Signoria, the site of Lucy's fainting spell. Anna is 'rescued' (much as Lucy is rescued in *A Room with a View*) by the murderer himself (played by Thomas Kretschman), but is later raped and attacked by him in her hotel room and, shortly after, when she comes to, witnesses his murdering another woman.

Anna manages to escape, returns to Rome, and begins to undergo psychological counselling, and then spends some time in her home town of Viterbo. Alfredo tracks her down there, and takes her to a cave, where he sexually assaults her once more. This time, however, she is able to fight back, wounds him fatally, and throws his body in the nearby river. Yet no one is completely sure if Alfredo is truly dead, since his corpse has not been recovered. All the while, Anna continues to demonstrate unstable behaviour, and after having rejected Marco, her former lover and colleague, she starts a relationship with a young French art student named Marie Bayle (clearly a reference to Stendhal's own real name, Marie Henri Beyle). The student is found murdered, and Anna maintains that Alfredo is the killer. By the end of the film, Alfredo's body has been fished out of the water network, and it becomes obvious that Anna has been behaving psychopathically, and that it was she who killed Marie. She then murders her psychologist when he confronts her with the truth, and immediately after kills Marco; the movie concludes with her apprehension by her colleagues.

While clearly the aims of a 1990s horror film are quite different from those of a nineteenth-century travelogue, or from those of an early-twentieth-century novel of social critique or of its cinematic adaptation of the 1980s, in *La sindrome di Stendhal* Argento evokes certain conceits that echo Stendhal, Forster, and the filmic version of the latter's novel. Undoubtedly Argento's film possesses its flaws, and obviously the fictional story can only have derived from Magherini's clinical book in terms of its exploiting the Syndrome as a plot device, yet one aspect the director effectively portrays is the sense of the omnipresence of art as oppressive. Apart from the visual explosion of art in the opening credits and in the initial sequences set in Florence's streets, on the Ponte Vecchio, in the Piazza della Signoria, and in the Uffizi, paintings, frescoes, sculptures, and prints pervade most other locales. For instance, there is a Michelangelo copy in Anna's hotel lift, a replica of his David in a snowball in her room, as well as a copy of Rembrandt's *Night Watch* on the wall. In the police headquarters in Rome paintings figure prominently, and Anna's apartment is covered with reproductions of various works. Even Alfredo's house is replete with art and sculpture, and the serial killer has singled out a poster of Narcissus that he thinks would appeal to Anna.

Exposed to this abundance of art initially in Florence, Anna Manni thus falls prey to the Syndrome. Unlike Stendhal, Lucy Honeychurch, or Magherini's patients, Anna is technically not a foreigner; she is in fact Italian, although her not being a native Florentine might perhaps allow her to be classified as a 'tourist,' a role reinforced, for instance, by the presence of a map and some postcards in her handbag. It would seem, however, that Argento has taken a fair amount of licence in his interpretation of the typical patient profile. And while the director may employ some interesting effects in terms of his representation of Anna Manni's reaction to Florence's art (e.g., her entering the paintings physically and even *becoming* a painting herself when she covers her entire body in oil colours), he liberally extrapolates on the after-effects of the Stendhal Syndrome, for the symptoms Anna Manni first exhibits in Florence do not end when she leaves the city. They continue both in Rome and in her home town.

An explicit link to Magherini's book is nonetheless found in a self-reflexive moment in the film, when Anna's psychologist informs her that she is suffering from the Stendhal Syndrome, as he authoritatively holds up a copy of what is supposed to be Graziella Magherini's text. (Incidentally, the psychologist acted as consultant for the film.) But Argento's version of the 'Stendhal Syndrome' does not lead to a positive outcome; it cannot possibly have an 'evolutionary' function, as Magherini terms it, since it presumably accounts for – or at the very least constitutes a prelude to – Anna Manni's psychopathic behaviour.

Anna's first indications of suffering from the Stendhal Syndrome occur almost immediately in the film's opening, and Argento's depiction of her succumbing to it blatantly exemplifies a mixture of the sensual and the horrific, so typical of the experience of the sublime. The initial sequences set in Florence's streets and in the Uffizi portray Anna as perturbed and breathless as she gazes on notable works of art (see figure 5). Piazza della Signoria's sculptures (the copy of Michelangelo's *David* and Baccio Bandinelli's *Hercules and Caecus*) seem menacing, just as they did in the film *A Room with a View*, which I cannot help but think must have influenced Argento's visual interpretation of this square. It is on entering the Uffizi that Anna Manni truly undergoes a sensory overload. First she gazes on a classic view of the Arno and the Ponte Vecchio through a large window, and as she enters the various halls she comes across *The Battle of San Romano* by Paolo Uccello, Botticelli's *Birth of Venus* and *Primavera*, and Caravaggio's *Medusa*,[19] all to the accompaniment of imaginary sounds elicited by the paintings and Ennio Morricone's haunting score (in a visual nod to the art-gallery scene in Hitchcock's *Vertigo*, as some critics have pointed out).[20] Furthermore, the crowds surrounding Anna are depicted as alienating, consisting of sightseers of all nationalities speaking in a variety of languages, such that one is initially led to think that perhaps Argento is critiquing mass tourism or a kind of 'foreign invasion,' while at the same time the standard scheme of depicting foreigners in Florence is reversed, inasmuch as Anna – an Italian – seems to feel alien in the surroundings where foreignness would instead appear to be the norm.

But the picture that is responsible for Anna's complete loss of consciousness is Breugel's *Landscape with the Fall of Icarus*, a work in reality not even housed in the Uffizi, but in Brussels. Anna stares at the surface of the water that wavers and she hallucinates that she is entering Bruegel's painting: she, like Lucy Honeychurch and Icarus, falls too, but then imagines that she is drawn underwater and kisses an enormous

Figure 5 Argento, *La sindrome di Stendhal*; Anna Manni in the Uffizi Gallery

fish. The sensual element witnessed in Stendhal and Forster thus resurfaces in Argento as well, and he later exaggerates the erotic aspect of the syndrome until it verges on the pornographic, indeed, the disturbing (for example, in the gory rape scene involving a razor blade after Anna Manni has imagined 'entering' the Rembrandt reproduction in her hotel room). During her collapse in the Uffizi Anna hits a table, cutting her mouth. The familiar motif of blood thus emerges early on in Argento's film, as in the other filmic and literary texts mentioned above. Obviously for Argento blood functions as an essential image, given the conventions of the horror-movie genre within which he is operating.

Yet genre constitutes an issue that remains blurred: *La sindrome di Stendhal* easily falls into the category of the horror movie, but at the same time can be considered a *giallo*, or detective film. *La sindrome di Stendhal* presents an intermingling of cinematic sub-genres as well, with certain elements recalling slasher movies, along with the rape-revenge film, or even film noir. This cross-contamination of genres brings to the fore a basic question in the film, namely, the permeability not only of such classifications as genre, but also the instability of other categories such as sexuality and identity.[21] Argento deliberately destabilizes borders between male and female, Self and Other, killer and victim, sanity and madness, reality and fantasy, life and art, thus reflecting, it would seem, the post-modern concern with questioning and undermining such categorizations.

The figure that incarnates this confusion of boundaries is above all Anna herself, and her transformations in appearance denote shifts not only in sexuality and personality but also in genre. Initially she is portrayed as stereotypically feminine, with flowing dark hair and a demure skirt and blouse. After her rape by Alfredo in Florence, she cuts off her long locks and changes her image, donning masculine attire (several times she is quizzed about her new look, and her brother tells her that she looks like a 'maschietto,' a tomboy). This change in hairstyle and apparel indicates a different phase in the film, in which Anna will be attacked again by Alfredo, but in which she brings about his demise. In her boyish guise, Anna recalls the standard figure of the 'Final Girl' in American slasher films as conceived by Carol Clover in *Men, Women, and Chainsaws: Gender in the Modern Horror Film*: that is, the young woman who (unlike the murderer's previous female victims) undergoes various trials but manages to survive and indeed defeat the killer. The Final Girl constitutes not the helpless victim but rather the hero. Clover contends that this androgynous figure allows for cross-gender identification, in that the target audience of most horror films, namely, young men, can relate to a woman when she is reconfigured under such a masculine guise: 'The Final Girl is ... a congenial double for the adolescent male. She is feminine enough to act out in a gratifying way, a way unapproved for adult males, the terrors and masochistic pleasures of the underlying fantasy, but not so feminine as to disturb the structures of male competence and sexuality' (Clover 51).

The tomboyish Anna succeeds in killing Alfredo only after he has abducted her and taken her to a cave covered in graffiti near some waterfalls outside Viterbo. The cave constitutes yet another example of an art source that sparks off hallucinations in Anna and is also a locus that fits Clover's description of the 'Terrible Place,' the location where much of the action is played out between attacker and victim in slasher films: 'Decidedly "intrauterine" in quality is the Terrible Place, dark and often damp, in which the killer lives or lurks and whence he stages his most terrifying attacks' (48). From the womb-like cave or 'Terrible Place,' where the 'Final Girl' eventually manages to defeat the serial rapist and murderer, a new Anna is born. Yet Anna's rebirth does not take place, like Lucy Honeychurch's, in Florence, where Forster's architecture of Piazza della Signoria holds sexual connotations also evoking the cave or the womb; Argento chooses to locate her reincarnation in her native town of Viterbo, and the new Anna is of a decidedly more troubling nature.

Back in Rome, before her bathroom mirror, Anna dons a long blond wig in an attempt to disguise a scar left by Alfredo's cutting her cheek with a razor, and adopts more conventionally feminine clothing (a white dress). This new look, complemented by dark glasses, recalls the femme fatale, and one scene in particular underscores this allusion, where Anna is depicted in Dottor Cavanna's office, announcing that she would now like to be called 'Luisa,' while wisps of cigarette smoke envelope her and the shadow of a Venetian blind is cast on her figure. Thus, another phase of the film is announced, one that stages Anna as the femme fatale in a film noir, with her blond wig recalling Veronica Lake's famous 'peekaboo' hairstyle that covered one eye.[22] The femme-fatale likeness has also been noted by Collette Balmain: 'In her final transformation, as iconic *femme fatale* (complete with blonde wig, red lipstick and high heels), Anna takes her violent revenge on the world of patriarchy: a world which insists on viewing her within the limits of image and desire and which ultimately fails her' (5).

In this latter section of the movie Anna is presented as eroticized and sexual, true to the tradition of the femme fatale: for instance, she and her new boyfriend Marie – the name clearly signals a play on standard conceptions of gender – kiss passionately and then make love in a park. At the same time, in this final part of the film, Anna perpetrates violence specifically against those men who care for her and have attempted to help her (Marie, Dottor Cavanna, Marco), which makes Balmain's claim that Argento's film is 'political' in its mission to 'provide a detailed and disturbing commentary on the consequences of violence on the female subject' (5) seem a difficult one to sustain. While one may sympathize with Anna throughout most of the film, by the end she has become a violent serial killer herself, equally capable of cruelty, especially towards the innocent. Her femme-fatale personality is the one that closes the film, and thus the 'definitive' version of her character presented is one that conforms to more established, indeed conservative, notions of femininity, rather than the androgynous 'Final Girl' of the earlier part of the film.

It is, in any case, problematic to contend that Argento wishes to comment on violence towards the female subject when *La sindrome di Stendhal* relishes in regaling the viewer with numerous bloodied, raped, dismembered, and lifeless female bodies, thus perpetuating rather than critiquing the problem.[23] Ultimately, Argento's film, rather than condemning violence against women, engages more with notions of the danger of art, and not just painting but cinema itself, especially the cinema of horror. When Anna undergoes her Stendhal Syndrome attacks and enters a series of artworks, the initially static canvasses begin to shift, waver, and transform themselves into surrogate screens. In these self-reflexive instances, the canvas has become a permeable membrane, signalling the interplay between art and life. All this is based primarily on the rhetoric of vision (sight constituting an even more important sense in Argento than in Stendhal or Forster): as the audience witnesses Anna looking at the canvas/screen and then entering it, we are reminded, in a metacinematic moment, of our own gaze in our role as spectators of the film itself.[24]

Alfredo, too, embodies the perils of gazing on art and, more seriously still, of gazing on Anna, of rendering her an object and violating her, metaphorically and physically. Repeatedly he comments on the power of art and, in Argento's book version, compares Anna directly to painting.[25] Forster's *A Room with a View* also plays with the equation between woman and art, as Lucy is frequently paralleled with painting, for instance, and she (successfully) struggles to break free from Cecil's classification of her as a Da Vinci figure in an attempt to reify her.[26] Anna, however, reacts more violently still to this objectification, indeed, violation on the part of the male: when she finally has the opportunity to avenge Alfredo's brutality towards her, she gouges out his eye with her finger, a move that echoes the rape-revenge movie, as described by Clover: 'It is no wonder, given the phallic associations of assaultive gazing, that rape-revenge films are so conspicuously concerned with vision and (hence) so frequently end with the blinding of the (would-be) rapist' (190). But Alfredo's wounded eye signals also a visual cue to the viewer, as Jean-Baptiste Thoret explains: 'Anche i primi piani di occhi, staccato *dall'orbita* e vero marchio di fabbrica argentiano, esprimono una volontà di indirizzarsi *direttamente* all'occhio dello spettatore, di connettersi a lui. L'occhio non è più superficie di proiezione ma d'impressione ...: metafora esemplare di una volontà di *impressionare*, costi quel che costi, lo spettatore' (96). [Even the close-ups of eyes, detached from their orbit and a true Argentian hallmark, express his desire to address the spectator's eye *directly*, to connect with him [sic]. The eye is no longer a surface of projection but rather one of impression ... an exemplary metaphor of the desire to make an impression on [in the sense of 'to shock'] the spectator, no matter the cost.] Thus, when Alfredo's eye is destroyed, the audience's eye is implicated as well, in a stratagem that exemplifies typical mechanisms of the horror film:

> Of course, horror films *do* attack their audiences. The attack is palpable; we take it in the eye. For just as the audience eye can be invited by the camera to assault, so it can be physically assaulted by the projected image – by sudden flashes of light, violent movement (of images plunging outward, for example), fast-cut or exploded images. These are the stock-in-trade of horror. (Clover 202–3)[27]

For Argento, the pairing of violence with paintings in his film serves, therefore, to alert the audience to the threat of art, and particularly of cinema, as the director himself elucidates: 'My overriding excitement concerned the fact that art can enrich our lives. Stendhal found out that wasn't true. It can also be debilitating. The possibility of Art being deadly really interested me. Violent images in film and on television are supposed to cause violence in viewers. The opening of *Suspiria* is often cited as causing people to faint yet this is art too. These are the questions I raise in *The Stendhal Syndrome*.'[28]

The director's treatment of art and its horrific connotations directly links his work, in particular *La sindrome di Stendhal*, to the sublime, as Thoret has also observed. According to this critic, Argento's use of gore in effect exemplifies the sublime in that it 'diventa ... l'espressione paradossale dell'immagine sublime, contemporaneamente affascinante (in superficie) e ripugnante (in profondità), violenta e pacata, crudele e seducente. La bella immagine seduce, l'immagine sublime affascina, la prima conserva la serenità al suo spettatore, la seconda lo scuote, lo turba, lo stravolge' (95). [becomes ... a paradoxical expression of the sublime image, simultaneously fascinating (on the surface) and repugnant (on a deeper level), violent and tranquil, cruel and seductive. A beautiful image seduces, a sublime image fascinates, the former preserves its spectator's serenity, the latter shakes him, disturbs him, distresses him.] For Thoret, too, Anna's mixed response of fascination and horror to art, in particular to the paintings in the Uffizi which she enters, is to be attributed to the notion of the sublime.[29]

While Argento's film clearly concerns itself with such rich and intriguing concepts of both the psychological and physical dangers of art and of the sublime, the director has evidently employed the Stendhal Syndrome as a multi-purpose device in his film, primarily to furnish an excuse to have the young police detective, like so many women in his films, become completely insane. By the end Anna Manni has metamorphosed into a schizophrenic killer, having adopted the identity of the serial murderer. Indeed, Anna represents the paradigmatic fractured self,[30] particularly evident in the frequent shots of her looking at her own reflection (for example, on numerous occasions in mirrors, as well as in the glass covering certain paintings – Botticelli's *Primavera* and Rembrandt's *Night Watch*), a filmic image often associated with the duplicitous woman. The monstrous Anna 'plays upon the *insecurity* of the boundaries between the "I" and the "not-I," between the real and the unreal' (Donald 237), much as monsters in horror movies typify life/death anguish. Furthermore, to quote Donald citing Robin Wood: 'The figure of the Monster *dramatises* "all that our civilization *represses* or *oppresses*" – that means ... female sexuality, the proletariat, other cultures, ethnic groups, alternative ideologies, homosexuality and bisexuality, and children' (236).

No wonder, then, that the provocative and aggressive Anna Manni, after having managed to kill not only the serial murderer but also three other men, is ultimately denied a role of agency; her insanity renders her impotent as she is captured by the police. As Janey Place puts it in her essay 'Women in Film Noir,' 'The ideological operation of the myth (the absolute necessity of controlling the strong, sexual woman) is thus achieved by first demonstrating her dangerous power and its frightening results, then destroying it' (45). The closing shots of *La sindrome di Stendhal* represent a defeated Anna, prostrate in the arms of the various policemen and detectives who have arrested her, in a pose that recollects Christ's Deposition and underscores the pathos of the scene.[31] The dynamic of violence towards women and their utter subjection in Argento's film, I would argue, is all part and parcel of the sociologizing of the Other, as Donald terms it (237). Argento's fascination with Otherness is incarnated by the female figure (an insane one at that), a woman who embodies his exploration of the boundaries of sexuality and identity, but whose agency, in the end, is negated, thus rendering his depiction of women essentially punitive.

In contrast, Forster offers a portrayal of a young heroine in a similar setting that is more nuanced and affirmative. Moreover, it is interesting that Forster employs this more positive female figure, rather than a man, in a novel that is concerned with a character's growing awareness of sensuality, an experience that takes place in an Italian context. Forster was reticent about his own homosexuality in his literary production, and Lucy Honeychurch thus allows him to express his own same-sex desire obliquely in her role as, to use Goldman's term, 'gay cipher' (132–4).[32] Like Palazzeschi, Forster employs a female stand-in for his own concern with sexuality, but his heroine – while at times being gently mocked – is depicted with more deference and respect than in the case of the comic-pathetic Materassi Sisters.

Although Lucy Honeychurch acts as a felicitous figure through which Forster explores sexual alterity, her contact with ethnic Others in Italy is enacted within limited boundaries. She clearly cannot communicate with Italians, given her lack of knowledge of the language, and she meets very few while in Florence, apart from the cart-driver ('Phaethon') and the man she witnesses being stabbed; even the hotel owner is from London. Nonetheless, Lucy responds to Italy's alterity – and Florence's sublime – with a mixture of fascination and trepidation. Stendhal, too, with his 'reverse racism,' depicts an enthusiastic reaction both to the sublime and to the Other – in this case the Italian Other – a phenomenon typical of much of his oeuvre. The Forsterian subject, moreover, is frequently caught in a dialectic wherein contact with the foreign causes an 'anxiety' that, to use Homi Bhabha's words, 'reveals a negotiation with the "irremovable strangenesses" of cultural difference' (37) and can lead to either dire or favourable consequences. Argento, on the other hand, has rendered Florence's impact on Anna Manni a hazardous contact with the sublime, designed instead to weaken her agency, exploring therefore primarily gendered Otherness, more than cultural or ethnic alterity.

Each one of these varied writers and filmmakers has chosen Florence as the locus that incarnates the dynamic between self and Other, between the sublime and the horrific, thus adapting the city's landscape in an almost startling way so as to illustrate their own individuated concerns. In these diverse accounts, the idealized monuments and artistic masterpieces of the Renaissance, a magnet for travellers throughout the centuries, hold hidden dangers – as well as the potential for regeneration – for the unsuspecting tourist.

5 'Going Native': Tuscan Houses and Italian Others in Contemporary American Travel Writing

Tuscan rural spaces, rather than Florence's historic centre, constitute the locus for negotiating cultural alterity and seeking to establish one's own identity in texts by contemporary American travel writers who have resettled in the countryside. The English-speaking world's attraction to Italy, and in particular central Italy, dates at the very least back to the days of the Grand Tour as well as to the nineteenth-century British colonization of Tuscany.[1] The central Italian regions' allure has endured up to the present, as witnessed in the phenomenon of the farming area of Chianti (tellingly dubbed 'Chiantishire' in popular parlance) functioning as a fashionable holiday destination, a trend exemplified by Tony Blair's highly publicized sojourns, as well as by those of countless other British tourists. This long-standing fixation on Italy's central regions, especially Tuscany, has consequently had its effect on anglophone authors, from the Brownings, Ruskin, Henry James, D.H. Lawrence, E.M. Forster, and Mary McCarthy to Michael Ondaatje and contemporary travel writers. In fact, since the mid-1990s there has been a veritable spate of travel literature on Tuscany that – in a formula along the lines of Peter Mayle's much disparaged books set in *Provence*[2] – extols the *dolce vita* in rural Central Italy.

These texts are usually penned by those who have been fortunate enough to afford to rent, and in many cases acquire, a house in the area (something that I begrudgingly acknowledge, given that I, and probably most readers, can empathize with the desire to actually own a Tuscan villa). This particular strain of travel literature generally does not involve the narration of a journey per se, in that the author recounts the personal experience of residing in one specific Tuscan locality, rather than outlining a voyage throughout the country. The writer may describe shorter day trips in the vicinity, but always returns to his or her adoptive home. As the following list attests, in recent years a plethora of these books has been published by a wide variety of English-speaking writers hailing from different countries such as Britain, the United States, Australia, and New Zealand: Phil Doran, *The Reluctant Tuscan: How I Discovered My Inner Italian* (2005); Isabella Dusi, *Vanilla Beans and Brodo: Real Life in the Hills of Tuscany* (2001) and *Bel Vino: A Year of Sundrenched Pleasure among the Vines of Tuscany* (2004); Paul Gervais, *A Garden in Lucca: Finding Paradise in Tuscany* (2000); Ferenc Maté, *The Hills of Tuscany: A New Life in an Old Land* (1998); Eric Newby, *A Small Place in Italy* (1994); Allan Parker, *Seasons in Tuscany: A Tale of Two Loves* (2000) and *Ciao, Tuscany* (2001); Tony Rocca, *Catching Fireflies: Capturing the Dream of a Tuscan Vineyard* (2004); and Matthew Spender, *Within Tuscany: Reflections on a Time and Place* (1993). The fascination for settlement literature situated in Tuscany is not limited to one particular nationality but rather has widespread appeal in the English-speaking world; indeed, the approach of these books towards the topic is quite similar, to the extent that they become repetitive.[3]

Typically, these Central Italian travel memoirs are found in the 'Travel Literature' section in most bookshops, an indication that, at least for marketing purposes, they are commonly perceived as pertaining to that category. And rightly so, I would argue, given that these narratives conform to a fundamental dynamic inherent to the genre: namely, the relationship between the Self and the Other. Casey Blanton, in her introduction to *Travel Writing: The Self and the World*, qualifies travel books as 'vehicles whose main purpose is to introduce us to the other'; and, she says, 'typically they [have] dramatized an engagement between self and world.' Blanton proceeds to state that, as far as the critical approach used in her volume is concerned, 'it was a matter of focusing on the various ways the observing self and the foreign world reverberate within each work' (Blanton xi).

Attempting to circumscribe the limits of travel writing as a genre any more than Blanton has done is virtually a futile endeavour: travel literature notoriously remains difficult to define.[4] Indeed, Peter Hulme, in his discussion of late-twentieth-century travel writing, points out that

> the parameters of travel are almost impossible to set. Xavier de Maistre wrote about a voyage around his bedroom, and there is no minimum length of stay laid down in the travel writer's handbook. However, most travel writing involves the experience of foreign cultures and languages,

and some travel writers practice a kind of deep immersion in the cultures they are visiting, acquiring the sort of intimate knowledge which gives them access to people and places unknown to short-stay travellers, let alone tourists. (Hulme 97)

Significantly, Hulme then cites Peter Robb's *Midnight in Sicily* – another travelogue set in Italy and penned by a long-term, non-native resident – as an example of the sort of travel writing involving an 'investment of time.' Hulme's observations, along with those of other critics, confirm that Robb's work, along with that of other writers who produce so-called settlement literature, has by now established itself as a sub-genre of travel literature.[5]

In the texts explored in this chapter, this spatial shift from narrative of movement to account of settled life in a new land frequently addresses the topos of life among the locals, and leads to an avid interest in the actual house itself, as well as its garden, and a detailed delineation of their reconstruction, all within the context of the author attempting to engage with foreign (in this case Italian) Otherness. For although the narrative in such texts remains primarily anchored to one geographical area, the kinds of remarks made regarding native culture and the relationships established with the local population follow schemas typical of most travelogues, with the author reiterating clichés easily traced in travel writing from various places and periods.

My analysis focuses on two relatively recent travel/settlement narratives (both by Americans but highly representative of the many set in central Italy by anglophone authors): one is the extremely successful *Under the Tuscan Sun: At Home in Italy* of 1996, by Frances Mayes, which became a *New York Times* bestseller and led to the follow-up *Bella Tuscany: The Sweet Life in Italy* (1999) and the coffee-table book *In Tuscany* (2000), and has even inspired the eponymous film, directed by Audrey Wells and starring Diane Lane and Raoul Bova (2003). Mayes has also published *Bringing Tuscany Home* (2004), which focuses on interior decorating, 'Tuscan style.' Her recent publications include the photobook entitled *Shrines: Images of Italian Worship* (2006) and a travelogue that wanders further afield: *A Year in the World* (2006). The second text I consider is the lesser-known *In Maremma: Life and a House in Southern Tuscany* (2001), written by David Leavitt (a recognized novelist in his own right) and his partner Mark Mitchell.[6]

In the two travel memoirs in question, the move to Italy signifies a change of lifestyle and a new beginning, in essence, a rebirth, a word so often associated with the proverbial 'Renaissance' Tuscany.[7] This trope of renewal is furthermore linked with the renovation (from *re + novare*, to make new again) of the recently acquired abode, and thus the house becomes an integral spatial figure in the writer's construction (literal and figurative) of his or her new 'Italianate' self.[8]

Mayes, a published poet and academic, recounts her experiences as a middle-aged American having undergone a divorce and deciding, along with her new partner, Ed, to buy and restore a house in the countryside near Cortona. Mayes continues to reside primarily in San Francisco, where she teaches, but regularly returns to Cortona for the summer months. Leavitt and Mitchell also move to Italy from the United States, purchasing and renovating a house in Maremma, an area in southern Tuscany less well known than the zones between Florence and Siena (the renowned Chianti wine-growing hills). Their book posits the move to Tuscany as essentially a permanent one, but Leavitt has since taken up a position at the University of Florida and so the couple divide their time between Gainesville and Maremma.

For Leavitt/Mitchell and Mayes, the move to Italy signifies having to adapt to new customs and habits and a coming to terms not only with Italian culture in all its ramifications (from food to art to bureaucracy), but also with Italians themselves. Yet the writers' rapport with Tuscany and Tuscans, and, by extension, Italy and Italians – Tuscany is assigned metonymic value by these writers, in that it becomes representative of the entire nation – is fundamentally conflicted.[9] On the one hand, they seem to want to maintain their sense of being foreign and thus continually categorize Italians as Others (a classification accomplished in various ways, as my study will point out); yet on the other there exists a desire to prove themselves 'Italian,' as fully acclimatized to and integrated into Italian society. Italians are thus represented as embodying an alien Otherness and yet simultaneously symbolize, for these foreign writers, a more 'genuine' way of life to which they aspire. Furthermore, the house (along with its trappings) becomes an extremely significant figure through which the writer can tangibly demonstrate his or her belonging to Italy, for, as Madan Sarup phrases it, 'the concept of home seems to be tied in some way with the notion of identity' (95).[10]

The Italians as Others

Just how do these travel writers characterize Italians? Through a number of (presumably unconscious) techniques Leavitt/Mitchell and Mayes repeatedly represent Italians as Others by endorsing stereotypes about the people and the culture that create a distancing effect between the authors and their objects of examination. The fact that the writers seemingly possess a less-than-expert command of the Italian language creates a lack of communication that surely must lead to certain misunderstandings of the people and culture. Mayes first arrives in Italy with almost non-existent Italian; Leavitt and Mitchell are in the process of learning it. Despite peppering their prose with Italian idioms and phrases – presumably for the effect of added authenticity – it would seem that none of the writers is particularly proficient in the language, at least at the time of writing their books, judging from the various mistakes made when providing Italian vocabulary or attempting to explain pronunciation (only so much can be attributed to careless copy editing).[11]

That travel writers should misrepresent or generalize about autochthonous populations is not remarkable or uncommon; in fact, it is virtually a trademark of the genre. But what interests me is specifically *how* the writers go about categorizing and what the resultant effects are. By endorsing stereotypes about Italians, they effectively construct them as Others, and in many cases Others who are perceived as belonging to another time, a time different from that of the writer. Distancing between the observer and the observed therefore occurs in two ways: (1) via generalizations about the observed expressed in the present tense, without explicit chronological references; (2) in comparisons between the observed and its past or its history.

Johannes Fabian, in his *Time and the Other*, has labelled such distancing 'the denial of coevalness,' or 'a persistent and systematic tendency to place the referent(s) of anthropology in a Time other than the present of the producer of anthropological discourse' (31). While Fabian is referring to the situation of the anthropologist vis-à-vis the subjects of his or her study, the techniques he describes also ring true for these travel writers, who find themselves in analogous circumstances with regard to the local population under their scrutiny and who, significantly, are working in a hybrid literary genre that owes much to anthropology.[12] While time references to Italians are certainly explicit in these two literary texts (as will be discussed shortly), the effect of 'allochronism,' as Fabian describes it (here in reference to an anthropological discourse), is not purely reliant on overt chronological distancing, but can be signalled instead by other markers:

> Physical time is seldom used in its naked, chronological form ... Labels

that connote temporal distancing need not have explicitly temporal references (such as *cyclical* or *repetitive*). Adjectives like *mythical*, *ritual*, or even *tribal*, will serve the same function. They, too, connote temporal distancing as a way of creating the objects or referents of anthropological discourse. (Fabian 30)

Thus, for Fabian, the subject can allocate a status of alterity to the object through the adoption of certain phrases connoting, for example, primitivism, even if the language of time is absent.

In Leavitt/Mitchell's and Mayes's texts, a relegation of Italians to the status of Others is at times effected without the explicit use of time indicators, but rather through reliance on essentialisms about Italians and the Italian character that create this distancing. Numerous textual incidences illustrate this tendency:

Like many Italian men, his cologne or aftershave surrounds him with a lemony, sunny aura only slightly dispelled by the cigarette smoke. (Mayes, *Tuscan Sun* 43)

I think there's a microbe in Italian painters' bloodstreams that infects them with the compulsion to paint Jesus and Mary. (Ibid. 164–5)

Italians seem to like this way of being at the beach. So many people to talk to! (Ibid. 183)

For though Italians are vocal in criticizing their government, the fact remains that Italians have more or less the system they have chosen, and perhaps even want. (Leavitt and Mitchell, *In Maremma* 71)

Francesco was tall and soulful and always wore a long white laboratory coat rather like a doctor's. (Italians love uniforms.) (Ibid. 74)

For some, social analysis is a bore. The longer one lives in Italy, the more it becomes an amusement. After all, the Italian adores holding forth, even on subjects about which he knows nothing. (Ibid. 93)

The only thing we find hateful about the Italians is their willingness to destroy their own patrimony – the Uffizi in Florence, the Teatro la Fenice in Venice, the church of San Giovanni Laterano in Rome – for the most selfish of motives. (Ibid. 120)

These essentialisms are frequently signalled by the use of the definite article before the noun of nationality, as well as by the verb (often a copula) being conjugated in the third person singular or plural, in the present tense. According to Fabian, 'the present [tense] unduly magnifies the claim of a statement to general validity' (80) and, he continues, 'at the very least ... the present tense "freezes" a society at the time of observation; at worst, it contains assumptions about the repetitiveness, predictability, and conservatism of primitives' (81); furthermore, 'the present tense is a signal identifying a discourse as an observer's language' (86). Stereotypes such as the ones cited above, therefore, relegate Italians to the role of (primitive) Other in the discourse engendered by these (and many other) travel writers as they observe Italian society.

Categorizations of Italians in Leavitt/Mitchell's and Mayes's texts are in other instances linked more directly to temporal referents. Italy and Italians are repeatedly compared to their ancient past, a relatively easy trope for writers to employ, given that Tuscany is replete with physical evidence of its history, from Etruscan and Roman ruins to the masterpieces of medieval and Renaissance art that abound in the region.

Thus, the compulsion to compare Italians to the country's ancient roots, to the mythological figures and the art of centuries gone-by, is almost irresistible. Russo Bullaro comments on Mayes's 'Romanticized' vision of Tuscany: 'Sacrificing the present to the past, Mayes defines places not by what they are today but by their history, thus reinforcing the Romantic tendency to exoticize the familiar. In Tuscany she is "haunted" by the Etruscans, Gela is where Aeschylus died' (8).[13] Textual examples of this emphasis on the past are numerous in *Under the Tuscan Sun*; when describing the son of one of the workers on the house, Mayes says, 'He looks like a little Medici prince, petulant and bored as he stands around listlessly kicking stones with the toe of his tennis shoe' (63). She also depicts a smith who works wrought iron in similar terms: 'The man who unfolds from Giuseppe's *cinque cento* [sic] could have stepped from behind a time shield of the Middle Ages ... My impression that he has stepped out of time strengthens. Where *is* Aphrodite, surely somewhere near this forge?' (68, 69). Mayes continually makes similar comments that in effect relegate Italians to their history: 'His slicked-back black hair, wanting to revert to curls, falls over his forehead. He looks like Caravaggio's Bacchus – only he has moss-green eyes and a slight slouch, probably from leaning into the speed of his Lancia' (43).

Mayes also seems to enjoy delving even further back in time in her statements about today's Italians, 'Qualities those of us with northern blood envy – that Italian insouciance and ability to live in the moment with gusto – I now see came down straight from the Etruscans' (187). Thus, according to Mayes, what she perceives as Italian *joie de vivre* is actually the result of an Etruscan legacy, and so she presents 'the Italian character' as being inextricably linked to its ancient origins.[14] Leavitt and Mitchell, too, do not hesitate to liken Italians to their artistic past: 'It was raining, and as Michele didn't have an umbrella, at the end of the evening he had to run home in order not to get drenched. How like a figure in a painting by Piero della Francesca he looked!' (Leavitt and Mitchell, *In Maremma* 108).

Not only are Italians inevitably linked to their history, they are perceived as having a unique relationship to time. Italy consequently is represented as a place where time slows down: 'I think most Italians have a longer sense of time than we do,' says Mayes when talking about having the work completed on her house. 'What's the hurry? Once up, a building will stand a long, long time, perhaps a thousand years. Two weeks, two months, big deal' (*Tuscan Sun* 45); and again: 'For once we don't start asking for the date of completion, the one thing we've learned to insist on to counter the enviable Latin sense of endless time' (ibid. 70).

Leavitt and Mitchell express similar feelings about Italy and time: 'We live in Maremma not by chance, not by default, but because it feels like home ... Living here is rather like being caught between the seventeenth and twenty-first centuries: Modern inventions make aspects of life easy, but remnants of ancient ways endure' (*In Maremma* 137–8). They also declare that 'the most useful thing anyone living in Italy can learn is how to be bored' (38), thus implying that time moves slowly there. Yet Leavitt/Mitchell's and Mayes's pronouncements about Italy's timeless quality are illustrative of their own perceptions, since in Tuscany they apparently are not tied to the sort of stressful work routine that would characterize their lives in the United States.

The attitudes revealed by Leavitt/Mitchell's and Mayes's prose are essentially nothing short of colonialist, and follow an established pattern in the discourse of travel in rural Europe, as observed by Joanne P. Sharp:

> Travel in the form of (semi-)permanent migration to rural areas is obviously based upon motivations and couched in expectations that differ from travel outside Europe. However, the parallel with the colonial traveller is often maintained, especially when the destination is the countryside. Despite the modern-industrial realities of much of the countryside

in Europe, it is predominantly represented in the English media as immediate, natural and timeless in contrast to the modernity and rationality of metropolitan life. (203)

While Sharp's comments are aimed specifically at British perceptions of rural continental Europe (her study concerns Peter Mayle's Provence books), the dynamic she describes certainly applies to the American reactions to the same context as witnessed in the texts I examine (and in those by other English-speaking writers on the same subject).

How the Writers See Themselves

This 'denial of coevalness' towards the Italians on the part of Leavitt/Mitchell and Mayes is ultimately paradoxical; while on the one hand there is a discernible colonialist stance of superiority towards the 'natives,' the writers themselves seem to desire, at least on a certain level, to integrate, to become Italian and 'go native' themselves.[15] Their endorsement of stereotypes reinforces this attraction-repulsion towards and from Italians, for, as Riggins explains, stereotypes 'are one of the major discursive strategies that ensure that differences between people are recognized. Through stereotypes, the Self expresses *ambivalence* toward Others, expressing not just derision but derision and desire' (Riggins 10). Clearly when commenting on Italy and Italians, these writers have been voicing their own identity crisis; as Fabian puts it, they have been 'hiding the self in statements about the Other,' since 'all statements about others are paired with the observer's experience' (91).

For instance, in her portrayal of time as being slower in Italy, Mayes is basically attempting to reinscribe her own relationship to time, and to slow down herself when living in Tuscany, a place where this is indeed more feasible for her, given that she is thousands of miles away from her demanding job as an academic in California. Her attitude is reiterated not only in her other books on Tuscany but also in an interview: 'The Italians know how to live. They have more fun than the rest of us. They inhabit time in a way that makes the day long. The cycle of seasons profoundly changes what they eat and what they do' (George).

On another level, the authors' insistence on Italy's timelessness, on its past, can also be interpreted as symptomatic of time relations that characterize our postmodern era. Urry's analysis of 'instantaneous time' identifies an increased nostalgia for (a sanitized version of) the past that ignores issues of social deprivation and inequality (Urry 218).

In his *Consuming Places*, the social theorist catalogues the characteristics that typify this amplified desire for the past, which for him include

> the belief that social life in the present is profoundly disappointing and that in important ways the past was preferable to the present – there really was a golden age; the increased aesthetic sensibility to old places, crafts, houses, countryside and so on, so that almost everything that is old is thought to be valuable whether it is an old master or an old cake tin; the need nevertheless for a certain re-presentation of the past – to construct a cleaned-up heritage look suitable for the gaze of tourists; the interpretation of history through artefacts, an artefactual history, which in part conceals underlying social relations. (219)

Mayes's and Leavitt/Mitchell's texts, then, reflect the current desire for times gone by, be it in their typecasting of Italians as their past, or in their presentation of their Italian houses with their historic features and various furnishings that constitute the artefacts of history.

Many statements in the texts concern the writers' own identity with respect to their adoptive homeland, and how they see themselves. The writers' vision of the new self oscillates between being either irrepressibly foreign or almost more Italian than the Italians themselves. This vacillation between feelings of being either assimilated or an outsider is, according to Holland and Huggan, a common thread in a genre where the sense of self is interrogated: 'In many travel narratives this instability is exacerbated, and … self-inquiries conducted by travel writers, even the most apparently unsophisticated, are often likely to reveal a conflicted sense of belonging and allegiance' (Holland and Huggan 14). Perhaps the impression of divided identity is heightened all the more in this particular sub-genre of travel writing (i.e., settlement literature), where the status of landowner in the foreign country could intensify the desire to assimilate, more than if the writer were merely passing through.

Textual examples of Mayes's wrestling with changeable identities are frequent. For example, her remarks about her partner's adaptability to Italian driving, conversation, and eating would indicate a kind of integration into the local culture: 'Ed is passing cars at 140 kilometers an hour; I'm afraid he has taken rather naturally to the blood sport of Italian driving' (*Tuscan Sun* 49); and in another instance: 'My idea of heaven is a two-hour lunch with Ed. I believe he must have been Italian in another life. He has begun to gesture and wave his hands, which I've never seen him do. He likes to cook at home but simply throws himself into it here' (129). Furthermore, when reflecting on herself and a group of ex-pats living in Tuscany, Mayes herself claims to feel virtually more integrated in Italy than in the United States:

> I feel immersed here; my 'real life' seems remote. Odd that we're all here. We were given one country and we've set ourselves up in another ... We feel so much at home, pale and American as we are. We could just stay here, go native. Let my hair grow long, tutor local kids in English, ride a Vespa into town for bread ... (*Stranieri*, foreigners, we're called, but it sounds more dire, more like strangers, an oddly chilling word.) (132–3)

On the other hand, she also has misgivings about ever being fully assimilated, replicating yet again stereotypes about Italy: 'How Italian will we ever be? Not very, I'm afraid. Too pale. Too unable to gesture as a natural accompaniment to talking' (194); and, later on: 'Splendid to arrive alone in a foreign country and feel the assault of difference. Here they are all along, busy with living; they don't talk or look like me. The rhythm of their day is entirely different; I am thoroughly foreign' (243).

This ambivalence about belonging to Italy pervades Mayes's text, and the following passage from a concluding chapter added to a later edition is worth quoting at length, given its reinforcement of the conflicting mechanisms that characterize *Under the Tuscan Sun*:

> The house and garden's changes over a decade ... parallel the changes in our lives among the Italians. Once we were the *stranieri*, the foreigners, who'd been crazy enough to take on a house abandoned for thirty years. Now we just live here. It is a commonly accepted idea that when Americans move to a foreign country, the local people never really accept them. Equally mistaken is the assumption that these expats regard all locals as amusing stereotypes. Cortona is home ... We have a tribe of Italian friends and everyone we know there is vividly singular. Our neighbors are as close as family. What luck – the intense sense of community that we once observed in this small hilltown now includes us. We are comfortable in a wider, deeper sense than I ever dreamed.
>
> My realization of the profound change in my life happened at the ceremony when I was made an honorary citizen of this noble town. No one does ceremonies like the Italians ... The events symbolized just how wildly unexpected my life had become. We are changed by place. I'm fascinated to the core to learn how fundamentally different Italy is; to

learn that the world is not small; that they are not like us. I am so happy for that. (293–4)

For Mayes, the parallel between her house's (and garden's) existence and her own is made explicit; the Italian house reflects the transformation, she maintains, that she and Ed have undergone, and has legitimized their belonging to Cortona in the eyes of their neighbours. Mayes asserts that, despite what might be common assumptions to the contrary, she and her partner have been accepted by the locals, and that she, in turn, does not portray the locals through stereotypes. Almost in the same breath, however, Mayes talks about having a 'tribe' of friends, employing language which is particularly telling, given the associations Fabian has pointed out for terminology figuring the indigenous as 'primitive.' Then, just a few lines further down, Mayes again applies the kind of generalization about Italians that is so frequent in her prose ('No one does ceremonies like the Italians').

Moreover, from Mayes's subjective stance, it is the *Italians* who are different, not the writer herself. Her statement 'they are not like us' endorses the Self/Other division through its language, for as Riggins reminds us: 'Expressions that are the most revealing of the boundaries separating Self and Other are *inclusive and exclusive pronouns and possessives* such as *we and they, us and them,* and *ours and theirs*' (Riggins 8). In *Under the Tuscan Sun* the reader is aware that the author has made friends with residents, but we are not privy to the locals' thoughts about her. Rarely are direct speech or extended dialogues with Italians themselves supplied, making the question of the perception of assimilation a complex one. Indeed, the privileged point of view is strictly Mayes's and the book revolves around *her* needs, around 'the attainment of individual desire,' as Jeffrey Folks phrases it (105). Mayes's text indicates a deep-rooted ambivalence about integration in Italy to the bitter end.

Leavitt and Mitchell seem to be wryly aware that they are foreigners in a foreign land, and so while they at times successfully pick up Italian habits and ways of thinking, they often revert to an American mode of being (take, for example, their craving for peanut butter [91]). When confronting the bureaucratic complexities of obtaining driver's licences in Italy, they comment:

> We think about it. We grow calmer. Of course the documents must agree, we acknowledge. There is no reason to be angry with the examiner. He had *ragione*. He was just doing his job. Only hours later, once we are back

at Podere Fiume, do we realize what really happened that morning: For a few moments we had been thinking like Italians. (66)

After this brief instance of 'thinking Italian,' another incident occurs that intensifies their sense of being American. At the Terme di Saturnia, the two men observe the other guests (for the most part Italians) who are bathing in the springs, and reflect on their own situation: 'As for us – the pleasure of being, as Byron wrote, "among them but not one of them"' (97). This elliptical statement provides a clear example of Riggins's pronominal dichotomy cited above.

Ultimately, however, the Italianization process seems to grab hold all the more strongly with Leavitt and Mitchell, and the book concludes with the following assertion: 'We moved here to capture a dream less of Italy than of being foreigners in Italy, figures in a Forster novel. And yet Italy has a way of refusing to remain only a background. It grows into you, just as you grow into it ... After seven years, in ways we could never have predicted, we have become Italian' (140). By the end of their narrative, Leavitt and Mitchell portray themselves as inevitably succumbing to the Italian way of life, and proclaim themselves fully integrated. What the locals might think of this assimilation is not indicated,[16] but clearly the physical entity and literary device that serves to anchor these three writers' identity all the more to the foreign land is the house itself.

Identity and Home

'Ah, the foreign self,' exclaims Mayes. 'The new life might shape itself to the contours of the house, which already is at home in the landscape, and to the rhythms around it' (*Tuscan Sun* 25). This process of pseudo-assimilation to Italian culture and society is embodied most of all through the figure of the house. The words 'home' and 'house' are in fact part of both texts' subtitles – *Under the Tuscan Sun: At Home in Italy* and *In Maremma: Life and a House in Southern Tuscany*[17] – and the distinction between the two words' significance is worth noting:

> The term 'house' is often paired with (or interchanged with) 'home' (German: *Haus und Heim*). These two terms describe distinct cultural constructions ... While 'house' implies a physical structure or shelter, 'home' defines a place of origin and retreat, such as one's natal village or birthplace, one's country or other native place. Home is a concept of place rather than space, implying emotional attachment and meaning beyond the

constraints of the physicality of any particular dwelling house ... 'Home,' thus, may take on the meaning of a territory, a physical reference point, a symbol of self, or a manifestation of family identity. (Birdwell-Pheasant and Lawrence-Zúñiga 6)

Both terms are relevant to this analysis, given that the texts in question focus on the physical entity of the house and, like most travel writing, address the opposition home-away.

Why then such insistence on the home/house as a key image in both Mayes and Leavitt/Mitchell? 'Home,' a complex, polyvalent signifier, has indeed been problematized by many writers, and James Clifford reminds us that 'the definition of "home" is fundamentally at issue here. In local/global situations where displacement appears increasingly to be the norm, how is collective dwelling sustained and reinvented? ... Binary oppositions between home and abroad, staying and moving, need to be thoroughly questioned' (Clifford 84). For Leavitt/Mitchell and Mayes, reconstructing a 'home' for themselves in a foreign land is intrinsically linked with their sense of Italy and Italians, as well as with their own identity and their attempts to refashion it. Mayes herself shows an awareness of the significance of the figure of the house: 'The house is a metaphor for the self, of course, but it also is totally real. And a *foreign* house exaggerates all the associations houses carry. Because I had ended a long marriage that was not supposed to end and was establishing a new relationship, this house quest felt tied to whatever new identity I would manage to forge' (*Tuscan Sun* 25).

The house therefore becomes an integral part of the process of 'constructing indigeneity'[18] in various ways for these writers, for it can be

- a fashioning of the house as self (symptomatic also of the trend of 'interior decorating'),
- the house as history,
- the house as part of the settler myth, or
- the summer house.

These categories are to an extent my own, and are also partially derived from Marjorie Garber's *Sex and Real Estate: Why We Love Houses*. Garber equates today's middle-class, middle-aged obsession with real estate to the fascination college students have with sex. She compares the process of 'grown-ups' buying a house in today's market to the dating game, and posits the house as object of the buyer's desire, and ultimately as his or her 'beloved.' That Leavitt/Mitchell and Mayes fall in love with Italy and, simultaneously, with their Italian houses, then, would seem logical.[19] What Garber's book critiques, however, is the consumer frenzy that surrounds the house. Given that her book addresses a topic about which there is sufficient interest to make it all the more marketable, she is, of course (along with the writers discussed), happily capitalizing on Western society's current obsession with interior decorating.[20]

Indeed, Mayes (like many others, including Leavitt and Mitchell, in her footsteps) has tapped into a winning formula, since her text presents itself as a 'lifestyle book' that appeals to those who read so-called shelter magazines (e.g., *House and Garden* or *Architectural Digest*), gardening manuals, travel guides, travel inserts and travel magazines, as well as upscale recipe books and food journals, or who watch the numerous television programs dedicated to these topics. Television series devoted to real estate or property makeovers have multiplied exponentially in the past few years, with at least one entire channel devoted to the subject in the United States and Canada (HGTV, House and Garden Television) and a minimum of two in the United Kingdom (Real Estate TV and Overseas Property TV). The property craze has spawned many other series, such as ABC's *Extreme Makeover: Home Edition* or *The Painted Room* (on the DIY network), and European counterparts *Relocation Relocation* (on Britain's Channel 4), *Escape to the Country* and *Love the Place You're In* (both on UKTV Style), *Property Ladder* (Discovery Travel and Living), and Ireland's *Househunters in the Sun*. Many of these television programs depend on the 'makeover' format, presenting a property in the 'before' and 'after' phases, a popular mode for portraying the renovation of gardens, houses, or even people themselves (for instance, British programs such as Channel 4's *Extreme Makeover* or *Love the Place You're In*, or *The Swan* and *Queer Eye for the Straight Guy* in the United States).[21] Such programs provide a 'quick fix' solution that plainly appeals to contemporary viewers, where by injecting money into places or people, one can effect rapid change, both in physical appearance and, consequently, it is presumed, in identity.

Mayes's books and assorted 'Tuscan Sun' accoutrements, moreover, cater to the materialistic desires of readers in their promotion of a new lifestyle and identity. *Under the Tuscan Sun* includes detailed descriptions of the house renovations, the cultivation of Mayes's garden, as well as the preparation of Tuscan food (she even includes recipes), all this in the context of the popular holiday destination, the 'exotic' (but not *too* exotic) Tuscany. Many shelter magazines, gourmet programs, cookbooks, and television shows are also fascinated with Italy, given its varied cuisine and landscape. Hampshire's guide *Buying a Home in Italy* sums up the qualities that, according to him, make Italy such a desirable location:

> Italy is one of the most beautiful countries in Europe, possibly the most alluring of all ... Few other countries in the world offer such an exhilarating mixture of beauty, culture, history, sophistication and style. When buying property in Italy, you aren't simply buying a home, but a lifestyle. As a location for a holiday, retirement or permanent home, Italy has few rivals, and in addition to the wide choice of properties and generally good value, it offers a fine climate for most of the year, particularly in the centre and south. (18)

Italy, then, embodies a 'lifestyle.' The media both promote and take advantage of the country's mystique, and popular culture seems obsessed with things Italian. A couple of examples suffice to illustrate this widespread phenomenon: Jamie Oliver's foray into Italian cooking, for instance, resulted in the television series *Jamie's Great Italian Escape* (Channel 4) and the associated recipe book *Jamie's Italy*. Magazines, too, frequently feature Italian themes: for instance, the November 2002 issue of *House and Garden* includes a piece on a Tuscan House, 'Before and After: Creating a Family Retreat in Tuscany – A Personal Account,' that is representative of so many other similar articles which typify the expat dream of buying a Tuscan house and giving it a makeover.

Mayes's books clearly cater to this desire for Italy, a civilization portrayed as exotic but not so foreign as to be alienating, either for her or for her readers. Her most recent books, which consist primarily of photos and text, serve to render Tuscany more accessible to the reader, and promote Mayes's idea of the 'Tuscan aesthetic,' as well as the associated consumer goods. The appearance of *In Tuscany*, for instance, essentially mimics the home magazine layout, with its carefully arranged shots of interiors and exteriors of her home (see figure 6).

Mayes's latest product in this vein is *Bringing Tuscany Home*, which advocates a 'Tuscan look' for interior décor, supplying pointers as to how to achieve this effect, and even going so far as to provide details on purchasing items, among them replicas of Tuscan antiques that Mayes owns and that have spawned her own line of furniture for Drexel Heritage. The name of the furniture company itself is revealing; in the passage quoted from Urry above (page 129), the theorist talks of the present-day attraction to the objects of history, of the promotion of 'a

Figure 6 Images of Mayes's house and garden, Bramasole, Cortona, from *In Tuscany*

cleaned up heritage look suitable for the gaze of tourists' that ignores, however, the 'underlying social relations.' Mayes's furniture line is based on antiques she has collected for her own home, whose origins presumably are in the Tuscan rural farming community. Yet questions of social inequality (both past and present) are for the most part glossed over by Mayes, while she and the furniture industry profit from the replicas they are producing. This blatant marketing of the 'Tuscan' phenomenon is clearly resulting in financial gain for Mayes and her publishers. Indeed, she has acquired sufficient capital to buy and restore yet another house in the countryside near Cortona, and delineates the vicissitudes of this latest project in *Bringing Tuscany Home*.

It follows, then, that Mayes's *Under the Tuscan Sun* as well as Leavitt and Mitchell's *In Maremma* deliberately cater to the interior-design element. Mayes recognizes her own fascination with domestic décor, and for her, the way in which the house is decorated is a reflection of the self:

> What is this thrall for houses? I come from a long line of women who open their handbags and take out swatches of upholstery material, colored squares of bathroom tile, seven shades of yellow paint samples, and strips of flowered wallpaper. We love the concept of four walls. 'What is her house like?' my sister asks, and we both know she means what is *she* like. (28)

Leavitt and Mitchell, too, openly voice their fixation with interior decorating and their love of 'shelter' magazines:

> In the month just after we had bought Podere Fiume and before the restoration work had begun, we got into the habit of buying and reading design magazines. Our favorites were *House and Garden* (the English version), *Homes and Gardens*, and *The World of Interiors*. Sometimes, however, such was our avidity to look at pictures of houses that after we had finished these we would also buy *Architectural Digest* and *AD*; *Elle Décor* (the French, Italian, and American editions); *Côte Sud, Côte Ouest*, and *Maison Madame Figaro*; *House Beautiful*; and *Country Homes and Interiors*. Once we had exhausted these, we would occasionally even turn to magazines in languages we could not read – Dutch or German – or periodicals treating of subjects we regarded with skepticism, such as *Feng Shui for Modern Living*. (72)

The link between the house narrative of *In Maremma* and the impact of house-and-garden magazines could not be stated any more clearly, leading one to question if the writers' desire for an authentic Tuscan home is influenced more by images promoted by the media or if it actually stems from direct contact with the local culture.

For Leavitt and Mitchell the foreign house in Tuscany constitutes a fundamental connection with history that, according to them, North Americans crave, and that seemingly explains the rationale behind their design choices:

> The artisans who worked on our house ... were often incredulous when we told them what we were interested in: a house from once upon a time (*una casa d'epoca*). (Isn't the whole point of living in Italy, though, to try to live – although one knows that one cannot – in a fairy tale?) We wanted rough terracotta floors, exposed beams, and a *pietra serena* fireplace because the United States does not have anything approaching the same depth of recorded history as Italy: Centuries are to Italy what decades are to us. In short, Americans want old houses because we do not have enough history, whereas Italians want new houses because they have too much of it. (*In Maremma* 16)

In this passage Leavitt and Mitchell once again reinforce the vision of Italy as tied to its past and as a country where time moves more slowly than in the United States (Italian centuries versus American decades). At the same time, the authors seem to emphasize that, because of their American origins, they presumably better appreciate this link with the past (even if it needs to be reconstructed) because it fulfils some sort of cultural lack, although they acknowledge, with a healthy dose of self-awareness, that they are attempting to live a 'fairy tale.' Mayes, too, devotes much time to outlining the origins of her house and its 'authentic' features, and is delighted that the wall on her property dates back to the Etruscans. Clearly, these houses fill a kind of lacuna for the writers, who up until now have felt deprived, they maintain, of tangible relics of history, and in this appropriation of these lost origins they manage to construct roots for themselves in foreign territory.

As mentioned earlier, for Leavitt/Mitchell and Mayes the house fits, in more ways than one, with the discourse of colonialism. An additional trope that demonstrates this stance is the equating of the Italian countryside with the American West, thus recalling the settler myth. What better way to conquer new territory, to discover the undiscovered, than to build (or rebuild) a house, and thus create a new home(land)? For Leavitt and Mitchell, the allegedly 'untamed' Maremma embodies this sort of dynamic and becomes, ostensibly, a more genuine space than the more usual Tuscan haunts:

> What made the Maremma appealing to us – what made us want to live here far more than in one of the areas that foreigners had colonized (Chianti, or more recently, Umbria) – was that it still felt like a frontier. We did not know exactly what we would find here, only what we would not find: lovely, but in their efforts to be the 'real' Italy, cartoon versions of hill towns (often ringed by factories); villages where it was possible almost never to hear Italian for all the English or German being spoken; the 'snobbism of place' you become aware of when you overhear someone begin a sentence, 'Of course, San Casciano dei Bagni was super-chic *last* year …' All of this seemed to us to defeat the point of living abroad: Although hiding in an enclave of one's countrymen is a way to be *in* a foreign land, it is not a way to be *part* of it. In Maremma, on the other hand, you could hear your own voice in the silence. (8)

In likening Maremma to the frontier, the unspoiled, Leavitt and Mitchell justify their desire to reside there, perceiving it as the more genuine Italian experience, while at the same time reiterating the settler myth, an emblem of American culture. While their inhabiting a place that to them seems as yet uncolonized (unlike the denigrated, more popular zones of Tuscany and Umbria) in a sense legitimizes their own colonization of the land, their subconscious metaphor of the frontier simultaneously situates the writers in the role of settlers.

In addition, how Maremma can be compared to the frontier is rather mystifying, for while parts of it might suggest wilderness (e.g., the Parco dell'Uccellina or the famous *butteri* [Italian cowboys]), it comprises both ancient towns (some with visible Etruscan ruins) and extremely developed areas, especially the seaside resorts or port towns (for example, San Vincenzo, Porto Ercole, Livorno, and Grosseto, among others). Yet interestingly, Mayes, too, finds parallels between this terrain and the frontier when visiting Massa Marittima:

> The Maremma keeps reminding me of the American West, its little out of the way towns the freeway missed by fifty miles, the shop owner staring out the window, the wide sky in his gaze. Certainly the piazza and the fabulous cathedral are nothing like the West – the similarity is under the skin of the place: a loneliness, an eye on the stranger. (*Tuscan Sun* 186)

Some presumably intangible quality of Maremma seems to have struck a chord with Leavitt/Mitchell and Mayes; perhaps it is merely the fact that it is a part of Tuscany less popularized by mass tourism and less likely to be written about by anglophone travellers (with the notable exception of D.H. Lawrence), and so the authors perceive it as uncharted territory.

Leavitt/Mitchell's and Mayes's fascination with the second residence is not unique to them: Garber, in a chapter entitled 'The Summer House,' provides a convincing analysis of the appeal of the second home, and of the rapport between owners and their summer houses, and perhaps supplies us with further clues as to why these writers, and consequently their readers, are so taken with the idea:

> Second homes and vacation homes can be like love affairs and second marriages. They're a chance to reinvent yourself, to start again – without the emotional and legal strain of divorce or disentanglement. There's no enforced monogamy in today's American dream of home-owning. A second home, even for some fortunate or profligate few a third home, fulfills the 'more the merrier' impulse to 'play around' without, well – playing around. So you can get both the moral points and the transgressive frisson. And take the other members of the household with you. (181)

Garber links the second home directly to a reinvention of the self, without any of the difficulties associated with more disruptive life changes.

In the book's conclusion, she again addresses the issue of the summer house as a kind of domestic utopia:

> The summer house, because it defines itself as a space for pleasure, comes to stand for that quest for the ideal 'place.' It is the ultimate 'romance,' the story we tell ourselves about who we are and who we wish to be. But this is really true for *all* the houses we allow ourselves to love. The house and all that it symbolizes is the repository of histories, memories, fantasies, self-images, aspirations, and dreams. That is why our romance with houses is – in every sense – such a consuming passion. (204)

This 'consuming passion' for self-definition via the house becomes all the more seductive when linked to the discovery of a foreign land and, in Mayes's case at least, has resulted in the gaining of actual revenue from the 'Tuscan Sun' phenomenon, which comprises various areas, ranging from books, to daily planners, to a Hollywood film, to a furniture line.[22]

The house itself has come to stand for the writer's own self-transformation in Italy and represents a late-twentieth-century consumerist attitude towards sojourns in Tuscany. Where once travellers in the nineteenth century might have felt happy to gaze on Tuscan archaeological ruins, now visitors to the same region (if sufficiently affluent) buy (quasi-) ruins, restore them, and modernize them to suit their taste.[23] Not content with a shared public space, the present-day traveller purchases the private sphere with a view to acquiring an 'Italianate' identity, but also, more significantly, to attaining the status that an ex-pat with that persona possesses, an identity consolidated, no less, by publishing a travelogue about the entire experience.

Leavitt/Mitchell's and Mayes's texts adopt a popular composite of such areas as interior decorating, gardening, cooking, and travel, thus exemplifying a contemporary manifestation of the hybridity of travel writing as a genre, yet not straying from the trademark 'othering' found in so much of it. In these writers' travelogues there is an absence of locals as agents of speech (only small dialogues or comments are supplied), and there are few, if any, references to actual Italian politics or social structures, with the result that the books portray primarily the authorial perceptions of the foreign culture and operate in a kind of vacuum as far as Italian current affairs are concerned, in a manner not unlike E.M. Forster's rather disengaged depiction of local Florentines in *A Room with a View*.

In their denial of Italians' subjectivity, the texts instead focus on the writers' reformulation of identity in a foreign context, and the concomitant feelings of ambivalence that Italian culture elicits in them. Yet these writers seem to uphold a kind of self-satisfied complacency about their relocation: clearly, for them, the Tuscan rural setting does not evoke the kind of personal crisis found in Forster's novel when Lucy Honeychurch is confronted with the cultural Otherness of her surroundings.

More than likely, it is the formulaic reiteration of stereotypes and the distancing of the Italian Other, along with an idealized narration of the house and the writer's own reconstruction of cultural identity, that contribute to the success of these recent American travel memoirs. For these contemporary travel writers, rural Tuscany and its residents are a resource to be tapped when they need workers, fresh produce, a new recipe, or a new 'look' for their houses and gardens: the reader learns little about current Italian culture or society, but rather more about the authors' own search for a new identity in a foreign setting. While in their travel writing Leavitt/Mitchell and Mayes eloquently describe their 'renewal' and 'rebirth' via the spatial tropes of their Tuscan homes, it is regrettable that they are unable truly to renovate the genre itself with more innovative insights about Italy and Italians.

6 The Tuscan Countryside: Nature and the (Non)Domestic in Elena Gianini Belotti

In the mid-1970s Elena Gianini Belotti bought and restored a house in the countryside near a small village south-east of Siena, an experience that forms the background to her book *Voli* (Flights, 2001). The concerns of this Italian feminist writer's text, for the most part, diverge quite radically from contemporary accounts of analogous situations, such as those authored by Mayes or Leavitt and Mitchell. Belotti is not a native Tuscan (her provenance is from Rome), so she, too, has to adapt to environs that are technically not her own, although obviously the culture shock in her case is not as pronounced as for the American writers (or for Stendhal and Forster's characters). She is resettling in a neighbouring region rather than visiting or starting a new life in a foreign country. In contrast to Leavitt/Mitchell's and Mayes's travelogues, rather than detailing the restoration of the house and describing the neighbours and their customs in stereotypical tropes, *Voli* concentrates instead on indigenous fauna and the natural surroundings. Thus, the writer's engagement with the area of Trequanda and its inhabitants is mediated above all through her contact with nature, and in particular with birds, as is indicated by the title.[1]

Most of Belotti's writings tackle women's issues overtly, as seen in such sociological and pedagogical publications as *Dalla parte delle bambine* (On Behalf of Girls, translated as *What Are Little Girls Made Of?* 1973), *Che razza di ragazza* (What Kind of a Girl, 1979), *Non di sola madre* (Not a Mother's Alone, 1983), *Amore e pregiudizio* (Love and Prejudice, 1988), *Prima le donne e i bambini* (Women and Children First, 1980); and in her fiction: *Il fiore dell'ibisco* (The Hibiscus Flower, 1985), *Adagio un poco mosso* (1993), *Apri le porte all'alba* (Open the Doors to the Dawn, 1999), and *Prima della quiete* (Before the Calm, 2003). *Voli*, by contrast, while autobiographical, stresses primarily the plight of animals in the face of environmental degradation; at the same time, the writer's presentation of nature is undoubtedly influenced by her feminism. Belotti has, in any case, always been dedicated to highlighting the circumstances of the oppressed, be they children, women, the elderly, migrants, animals, or nature: all are victims of Western patriarchal society's dictates.[2] Her most recent fiction addresses both emigration and immigration, with *Pane amaro* (Bitter Bread, 2006), the narrative based on her father's experience as labourer and musician in the United States in the early twentieth century, and *Cortocircuito* (Short Circuit, 2008), a series of short stories centred on the figures of foreign workers in contemporary Italy.

Belotti's commitment to denouncing the oppression of women, the environment, and the Other in general, is in line with the tenets of Ecofeminism. While the writer is not a professed 'ecofeminist' per se, her feminism and dedication to writing about ecological issues conform with the movement's ideology, as outlined by Mellor: 'Ecofeminism is a movement that sees a connection between the exploitation and degradation of the natural world and the subordination and oppression of women' (1).

Val Plumwood provides an even more detailed account of Ecofeminism and its contribution:

> A feminist account of the domination of nature presents an essential but difficult further frontier for feminist theory, all the more testing and controversial because the problematic of nature has been so closely interwoven with that of gender. Because 'nature' has been a very broad and shifting category and has encompassed many different sorts of colonisation, an adequate account of the domination of nature must draw widely on accounts of other forms of oppression, and has an important integrating role. Ecofeminism has contributed a great deal both to activist struggle and to theorising links between women's oppression and the domination of nature over the last two decades. (1)

Such issues are particularly relevant in Belotti's earlier novel *Apri le porte all'alba*, where the protagonist, Doris, comes across countless examples of ecological devastation and finds solidarity within her friend Irene's feminist group, which is exploring the social cost of violence perpetrated by men against the environment. In a note to me in response to an essay of mine on the novel,[3] Gianini Belotti expresses her agreement with Plumwood's ecofeminist philosophy:

Sono d'accordo con Val Plumwood: non lo dico esplicitamente, ma il degrado ambientale divenuto ormai imponente è frutto del dominio, dello sfruttamento, della violenza, dell'avidità e cecità della parte maschile della società. È analogo all'oppressione sulle donne, e in stretta correlazione con la ricerca sul costo sociale degli uomini condotta da Irene e dal suo gruppo di donne nel seguito del romanzo. Basta fare l'esempio delle distruzioni e violenze di ogni genere connesse con le partite di calcio e delle somme enormi che costano a tutti noi. Quello che racconto ha volutamente aspetti paradossali ma è vero.

[I agree with Val Plumwood: I don't say it explicitly, but the environmental degradation that has by now become daunting is the fruit of dominance, abuse, violence, avidity, and blindness on the part of male society. It is analogous to the oppression of women, and is closely correlated to the research on the social cost of men conducted by Irene and by her group of women in the rest of the novel. All it takes is the example of all the different kinds of destruction and violence connected with soccer matches and the huge sums of money that they cost us all. What I narrate deliberately has its paradoxical aspects, but it's true].

In *Voli*, Belotti's ecological concerns come to the fore in her attention to the zoological and botanical life around her house and in her denunciation of environmental destruction. While her critique is not necessarily as forceful or exaggerated as that voiced by her fictional characters in *Apri le porte all'alba*, a clear ecofeminist agenda emerges.

Another aspect that indicates a new direction with respect to Belotti's previous production is the question of the genre classification of *Voli*. Her other writings are, for the most part, either essays, novels, or short stories. *Voli* instead could be categorized as nature writing in its privileging of animal subjects, but at the same time the text resembles a memoir in its personalized narration of the author's encounters with zoological activity on her rural property, episodes that frequently evoke childhood recollections of her dealings with animals.

The Tuscan Farmhouse: Spaces of a History of Hardship

In contrast with Mayes, Leavitt/Mitchell, and other writers like them who narrate the vicissitudes of their new life in Tuscany, Belotti pays (refreshingly) little attention to the house itself. The reader is informed that its restoration has taken several years to conclude, but the physical structure of the house and its décor are, by and large, glossed over in

Nature and the (Non)Domestic in Belotti 145

the text. Moreover, the description that opens *Voli* concentrates above all on the house's geographical and historical contextualization within its socio-economic origins, as Belotti meditates on the poverty that must have typified the original inhabitants' living conditions:

> Se torno con la memoria alla prima volta in cui ho visitato la casa diroccata ... ho la visione di una fuga di stanze una dentro l'altra, come usavano i contadini, e di un angusto, rudimentale gabinetto in fondo a un corridoio di nudi mattoni forati. Nella vasta cucina con i muri anneriti dall'asmatico tiraggio del focolare, la cappa era crollata e dall'apertura si affacciava un rettangolo di cielo. Il sale aveva corroso il pavimento di terracotta di una stanzetta attigua fino a scavare fosse frastagliate ancora orlate di salsedine, sulle travi restavano i chiodi arrugginiti ai quali pendevano a stagionare i prosciutti. Era disabitata da almeno quindici anni, i mezzadri si erano spostati nella valle al seguito delle fabbriche sorte da poco e l'avevano costipata di banali casette prive di ogni grazia e però fornite di luce elettrica, acqua corrente e servizi igienici. Una fuga, più che un trasferimento, perché tutto quello che s'erano lasciati alle spalle parlava di cupa miseria e di durissima fatica, di crudi geli invernali, di solitudine e isolamento che la bellezza dei luoghi non era mai riuscita a compensare. (*Voli* 9)

> [If I go back in my memory to the first time I visited the ruined house ... I have the vision of a succession of rooms one inside the other, as was the peasants' habit, and of a narrow, rudimentary bathroom at the end of a hall of bare, hollow brick. In the vast kitchen with its walls blackened by the asthmatic draw of the fireplace, the hood had caved in and a rectangle of sky peeked through the opening. The terracotta floor of the adjoining room had been so corroded by salt that it had ragged grooves carved out in it, still edged with salt stains, and on the beams you could still see the rusty nails from which the legs of prosciutto used to hang to cure. It had been uninhabited for at least fifteen years, and the labourers had moved to the valley, where factories had recently emerged, and had stuffed it with banal, graceless little houses that, however, had electricity, running water, and modern conveniences. More of an escape than a house relocation, because everything they had left behind bespoke darkest poverty and hard work, harsh winter frosts, loneliness and isolation, for which the beauty of the area was never able to compensate.]

Belotti's verbal report of the rough conditions of the house reveals an awareness of the circumstances in which its occupants lived and empathizes with their reasons for abandoning it. Belotti does not resort to the idealized (and commercialized) vision of the Tuscan villa endorsed by Mayes and others like her. Instead of detailing the home improvements and interior decorating styles she will adopt, the writer traces the visible signs of hardship etched in the house and reflects on their significance. While Mayes and Leavitt/Mitchell are on a quest to discover or uncover the 'authentic' Tuscany via their houses' restoration, Belotti's sensitivity and class consciousness lead to more reflective and informed comments on the house's structure and its origins. This may be due in part to Belotti's first-hand knowledge of the hardships that manual labourers and farmers undergo, given her father's grim experience of migrating to the United States, and his return to Italy to make his living as a builder and on a farming plot in the Agro Romano.[4]

The above passage also acknowledges a common phenomenon of mid-twentieth-century Tuscany: that of the migration of the *mezzadri* – those labourers tied to the agricultural system of sharecropping – from a rural environment to more practical modern residences found near towns and cities. Anthropologist Jeff Pratt explains: 'The collapse of the *mezzadria* also created major fractures in rural society. In some provinces the exodus left a desert of abandoned farms and estates, which after a long hiatus became the locus for investment in specialist agriculture, especially wine. Most of the rural workforce are now wage-labourers, and live in the villages' (1–2).[5] Belotti's visual reading of her house, therefore, does not fail to take into consideration the socio-economic history of place.

Furthermore, Belotti is also aware that the enjoyment of the area's beauty is a luxury reserved for those who have the time and money to reflect on the appearance of their surroundings, unlike the former inhabitants of her house:

> La nudità dell'aia narrava di una miseria senza respiro, di fatica senza sosta dall'alba al tramonto: se una sosta fosse stata contemplata, l'ombra di un albero sarebbe stata necessaria per addolcirla. Gioire della bellezza di un paesaggio o di un glorioso tramonto è un privilegio di chi possiede già molto altro, coltivare fiori o piante ornamentali è un'occupazione per chi ha tempo libero da quelle necessarie per sopravvivere. I contadini non alzavano gli occhi per ammirare le nuvole incendiate dal sole che cala, se mai scrutavano il cielo alla ricerca dei segnali della tempesta di grandine che distruggerà il raccolto o della pioggia benefica che lo salverà. Io godevo di molti privilegi e la calvizie del luogo che mi riconduceva

alla estrema penuria dei contadini, me ne faceva vergognare come di una colpa. (15)

[The yard's nudity told of unrelenting misery, of ceaseless toil from dawn till dusk: if a break had been contemplated, the shade of a tree would have been necessary to sweeten it. The enjoyment of the beauty of a landscape or of a glorious sunset is the privilege of those who already possess a great deal more, the cultivation of flowers or ornamental plants is an occupation for people who have free time to spend away from those occupations that are necessary for survival. Farmers wouldn't have lifted their eyes to admire clouds enflamed by the setting sun; if anything they would have scoured the sky looking for signs of a hailstorm that might damage the crops or of a beneficent rainfall that might save them. I enjoyed many privileges and the baldness of the place brought me back to the farmers' extreme penury and made me ashamed, as though guilty.]

The condition of the former inhabitants is mapped out on the surroundings: Belotti notes the lack of vegetation or a garden around the house, conscious that decorative horticulture is an advantage of affluence. Her comments connote a sense of respect but also of empathy for the farmers who resided in her dwelling, and the picture she paints is based on her informed knowledge of the living conditions, not a romanticized vision of peasant life.[6] For Belotti, the house evokes a past of adversity that she acknowledges; her observations on the house's history bear no resemblance to the kind of romantic reverie on farming penned by Mayes.

'Amore e rabbia' (Love and Rage), another thoughtful piece by Belotti, is included in a collection of writings by women about Tuscany. In the essay the writer makes similar observations about the aesthetics of place and reiterates her sympathy for the emigration of the *mezzadri* to more densely populated areas, outlining the hardships they endured and the understandable drawing power that modern conveniences would have had. Rather than their abandoning old farmhouses in favour of unattractive newly constructed houses in town, Belotti contends, financial incentives would have solved the problem of overdevelopment:

Dovevano passare trent'anni prima che i loro figli o nipoti si rendessero conto che genitori e nonni avevano rinunciato a qualcosa che nel tempo aveva acquistato valore e significato. E qui entra in campo la politica nazionale e quella delle amministrazioni locali. A che serve la politica se non a indirizzare le scelte dei cittadini, a illustrarle con ragioni convincenti, a stimolarle con incentivi economici o sgravi fiscali? Ammesso, ovviamente, che sindaci e consiglieri per primi ne siano persuasi. Sarebbe bastato che al tempo giusto i comuni offrissero opportune condizioni che favorissero e agevolassero il restauro delle antiche case dei centri storici adeguandole a moderne legittime esigenze, per rendere antieconomico costruire villette nuove di zecca. ('Amore e rabbia' 19)

[It took thirty years before children or grandchildren were to realize that their parents and grandparents had given up something that, over time, had acquired value and meaning. And this is where national and local administrations' politics come into play. What use is politics if it doesn't guide citizens' choices or illustrate them with convincing reasons, or stimulate them with economic incentives or financial relief? On condition, obviously, that mayors and councillors are the first to be convinced. All it would have taken, at the right moment, would have been for local councils to offer advantageous conditions that favoured or facilitated the restoration of old houses in historic town centres, and their conversion to suit legitimate modern needs, to render the construction of brand new houses anti-economical.]

Whether or not the solution she puts forward would indeed have deterred the construction of new houses in Tuscany is impossible to determine, but Belotti at least demonstrates a political engagement that is symptomatic of her committed attachment to place and to the preservation of landscape.[7]

Landscapes, Nature, and Animals

The writer's concern with landscape is witnessed in the topographical delineations in *Voli*, but these passages are not numerous, as the text centres primarily on wildlife and nature. Indeed, when landscape portraits do appear, they often contain elements that deviate from canonical depictions of locale. In one particular instance the writer paints an unusual picture of place that homes in literally on animal tracks:

Da quando ho comprato un manualetto che insegna a identificare le tracce e le impronte degli animali, vado in giro a perlustrare la campagna a muso basso come un segugio. Sui bordi delle pozze dal fondo di argilla impermeabile in cui l'acqua ristagna, c'è un ricco assortimento di zampe, zampine e zamponi dei molti animali che vanno ad abbeverarsi. Segni del loro passaggio o delle loro soste si trovano ovunque, nei boschi come nelle radure. Le più numerose sono quelle dei corpulenti cinghiali che si muovono in branchi insieme alla prole. Gli zoccoli fessurati incidono profondamente la creta e, poiché appoggiano la zampa posteriore nel punto in cui hanno posato quella anteriore, le orme risultano pressoché sovrapposte, con un lievissimo scarto che dà loro un disegno leggiadro ad ali di farfalla. Quando si incontrano tronchi dalla corteccia intaccata o strappata, significa che un maschio ha marcato il territorio con le sue zanne affilate. I cigli melmosi degli stagni sono spesso sconquassati dai tumultuosi bagni di fango dei cinghiali che vi si rotolano a zampe all'aria con fragorosi grugniti. Dopo il bagno, si strigliano strofinandosi contro gli alberi e l'energica grattata lascia sulla corteccia setole e croste di mota. I loro escrementi sono identici a quelli dei maiali: grosse, rotonde polpette, brune e compatte. (101)

[Since buying a little manual that explains how to identify animal traces and prints, I wander around scouting the countryside with my head bowed down like a hound. On the edge of puddles with impermeable clay bottoms where the water stagnates, there is a rich assortment of paws, small and large, of the many animals that go there to drink. Signs of their passing through or of their rest can be found everywhere, both in the woods and in the clearings. The most numerous are those of the corpulent boars who move in herds along with their young. Their cloven hooves cut deeply into the clay and, since they place their back foot in the same spot where they placed their front one, their prints appear almost superimposed, with a slight shift that gives them a graceful design like butterfly wings. If you come across tree trunks with bark that is notched or torn, it means that a male has marked his territory with his sharp tusks. The slimy borders of ponds are often smashed up by the tumultuous mud baths of boars who roll around in them, with their hooves in the air and grunting noisily. After their bath, they groom themselves by rubbing against trees, and their energetic scratching leaves bristles and crusts of mud on the bark. Their excrement is identical to that of pigs: fat, round balls that are dark and compact.]

The writer scrutinizes the geography and vegetation, searching for evidence of faunal activity. After the comments on the impact of the wild boars, the delineation continues for another two pages, in which Belotti covers other animal tracks and droppings within her surroundings, including those of deer, porcupines, rats, dogs, cats, mice, and foxes. Her attention to the earthier aspects of faunal life gives rise to landscapes that are the antithesis of romanticized visions of Tuscan rurality such as those authored by Mayes, Leavitt/Mitchell, and similar writers; instead of praising emblematic olive groves, cypresses, and vineyards, Belotti enters into an excursus on the scenery's scatological elements, employing language that is explicit without descending into coarseness.

Apart from the first-person narrator, the protagonists of *Voli* are the animals themselves. Each chapter is devoted to one or more episodes recounting the writer's contact with animals within or in the proximity of her Tuscan house, encounters that often draw out reminiscences from her past, and particularly of her childhood dealings with animal life on her parents' rural property. The human–animal relationship is thus key for Belotti, and a large portion of her book deals with this specific issue. At the same time, it is useful, indeed essential, to remember that Belotti's portrayal of animals is precisely that, a representation mediated by her preconceptions and ideology. This is illustrated, for example, in her anthropomorphization of animals and in her feelings of tenderness towards them (in particular the young), impulses that in various instances, paradoxically, superimpose metaphors of human relationships and domesticity on to the animal kingdom.

Throughout *Voli* Belotti takes pains to point out that she considers animals in their own right, not as humanized creatures, and that if anything, what counts is to acknowledge that human characteristics derive from those of animals: 'Non si tratta di proiettare qualità umane sugli animali, ma proprio il contrario, e cioè riconoscere quanto sia ancora forte e profonda l'eredità animale nell'uomo' (56) [It isn't a question of projecting human qualities on to animals, but in fact the exact opposite, that is, recognizing how strong and deep the animal inheritance is in mankind]. Yet many of the writer's statements would seem to undermine her intentions; repeatedly she remarks on animals' habits in a manner that evokes their similarities to humans.

For instance, when baby swallows have hatched in the nest in her loggia, she speculates as to how the elder siblings will react to seeing their parents caring for the hatchlings: 'Mi chiedevo se provassero i sentimenti di ansiosa aspettativa mista a gelosia che sperimentano i bambini all'annuncio della nascita di un fratellino' (187) [I wondered if they experienced the same feelings of anxious expectancy mixed with jealousy that children feel at the announcement of the birth of a baby brother]. When she witnesses two swallows becoming agitated, she construes the scene in human terms: 'Tra i due coniugi si era scatenata una furibonda discussione, un battibecco concitato in cui parlavano l'uno sull'altro senza ascoltarsi a vicenda, come se ciascuno si accanisse a far valere a tutti i costi il proprio punto di vista. Mi sembrava di assistere a una litigata fra marito e moglie che dissentivano sulla più opportuna collocazione del frigorifero o del fornello a gas nella nuova cucina' (201). [A furious discussion had erupted between the two spouses, an agitated squabble in which they both spoke at the same time without listening to each other, as if each one was bent on having his or her point of view prevail at all costs. I felt like I was watching an argument between a husband and wife who disagreed on the best place to put the fridge or the gas stove in a new kitchen.]

The interpretation of animal conduct through human parameters is a common enough phenomenon, but Belotti takes this inclination even further, since fauna often elicit her parenting instincts. When caring for a young abandoned blackbird, she responds to its cries and calls it a 'poppante' [nursing baby] (as well as her 'figlioccio' [godson]), employing a discourse usually applied to infants: 'Intanto lo vezzeggiavo, come si fa coi lattanti, "bravo piccolo," gli dicevo, "come sei bravo, se mangi tanto crescerai e diventerai grande e robusto"' (73). [All the while I stroked him, as you do with nursing infants, 'good little boy,' I would say to him, 'what a good boy, if you eat lots you'll grow big and strong.'] Belotti clearly is conscious of the feelings animals can elicit in people, describing the blackbird as 'un esserino così minuscolo, grazioso, inerme e dipendente, proprio perciò era capace di risvegliare quella disposizione allevante che sonnecchia nella maggioranza di noi.' (76) [a being so tiny, so sweet, helpless and dependent, and for these exact reasons capable of reawakening that parenting disposition that lies dormant in most of us.] It is above all young animals that conjure up the parenting impulse in the author, and her reaction is typical of the phenomenon of neoteny, whereby infantilized features (be they human or animal) spark off the nurturing instinct in people.[8]

Significantly, these and other comments of Belotti on ornithic behaviour frequently draw on familial paradigms, linking the birds with anthropological structures of kinship and the domestic environment, and often placing the writer herself in the role of surrogate parent. Many of Belotti's observations on birds revolve around the activity of nest-building, which takes place either in or just outside her house. Nesting, as Bachelard indicates in *The Poetics of Space*, evokes a sense of refuge (91), and is strongly connected to our concept of the house. Furthermore, he claims that viewing nests returns us to our childhood, 'in our capacity to recapture the naive wonder we used to feel when we found a nest' (93), a reaction that undoubtedly applies to Belotti's narration of her watching birds constructing nests on her property and in her home. At the same time, the concept of instinct is regularly interrogated by Belotti, in her repeated affirmation that 'l'istinto non è infallibile' [instinct is not infallible], a statement evoked, for instance, when she sees an impractical, exposed nest built by inexperienced swallows (194–5).[9]

The writer's musings on avian activity (in particular, nesting) invariably draw out recollections of her own family's interactions. In *Voli*, Belotti's parents are portrayed in schematic, Manichean terms, whereby the mother represents coldness and interdiction and the father – the more nurturing of the two – is the one who fosters the writer's love for animals, in particular through encouraging her help in raising their chicks. In fact, the writer's first experience of surrogate mothering of animals is caring for the chicks that have hatched from an incubator. These animals follow her around devotedly, an attachment, she later learns, that is due to the phenomenon of imprinting (52). For Belotti, the winged creatures' affection for her is completely selfless, and she claims that they, in turn, exerted their imprinting on to her, as illustrated by the impact they had on her formation.

Clearly, the writer possesses a quasi-obsessive interest in birds, a point the book makes repeatedly, and perhaps her strong connection with animals can be attributed to a compensation for the presumed lack of maternal warmth during her childhood. Yi-Fu Tuan considers Western society's history of displaying fondness for domestic animals:

> This highly sentimentalized view of animals was uniquely developed in western Europe ... What were the contributory causes? One general cause was simply the growing distance between people and nature. Wild animals and even farm animals were becoming less and less the common experience of men and women in an increasingly urbanized and industrialized society. It was easier to entertain warm feelings toward animals that seemed to have no other function than as playthings. Moreover, humans needed an outlet for their gestures of affection and this was becoming more difficult to find in modern society as it began to segment and isolate people into their private spheres, to discourage casual physical contact. (112)

Belotti's affinity for avian creatures (along with that for other animals) demonstrates her belief that the animal world and the human environment can and should interact. While at times she might find the presence of certain animals in or near her house in Trequanda intrusive, she is aware that the boundaries between herself and the animal Other cannot be rigid; in fact, under certain circumstances, she encourages their intermingling. This is brought to the fore in one particular incident, when she allows a pair of swallows to build a nest in her living room, forcing her to keep the window open and live with these avian presences for several weeks, along with the off-putting side-effects that such a cohabitation implies (the malodorous droppings, to name but one).

During an earlier attempt of another swallow couple to build a nest in her kitchen she is torn, and considers the permeability between her abode and the natural world: 'Va bene, mi dicevo, sono in campagna, non nel grattacielo di una metropoli, perciò devo aspettarmi che gli animali sconfinino dai loro territori per accamparsi nei miei, una contiguità che può avere aspetti piacevoli' (168) [That's okay, I said to myself, I am in the countryside, not in a metropolitan skyscraper, and so I should expect animals to stray from their territory so as to camp out in mine, a contiguity that can present pleasant aspects]. Precisely because she is living in a rural rather than urban environment, she reflects, her space and that of animals will overlap.[10] This weakening of the borders between inside and outside characterizes much of Belotti's text, as her inhabiting a restored Tuscan farmhouse implies a connection with nature and animal life. The porous quality of these limits between the house and its surroundings denotes a bonding with animal alterity in her case. For Palazzeschi, the liminality of the window is a key trope that erodes notional categorizations (between inside and outside, male and female, country and city, among others); yet the Florentine author, I would suggest, draws on this figure of liminality as a convenient iconographical metaphor. For Belotti, by contrast, the permeability of her house's confines has an impact on the day-to-day reality of living within the four walls, as she ends up by sharing her abode with the nesting swallows.

Belotti's fascination with the animal Other, however, does not preclude her imposing limits; on various occasions she reaffirms that the house is *hers*, that it does not belong to the invasive animals in question. (Regarding the swallows nesting in her living room, she says: 'Di tanto in tanto lanciavano un unico grido, un'esclamazione che io, incalzata dal senso di colpa, interpretavo come protesta per la mia presenza. Belle pretese, mi ribellavo, non vi ho invitato io, dopotutto esisto e questa è casa mia da molto prima che arrivaste voi' (210) [From time to time they would emit a single shriek, an exclamation that I, spurred by a sense of guilt, interpreted as a protest against my presence. Some cheek, I countered, I didn't invite you; after all, I exist and this house was mine long before you arrived].) That said, her spatial possessiveness, her 'colonization' of the land, is not of the same stripe as Mayes's and Leavitt/Mitchell's since it is less self-involved: Belotti fosters interactions with the animal Other, even at her own expense. While the author clearly maintains a sense of entitlement to her space and her property, she appreciates the animals who appear or dwell on her land, even permitting them to share 'her' territory under circumstances that most would likely find unacceptable:

> Dopo il primo sgomento, avevo provato uno smisurato orgoglio e sconfinata gratitudine per il privilegio che le rondini mi accordavano scegliendo di nidificare nella mia casa. Era un segno rinnovato di stima verso la mia persona, la dimostrazione che non esitavano ad affidarsi a me, sicure di essere benvolute e protette. (207)

> [After my initial consternation, I felt a boundless pride and limitless gratitude for the privilege that the swallows had accorded me by choosing to nest in my house. It was a renewed sign of respect towards me, the demonstration that they did not hesitate to place their trust in me, certain of being well liked and protected.]

Conversely, Belotti does not hesitate, in turn, to encroach on the space of the animal Other: for instance, she regularly puts her hand in a swallows' nest in her loggia so as to caress the hatchlings:

> Tutta quella vitalissima agitazione di creaturine appena venute alla luce, fragili, inermi eppure piene di energia e di pretese, la loro aspettativa di essere nutriti anche da me benché non somigliassi neppure lontanamente a una rondine e il loro evidente piacere di starsene accucciati sotto la conca tiepida della mia mano, mi regalavano una commozione intensa. Ogni volta che transitavo per la loggia mi fermavo a salutarli con un'affettuosa palpatina. (177)

> [All that lively agitation of newborn creatures, fragile, helpless, yet full of energy and expectation, their presumption of being nourished by me even though I didn't remotely resemble a swallow and their evident pleasure in huddling up under the warm hollow of my hand, touched me deeply. Every time I passed through the loggia I stopped to greet them with an affectionate little pat.]

Nature and the (Non)Domestic in Belotti 155

Clearly, the author finds the baby swallows' snuggling up to her hand gratifying, an act that obviously conjures up her surrogate parenting impulse. In fact, she continues to 'invade' the birds' nest, even though she fears this might cause the parents to reject the offspring, an occurrence that fortunately, she realizes, does not come to pass.

Spaces of Fear and Alterity

There are occasions, however, when the animal incursions on the writer's territory can cause her uneasiness, as evidenced by the fox episode recounted at length in chapter 5. When she finds a dead snake on her front steps, she interprets it as a threat by some neighbour or local hunter whom she has unwittingly annoyed. Her anxieties peak again when she comes across the head of a rat on her doorstep some time later. After many conjectures and after being on the verge of abandoning her house, Belotti finally establishes the identity of the mysterious intruder. She and a friend spread talcum powder on her steps one night, and the next morning she easily identifies the vulpine pawprints and surmises that the fox is bringing her gifts, much in the manner of some domestic cats with their owners.

The entire fox encounter (or lack thereof) has several ramifications in *Voli*: it causes the author to reflect on her status of being a female homeowner who lives on her own (along with the vulnerabilities that this can imply), and she also develops a sense of fear of being antagonized by the locals, the native Others, a perception that turns out to be unfounded. Her anxieties about being targeted lead in fact to her perception of place and of the local Others being altered. When recounting her qualms about returning home at night on her own, she explains how her property and the area around it acquire a menacing air: 'Conosco la strada a menadito, eppure ogni tronco di quercia illuminato dai fari assume sembianze sinistre, ogni cespuglio di ginestra, di scopa, di sanguinella, di ginepro, sembra agitato dal passaggio di qualcuno che è appena stato lì e si è rintanato nei pressi, una roccia calcarea che appare dopo una svolta pare un torso d'uomo coperto da una camicia bianca' (116) [I know the road like the back of my hand, and yet every oak tree trunk lit up by my headlights takes on a sinister appearance, every bush of broom, tree-heath, dogwood, juniper, seems agitated by the movement of someone who was just there and has hidden nearby, a limestone rock which appears after a bend looks like a man's torso covered by a white shirt]. Even when opening the gate to her drive and parking her car the author has the impression of imminent ambush. Thus, the vegetation and geographical features that normally would form part of a familiar picturesque setting contribute, in this context, to a nightmarish vision.

While presumably threatening circumstances alter the writer's sentiments and perception of her space, her views on the locals undergo a change as well. It is precisely in the moments when Belotti believes herself to be in danger that she engages in typecasting the locals, adopting tropes that at times recall those found in Mayes or Leavitt/Mitchell. When her friend Athos, a local, comes to see her about the dead snake, she reacts angrily to his asking her whether she could have bothered someone in the area:

> mi inalbero con lui, che è perfettamente innocente, solo perché è disposto ad accettare che un qualsiasi fastidio da me causato sia sufficiente per piazzarmi un serpente sulle scale. 'Ma che razza di selvaggi vivono qui intorno?' osservo bellicosa, riesumando all'istante antichi fraintendimenti e qualche rancore. 'E quale mai potrebbe essere l'offesa ai vostri imperscrutabili codici capace di provocare una simile reazione?' (114)

> [I get angry with him, even though he is perfectly innocent, simply because he is willing to accept that any sort of annoyance caused by me could be sufficient to have a snake land on my steps. 'What sort of savages live around here?' I observe, in a bellicose tone, resurrecting on the spot ancient misunderstandings and rancor. 'And what sort of offence to your inscrutable codes could possibly be capable of provoking such a reaction?']

In these comments Belotti primitivizes the local residents, dubbing them 'selvaggi' [savages], a trope that recalls Fabian's theories and echoes the declarations about Tuscan neighbours made by Mayes and Leavitt/Mitchell. She refers to local codes as 'inscrutable': so obscure, so uncivilized, as to be impenetrable by an educated urbanite, implicitly reiterating the commonplace of the country-city opposition.

To be fair, however, when Belotti realizes that it was indeed the fox who had been her invisible visitor, she recognizes her own prejudice and discloses a healthy degree of self-knowledge:

> Ora tutto torna, con una semplicità e una naturalezza così sconcertanti da farmi sentire un'idiota. Come ho potuto costruire un castello di ipotesi tanto arzigogolato, senza dubitare nemmeno per un secondo che il

visitatore notturno non fosse un essere umano? Come è stato possibile un simile accecamento? Quali pregiudizi coltivo a mia stessa insaputa, per saltare automaticamente a certe conclusioni ed escluderne altre? Quali malintesi hanno generato tanto radicate diffidenze verso il vicinato, fino a guastare la mia percezione della realtà e ad avvertire minacce dove non ci sono? Quelle impronte stampate sul talco rappresentano una disfatta della ragione. (126–7)

[Now it all makes sense, with a simplicity and a naturalness so disconcerting that I feel like an idiot. How could I build such an elaborate castle of hypotheses without stopping to think for just one second that the nocturnal visitor might not be a human being? How was such blindness possible? What prejudices do I nurture, unbeknownst to me, so as to jump automatically to certain conclusions and to exclude others? What misunderstandings have generated such deep-rooted diffidence towards my neighbours, to the point of spoiling my perception of reality and of my sensing threats where there are none? Those tracks imprinted on the talcum powder represent a defeat of reason.]

The writer is forced to confront her own biases and question her preconceptions when she comes face to face with evidence that contradicts her previous conclusions. She admits to herself, and to her readers, that she has been guilty of nurturing prejudice against her neighbouring residents.

Another effect of the fox incident is that the writer, in her sensation of vulnerability, meditates on her status as a single female homeowner in the area, a situation that deviates from the norm. During the period in which she feels under attack, her domicile, too, is transformed from a locus that once enabled her to feel in control into a restrictive space:

Dopo tanti anni, all'improvviso mi sento vulnerabile quassù, esposta a rischi cui non avevo mai pensato: col tempo la campagna qui intorno mi è diventata così familiare da sentirla come un guscio protettivo, amichevole e rasserenante. Riconosco ogni albero, ogni cespuglio, ogni pietra, ogni suono. Mi pare di abitare in un castello fortificato sulla cima di un'altura, da cui domino le terre intorno e controllo chi va e chi viene. Ora il castello fortificato minaccia di trasformarsi in una prigione. (114)

[After so many years, I suddenly feel vulnerable up here, exposed to risks that I had never considered before: with time the countryside around here has become so familiar to me that it feels like a shell that is protective, friendly, and reassuring. I recognize every tree, every bush, every stone, every sound. I feel as though I live in a fortified castle on a hilltop, from which I dominate the surrounding lands and monitor who comes and goes. Now the fortified castle risks turning into a prison.]

Previously, the countryside seemed to provide a kind of protection for the author, as she recounts her former sensation of being in command in her home, of having literally the 'higher ground' ('quassù' and 'sulla cima di un'altura'). This elevated vantage point recalls the 'monarch of all I survey' gaze as described by Mary Louise Pratt, a stance typical of the colonizer's sense of superiority towards the land and its inhabitants (a visual strategy that highlights 'the relation of mastery predicated between the seer and the seen,' 204). Yet for Belotti – a woman – this feeling of dominance has dissipated in light of the recent events; a proprietary gaze such as that of the male colonizer is untenable, as the house risks metamorphosing into a prison, echoing a quasi-standard trope of female domestic space as confining.

Thus, in the subversion of Belotti's colonizing impulse, what is disclosed instead is her own sense of oppression under the circumstances. Precisely because she is female, her claim to legitimacy of home ownership is one on which she deliberates, especially when living in a state of apprehension:

> Devo accettare l'amara realtà che, dal momento in cui pretendo di vivere da sola e così isolata, perdo ogni comprensione verso le mie fragilità e paure, ogni diritto a una protezione. Qui le donne non ancora sposate abitano in famiglia, quelle rimaste sole, dentro il paese. Io sono anomala, mi permetto di trasgredire queste regole basilari, perciò tutto sommato ho quel che mi merito. Sono disorientata e scoraggiata, la mia bella spavalderia è svanita. Osservo il pacifico, soleggiato paesaggio che conosco così bene, tutto appare in ordine, eppure un segreto disordine l'ha turbato, è come un'unghiata che ha lasciato un segno che non si cancella. Ho la gola stretta, dopo quella minaccia, niente sarà mai come prima. (115)

[I have to accept the bitter reality that, from the moment in which I expect to live isolated, on my own, I lose any sympathy for my fragility and my fears, any right to protection. Around here, unmarried women live with their families, those who have been left on their own, in town. I am an anomaly; I allow myself to transgress these basic rules, therefore, and when all's said and done, I get what I deserve. I feel disoriented and discouraged;

my beautiful boldness has vanished. I observe the peaceful, sunny landscape that I know so well, everything looks in order, and yet a secret disorder has disturbed it, like a scratch that has left a mark that cannot be erased. I feel a tightness in my throat; after that threat, nothing will be the same as before.]

Belotti shows a particular sensitivity to her own presence within the local vicinity and tries to imagine how those around her might view her decisions about living on her own in a rural area, a status that underscores her alterity in her divergence from expected practice. Again, her perception of her physical surroundings is affected by her own disquiet, as if the harmonious countryside has acquired the air of harbouring a dark secret. She surmises, moreover, that she might be breaking some local unspoken laws with her unorthodox presence, as if her ownership were illegitimate,[11] and is angered as well as demoralized by the thought that she is being victimized purely because her presence as a woman is *non grata*.

In fact, Belotti articulates her fears as typifying the oppression of the female, especially one who is no longer young. She surmises what the desired effect of the dead snake might be, and wonders what she could have done that would provoke such an action:

So che è un serpente del tutto innocuo anche da vivo, ma rifletto che i rettili, vivi o defunti che siano, spaventano a morte le donne, tutti sanno che vivo sola in una casa isolata, perciò quel regalo ha tutta l'aria di un'intimidazione ben calcolata, mirata a una paura tutta femminile. Per quale motivo? A quale scopo? Quali torti ho inflitto senza volerlo, quali regole ho trasgredito senza saperlo? (106).

[I know that it is a perfectly innocuous snake, even when alive, but reptiles, I reflect, be they alive or dead, frighten women to death; everyone knows that I live on my own in an isolated house, so the gift has the air of well-calculated intimidation, aimed at entirely feminine fears. For what reason? To what end? What wrongs have I inflicted without wanting to, what rules have I broken unwittingly?]

While the presence of the water snake turns out in due course to be benign and not in the least symbolic, given its donor, Belotti's interpretation of it constitutes a comment on her own status as an unattached woman, an outsider, someone who does not conform to societal norms and is therefore considered Other by her neighbours.

Her friend Giordana, too, remarks on Belotti's unorthodoxy: '"Sei una donna sola non più giovane, ti lasciano in pace se ti adegui alle regole della tua età e della tua condizione, ma se le trasgredisci te la fanno pagare"' (114) ['You are a woman living on her own, no longer young; they leave you alone if you adhere to the rules appropriate to your age and your condition, but if you transgress, then they make you pay']. Her words evoke a theme common to much of Belotti's prose, which analyses the circumstances of aging women and the prejudices against them.[12]

Significantly, however, Belotti's fears are not entirely unfounded, for although the fox episode is entirely benign, in another incident, several years earlier, she was subjected to harassment expressly by men. After her reflection on her erroneous conjectures about the fox's gifts, in which she mulls over what sort of 'misunderstandings' (*malintesi*) could possibly have generated her prejudices towards the locals, she reconsiders her previous statement more carefully: 'Non solo di malintesi però si trattava. L'entusiasmo fanciullesco, l'umore fiducioso con cui avevo iniziato ad abitare la casa in quel lontano agosto di vent'anni prima, sentimenti intensi, ma delicati e fragili come un velo di tulle, a quel tempo erano stati lacerati da un'unghiata selvaggia e lo strappo non era stato più ricucito' (128) [It wasn't just a question of misunderstandings, though. The childish enthusiasm, the trusting mood that I had had on first living in the house in that distant August of twenty years ago, intense emotions, but delicate and fragile like a tulle veil, at that time had been ripped apart by savage claws and the tear was never sewn up]. The author then recollects a much earlier episode in which one evening, after going to bed, she is disturbed by the sound of cars and male voices outside her home. Some drunken louts decide to make a ruckus and intimidate her, and she believes them to be a group of youths who hang about the town piazza and who regularly observe her leaving the local trattoria: 'Dovevo aver infranto qualche rigoroso codice di comportamento femminile e avevano deciso di darmi una lezione' (128) [I must have broken some rigid code of female behaviour and they had decided to teach me a lesson], she deduces. When, the following day, she decides to report the incident to the police, she is warned by other residents that this course of action would be unwise, as the perpetrators would only make her suffer all the more for it.

Ecology and the Tuscan Countryside

Just as Belotti is a casualty of patriarchal mores and oppression, so, too, is the environment victimized by Western, male-dominated society.

While Belotti does not draw a parallel directly between the two forms of domination in this text, it is significant that both should receive such attention. Belotti frequently remarks on (male) hunters' violence towards animals – even those that are not strictly their quarry – such as, for example, pets that might be deemed as interfering in their activity. (Belotti recounts the fate of her friend's particularly loud and boisterous puppy, which ends up being poisoned.)

Local farmers are also blamed for excessive use of pesticides, which damage the environment to such an extent that fauna disappear, as was the case for swallows in the past. The author explains how, after an adjoining olive grove is destroyed by a farmer, the birds vanish for several years:

> Più tardi, dopo la mattanza degli olivi, quando sul campo arato erano stati sparsi a quintali pesticidi e concimi chimici, per anni le rondini erano sparite perché quei veleni avevano ucciso gli insetti e dunque non trovavano di che sfamarsi. Sono tornate dopo che il grande prato, e altri all'intorno, non sono stati più coltivati, ma lasciati al pascolo delle vacche chianine, perennemente assediate da nugoli di mosche e tafani. Le rondini sfrecciano rasenti alle candide groppe degli animali, un turbinio di ali e code nere in voli eleganti e precisi, e a ogni passaggio se ne riempiono il becco. (70)

> [Later on, after the slaughter of the olive trees, when tons of pesticide and chemical fertilizers were spread on the ploughed field, for years the swallows disappeared because those poisons had killed the insects and so they couldn't find anything to eat. They returned after the large field and others nearby were no longer cultivated, but were used instead as pasture for the Chianine cows, perennially besieged by swarms of flies and horseflies. The swallows whiz by the white backs of the animals, in a whirl of black wings and tails, in elegant, precise flights, and with every swoop they fill their beaks.]

The ecological issues that deter the presence of the swallows are complex, and Belotti then factors in a number of other contributors to the problem, such as changing agricultural techniques (artificial fertilizers, animals being bred indoors) and structures (industrial livestock farming, the absence of traditional barns where swallows roost) and lack of marshlands (70).

In various instances Belotti comments on anti-ecological practices that contribute to the demise of avian populations, or at least account for their no longer frequenting certain zones. Fostering the building of the swallows' nest in her living room (apart from its undesirable effects on her living conditions) is, in reality, her contribution to safeguarding the species:

> Avevo adempiuto al mio compito di protezione e ai miei doveri di accoglienza, sopportato i fastidiosi inconvenienti di una convivenza tanto insolita e prolungata, offerto il mio contributo disinteressato alla conservazione di una specie in continuo calo per le colpe di noi umani (rimediando solo in milionesima parte alla nostra collettiva insipienza), con quella famigliola avevo ricostruito le fondamenta della fiducia e delle speranze del loro ritorno. (222)

> [I had fulfilled my task of protecting them and my duty to welcome them; I had put up with the annoying inconveniences of such an unusual and prolonged cohabitation; I had offered my disinterested contribution to the preservation of a species in constant decline due to our faults as human beings (making up for only one millionth part of our collective ignorance); and with that family I had rebuilt the foundations of trust and of hope for their return.]

The adventure of cohabiting with the nesting swallows and their hatchlings, then, is evidently an effort on the part of Belotti to attempt to compensate, albeit minimally, for the environmental injustices perpetrated against these avians.[13]

Elena Gianini Belotti's book is a celebration of nature and local fauna, not a self-promoting advertisement for her house and garden. In *Voli* Belotti makes a strong case for the protection of animals, and in her nature writing/memoir she deliberately chooses to address chiefly the faunal rather than the anthropological aspects of community. Thus, while she at times 'others' her Tuscan neighbours, her treatment of the animal Other indicates an ethical engagement with place, as is evidenced not only by her actions but also by her depicting a house that embodies a permeability between the domestic and the natural spheres. Belotti's account of settled life in a Tuscan house does not paint an untarnished georgic idyll, nor does it revolve around her own consumerist desires. While the writer's colonizing impulse does occasionally emerge in the text, her own (subordinate) 'Othered' status, as a mature woman living on her own, prevents her from fully mastering the landscape around her. With its concern for ethical issues such as the environment and the plight of animals or the living conditions of her house's former inhabitants, and its underlying ecofeminist ideology, *Voli* is, ultimately, a much more socially and politically engaged representation of rural Tuscany than Mayes's or Leavitt/Mitchell's, which disclose, in the end, the writers' appropriation of place for their own personal pleasure, a colonization more heavily involved with the Self than with the Other. Belotti's innovative portrait of place avoids, for the most part, trite observations about the residents and the environs and supplies instead an original and by and large sensitive interpretation of life among the locals, be they human or animal.

Afterword: Further Tuscan Spaces of Alterity

In *The Structure of the Artistic Text* Lotman states, in reference to Tjutčev's poetry: 'We are interested in stressing that the spatial order of the world in these texts becomes an organizing element around which its non-spatial features are also constructed' (220). The same can be said of the texts, both literary and filmic, analysed in this volume; at the same time, it can be argued that each writer or filmmaker inflects the spatial environments depicted in a such a manner as to mirror or underscore specific themes explored in the work. In essence, the spatial and the thematic are tightly intertwined and mutually influence each other. The texts examined here have all been chosen because they concern spaces located in the region of Tuscany and contribute – with a greater or lesser degree of originality – to the representation of the region in modern and contemporary culture. Furthermore, the spatial constructions considered all reflect the authors' exploration of alterity, in particular alterity that hinges on ethnicity, gender, or sexuality.

In some cases, the Tuscan milieu fosters common reactions, for example, the dramatic responses penned by those writers who portray the Florentine sublime and characters who succumb to the Stendhal Syndrome in their encounter with cultural or sexual alterity (Stendhal, Forster, Argento). In other instances, analogous settings, such as a restored villa in the Tuscan countryside, can elicit platitudes about the local residents on the part of the expatriate travel writer while grounding his or her sense of new-found identity (as is the case for Leavitt/Mitchell and Mayes), or else can foster a unique relationship with the natural surroundings, eroding the boundaries between the domestic and the external worlds (as in Gianini Belotti's *Voli*).

Throughout this study I have endeavoured to indicate other points of contact between the various portrayals of space and place in the different genres examined, yet the basic fact remains that each writer or filmmaker depicts the chosen locale in terms that suit his or her poetics. In the majority of texts analysed, the result is an individuated and innovative representation of Tuscany. The most notable exceptions to this are the travel/resettlement narratives of Mayes and Leavitt/Mitchell, whose reiteration of stereotypes about local residents sheds little light on the places and the culture in question; although, to be fair, it should be remembered that this kind of formula typifies the genre within which they are operating.

Another area that could be opened up to interpretation is the possibility of native Italian literary and cinematic self-fashioning as conditioned by or reflecting general stereotypes, a process that thus re-inscribes the Other's hegemonic view in one's own perception of self and place. Do foreigners' categorizations about Tuscan Others filter through and influence native writers and filmmakers? Are the region's physical landmarks portrayed in such a way as to reiterate visual conventions that have come to emblematize the location? An instance of such a mélange of 'Italianness' and 'foreignness' set in a Tuscan locale is Bertolucci's film *Io ballo da sola* (Stealing Beauty, 1996) – filmed in the Brolio Castle and the surrounding Ricasoli Estate – which centres on the English-speaking community in the countryside near Siena and clearly presents the landscape of 'Chiantishire' in a highly aestheticized manner that caters to a non-Italian audience.[1]

Obviously, any critical study must perforce limit itself in terms of the number of works taken into account. For most of the writers included in this volume, other texts of theirs could also be examined. For instance, Palazzeschi portrays the Florentine skyline and landmarks in various modes in much of his oeuvre, from his poetry to his short stories to *La piramide* or *Stampe dell'800*; a detailed investigation of these would certainly reveal still more about his spatial practices and personalized sense of difference. Palazzeschi's portraits of foreigners in Florence, such as those found in the section 'Vecchie inglesi' (Old Englishwomen) in *Stampe dell'800*, would also serve as a fruitful counterpoint to the texts authored by English-speaking writers, past and present, who 'colonize' Tuscany. Palazzeschi's foreign figures are frequently depicted as eccentric, in keeping with his vision of difference, incarnated in his *buffi*. To take another Florentine example, Pratolini's *Il Quartiere* is heavily involved in questions of space, place, and alterity, given the centrality of the neighbourhood as representative of collective opposition to Fascism and the writer's concerns with (adolescent) sexuality. The same can be said for his most successful novel, *Cronache di poveri amanti*.

However, if one were to open up the question of Tuscan space further still and take into account other writers from the region, one could consider Piero Calamandrei (1889–1956), Gianna Manzini (1896–1974), Romano Bilenchi (1909–89), or Carlo Cassola (1917–87) – to name but a handful out of a host of Tuscan writers roughly contemporary to those major figures, such as Tozzi, Palazzeschi, and Pratolini, already included in this volume. For instance, parallels could be drawn between Tozzi's Siena and the Tuscan environment depicted in Bilenchi's novel *Conservatorio di Santa Teresa* (St Teresa's Conservatory, 1940), particularly in terms of the young male's sense of exclusion. Cassola's portrayal of rural life in Maremma in *Il taglio del bosco* (The Cutting of the Woods, 1954) or *La ragazza di Bube* (translated as *Bebo's Girl*, 1960) or *Paura e tristezza* (Fear and Sadness, 1970) is also of interest, in particular in relation to questions of gender. Gianna Manzini's *Tempo innamorato* (Time in Love, 1928, revised and republished in 1943) also constitutes a rich exploration of gender and space (again the trope of the window appears, an aspect to be contrasted with Palazzeschi's use of the icon), yet the 'Tuscan' quality of setting is virtually absent, given that toponyms are supplied only in the vaguest of terms. Calamandrei's memoir about his childhood in the countryside (*Inventario della casa in campagna* [Inventory of a Country House], 1941) nostalgically focuses on nature and wildlife, and can perhaps be seen as a precursor to Belotti's nature writing in *Voli*.

A new generation of Italian writers is also choosing to set novels in the Tuscan countryside, the most notable example possibly being Benedetta Cibrario's *Rossovermiglio* (Vermillionred, 2007), winner of the Premio Campiello in 2008, which again evokes the icon of the Tuscan villa. Cibrario's book, while attempting to subvert commonplaces by foregrounding as protagonist a separated woman who acquires a Tuscan vineyard during the Fascist period and continues to reside there after the Second World War, ultimately reproduces an unoriginal, sentimentalized portrait of the upper bourgeoisie in a quintessentially picturesque rural context.

Foreign writers who depict Tuscany are too numerous to be catalogued; it seems that the region's charms have spawned countless novels, short stories, and travelogues running the gamut from literary masterpieces to dross. One of the most evocative representations of

Tuscany to have emerged is Michael Ondaatje's *The English Patient* (1992), a novel heavily involved in questions of identity and alterity. The Canadian writer presents a Tuscany resonant with ruins such as those depicted in Neorealist portrayals of Second World War Italy (e.g., Rossellini's *Paisà*) and at the same time reflects his fascination with the region's Renaissance past, contrasted with the history of the exploration of the Libyan desert, the location that constitutes the focus of most critical studies of the novel's setting. Yet the landscape of Ondaatje's Tuscany, while embodying the physical and psychological wounds of the novel's characters and the trauma of the war, provides them with a cross-cultural meeting place and locus of temporary regeneration (again the familiar theme of 'renewal') and, ultimately, signifies the writer's postmodern concern with nomadic or hybrid identities. Although in some ways romanticized, Ondaatje's Tuscany constitutes a much more perceptive exploration of identity than that presented by travel writers such as Mayes or Leavitt and Mitchell. At the same time, like these travel writers and Forster's Lucy Honeychurch, his characters' interactions with native Italians are quite restricted, hinting at the fact that perhaps the setting has been selected more for its visual impact and artistic patrimony than for the actual residents themselves.

Further examples of anglophone travel writing on Tuscany could potentially be considered, yet most of the texts published in the last couple of decades along these lines, as mentioned in chapter 5, have little to contribute in terms of innovation in the presentation of place, and for the most part follow in the footsteps of the formula spelled out by Mayes in her bestseller. One noteworthy travel narrative that deviates from this prototype is Gary Paul Nabhan's *Songbirds, Truffles, and Wolves: An American Naturalist in Italy* (1993), an informed and informative examination of central Italy that expertly blends personal reflection and direct contact with local Italians in the author's account of a Franciscan pilgrimage/walking tour. Nabhan's interest in the Other, his awareness of his own alterity (as a Lebanese-American, which he discusses in this text and elsewhere), and his insistence on Mediterranean and Trans-Atlantic exchanges lead, on the whole, to unique observations about place and help create a text that allows readers to gain knowledge about Tuscany and Central Italy.

Florence's association with the horrific is another area that would merit additional attention, especially in other genres such as detective fiction. Authors and filmmakers are seemingly inspired by the city's artistic patrimony, but simultaneously correlate the urban landmarks with the terrible, in a move typical of the dynamic of the sublime. Thomas Harris's horror novel *Hannibal* (1999) and the eponymous film derived from it (directed by Ridley Scott) recall Florence's history of factionalism and conflict, and, like Stendhal, Forster, and Argento, the director Scott stages disturbing (indeed, violent) scenes in the city centre. Several detective novels, moreover, have been published that draw at least in part on actual tragic events that took place in the countryside near the Tuscan capital, namely, the gruesome murders perpetrated by the *mostro di Firenze* (the monster of Florence) in the 1970s and 1980s. The most famous of these is probably Magdalen Nabb's *The Monster of Florence* (1996), but others penned by Italians include Michele Giuttari and Carlo Lucarelli's *Compagni di sangue* (1998), or Douglas Preston and Mario Spezi's *The Monster of Florence* (2008), among others.

Another intercultural aspect of the Florentine (sub)urban landscape is presented in an essay by the novelist Antonio Tabucchi in his *Gli Zingari e il Rinascimento: Vivere da Rom a Firenze* (1999), which deals directly with the spatial and social exclusion of the Rom community. Tabucchi's short text, which combines personal reflection and reportage, contrasts Florence's reputation as the cradle of the Renaissance and its capitalizing on this image for commercial purposes with the plight of the marginalized Rom living in camps on Florence's outskirts (and here parallels can be drawn with Pratolini's depiction of the Greek immigrant community outside Rifredi). While attempting to dispel common misconceptions about Rom, Tabucchi indicts the rhetoric of Florence as Renaissance capital employed by politicians and the media, and thus subverts the figure of the Medicean city. Nonetheless, Tabucchi on occasion resorts to generalizations about Florentine character and attitudes (e.g., portraying Florentines as conservative, or interested only in fatuous yet lucrative enterprises such as the fashion industry), thus reinforcing stereotypes about the local residents, despite his sensitivity towards the dangers of ethnic categorizations and his agenda of highlighting the local/outsider opposition common to anti-Rom propaganda.

To continue in this vein, the study of migrant writing in Italian (which is increasingly gaining recognition) set in Tuscany would enable readers and critics to access the voices and responses to place of those who are often 'Othered' by the dominant culture. Greater sensitivity towards questions of alterity and space can be gained by examining a plurality of viewpoints. These additional possibilities for the analysis of Tuscan places mentioned thus far attest to the wealth of texts inspired by the region, and to the usefulness of examining literature in light of its spatial constructions.

Raising readers' awareness about and familiarity with textual setting and spatial practices can only benefit literary analysis. Bal explains the crucial role of spatial setting to the text:

> In many cases ... space is 'thematized': it becomes an object of presentation itself, for its own sake. Space thus becomes an 'acting place' rather than the place of action. It influences the fabula, and the fabula becomes subordinate to the presentation of space. The fact that '*this* is happening here' is just as important as 'the way it is *here*,' which allows these events to happen. (95–7)

An exploration of a literary or filmic text through the filter of space, rather than being prescriptive, can in fact serve to access insights that might otherwise remain less evident, can aid in undermining commonly held assumptions about a work, and ultimately strengthens its critical interpretation.

Notes

Introduction

1 'The border may be viewed in very different ways by those to whom it has relevance ... Even where borderlines are already established and relatively stable, the borders themselves, and the identities of those who live there, may be characterised by continual change and negotiation; the boundary line itself may not shift, but the relations across it as well as within it – between a border people and their political core – may be subject to repeated definition' (Wilson and Donnan 21) and 'Whether borders are old or new, their frontiers are volatile social and cultural spaces' (24).
2 'It is a characteristic of the region to have neither a definition nor an outline. The empirical criteria which allow the socio-economic entity to be recognised as sufficiently homogeneous and distinct, are vague and mixed' (Smouts 30–1). Smouts continues: 'The "region" category regroups disparate aggregates and the same term serves to denote sub-national formations, intermediaries between the local and the national levels within the state (Bavaria, Catalonia, Lombardy, Aquitane), various co-operation zones, including states, indeed, entire subcontinents (the South-American cone, North America, the Pacific region), and trans-border areas between several sub-national regions belonging to different states (Neisse, the new economic development zones in East Asia).'
3 Two geographers, Fonnesu and Rombai, supply a comprehensive overview of Tuscany's geography and its representation in literature in their useful and informative *Letteratura e paesaggio in Toscana: Da Pratesi a Cassola* (2004), which is somewhat anthological in approach. The authors are preoccupied more with fiction's capacity to record topographical characteristics rather than with literary analysis.

4 Becattini cautions against accepting unquestioningly the *mito toscano* which promotes the image of a harmonious, gentle landscape and an emphasis on the region's 'illustrious past' (903).
5 'È in ogni caso indiscutibile che i piú prestigiosi, i piú imponenti ed i piú appariscenti "artifici dell'uomo" erano quei borghi e quelle città ... le cui strutture materiali rappresentavano già di per sé la testimonianza di una civiltà fra le piú alte che la storia del genere umano avesse conosciuto e, insieme, di una fissità che ne rivelava malinconicamente la bellezza unica ed una illusione perduta. Prestigioso, imponente ed appariscente non sono comunque aggettivi sprecati o retorici per Firenze, Lucca, Pisa e Siena, ma anche, se si dovesse fare qualche altro nome, per Pienza, per Arezzo, per Montepulciano, per Volterra, per Massa Marittima, per San Gimignano, per Cortona, per Pistoia le quali, singolarmente e nell'insieme, costituivano una molteplicità di situazioni ambientali e artistiche, ma anche residenziali e sociali di grande momento' (Mori 7). [It is in any case indisputable that the most prestigious, imposing, and striking 'artifices of man' were those towns and cities ... whose material structures represented in themselves proof of one of the highest civilizations that the history of mankind has known and, at the same time, proof of a fixity that melancholically revealed their unique beauty and lost illusions. Prestigious, imposing, and striking at any rate are not gratuitous or rhetorical adjectives when used for Florence, Lucca, Pisa, and Siena, but also – if we are to mention some other names – for Pienza, Arezzo, Montepulciano, Volterra, Massa Marittima, San Gimignano, Cortona, Pistoia, which, individually and as a group, comprised a multitude of environmental and artistic, as well as residential and social, situations, of a great moment]. Also worth mentioning is that several Tuscan locations have been deemed world heritage sites by UNESCO: Florence's city centre in 1982; the Piazza del Duomo, Pisa, in 1987; San Gimignano in 1990; Siena's historic centre in 1995; Pienza in 1996; and Val d'Orcia in 2004 (UNESCO).
6 Lasansky's *The Renaissance Perfected* (2004) is a fascinating study of the propagandistic use the Fascist regime made of (in particular Tuscan) medieval and Renaissance architecture and culture and how this has contributed to current stereotypical constructions of these periods.
7 It was under Medici rule that the Republic ended and the 'Granducato' began for Tuscany, the title of Grand Duke being obtained for Cosimo I from Pope Pius V in 1569. The 'Granducato' lasted until Italian unification. See *Guida d'Italia: Toscana*, Touring Club Italiano, 53.
8 Obviously Florence was the central axis for the majority of these events and therefore there exist far too many accounts of its historical role across

the centuries and in specific periods to furnish a comprehensive bibliography here. For this reason I will limit myself to indicating a couple of volumes exclusively on Florence that paint an overall picture of the city's role: Spini and Casali's *Firenze* (1986), as well as Vannucci's *Storia di Firenze* (1986), translated as *The History of Florence* (1988).

9 Marcello Vannucci's *L'avventura degli stranieri in Toscana* (1981) gives a lively account, written and photographic, of the presence of the non-Italian community in Tuscany in the nineteenth and twentieth centuries.

10 For more on the inter-war period and the *caffé letterari*, consult *La cultura a Firenze tra le due guerre* (1991), by Pier Luigi Ballini et al., which supplies an informative overview; see also Walter L. Adamson, *Avant-garde Florence* (1993), for an examination of the Futurist movement and Florence, as well as of many other key players in the city's cultural scene.

11 Some critical works on literature and Tuscany (or, more specifically, Florence) have been published, but they do not cover the same area or use the same approach as the present study; included among these is *The Poetics of Place: Florence Imagined* (2001), edited by Marchegiani Jones and Haeussler, which encompasses a number of essays centring exclusively around Florence; the contributions span various periods (from the eighteenth century to the present) and a range of literatures (English, German, French), while only one relates to Italian literature. Lanuzza's *Firenze degli scrittori del Novecento* (2001) also limits its focus to the Tuscan capital and provides a historical overview of Italian writers' reactions to twentieth-century Florence, while performing limited critical analysis of their works. Luti's *Cronache dei fatti di Toscana: Storia e letteratura tra Ottocento e Novecento* (1996) consists of a broad overview of numerous modern Tuscan writers, but addresses neither the question of regional space nor the foreign literary interpretations of the region. The conference proceedings edited by Savellini, *Firenze nella cultura italiana del Novecento* (1993), concern the issue of Florence as cultural milieu, but do not examine the theme of geographical locus, nor do they extend to the entire region of Tuscany. Michael Ross's *Storied Cities: Literary Imaginings of Florence, Venice, and Rome* (1994) focuses primarily on British and American writers' approaches to the three Italian cities, and *Firenze dei grandi viaggiatori*, edited by Paloscia (1993), examines the perceptions of foreigners in Florence, in particular those on the Grand Tour, but not Tuscany in general.

12 Cresswell's *Place: A Short Introduction* provides a particularly cogent overview of the concept of 'place' and its evolution in geographical theory. The bibliography on the notions of space and place is vast; some notable recent contributions in the area of human geography include Crang and

Thrift, eds, *Thinking Space* (2000), Holloway and Hubbard's *People and Place: The Extraordinary Geographies of Everyday Life* (2001), Hubbard, Kitchin, and Valentine, eds, *Key Thinkers on Space and Place* (2004) and Massey's *for space* (2005).

13 'Stories thus carry out a labor that constantly transforms places into spaces or spaces into places. They also organize the play of changing relationships between places and spaces' (de Certeau 118).

14 Literature on landscape theory is extensive and much of it concerns visual representation (for instance, in art or photography) or analyses it from an architectural point of view; some works include Romani's *Il Paesaggio: Teoria e pianificazione* (1994), Socco's *Il paesaggio imperfetto* (1998), and Assunto's *Il paesaggio e l'estetica* (1973), among many others.

15 Cloke, Philo, and Sadler 58. The three geographers define the parameters of humanistic geography as follows: 'The bottom line for humanistic geography lies in the objective of *bringing human beings in all of their complexity to the centre-stage of human geography*: and this is an objective pursued explicitly, in a sustained fashion and in conscious opposition to the curiously "peopleless" character of much that had previously passed off as "human" geography ... We ascribe considerable importance to this heightened awareness of the intimate emotional, practical, political and other attachments people usually possess about the places containing them, and as such we are prepared to talk about an emergent and innovative *geographical humanism*' (58–9).

16 Raymond Williams discusses the historical opposition between the two: 'On the actual settlements, which in the real history have been astonishingly varied, powerful feelings have gathered and have been generalised. On the country has gathered the idea of a natural way of life: of peace, innocence, and simple virtue. On the city has gathered the idea of an achieved centre: of learning, communication, light. Powerful hostile associations have also developed: on the city as a place of noise, worldliness and ambition; on the country as a place of backwardness, ignorance, limitation. A contrast between country and city, as fundamental ways of life, reaches back into classical times. Yet the real history, throughout, has been astonishingly varied. The 'country way of life' has included the very different practices of hunters, pastoralists, farmers and factory farmers, and its organisation has varied from the tribe and the manor to the feudal estate, from the small peasantry and tenant farmers to the rural commune, from the *latifundia* and the plantation to the large capitalist enterprise and the state farm. The city, no less, has been of many kinds: state capital, administrative base, religious centre, market-town, port and mercantile

depot, military barracks, industrial concentration. Between the cities of ancient and medieval times and the modern metropolis or conurbation there is a connection of name and in part of function, but nothing like identity. Moreover, in our own world, there is a wide range of settlements between the traditional poles of country and city: suburb, dormitory town, shanty town, industrial estate. Even the idea of the village, which seems simple, shows in actual history a wide variation: as to size and character, and internally in its variation between dispersed and nuclear settlements, in Britain as clearly as anywhere' (Williams 1).

17 For Dainotto, regional literature is antithetical to Marxism and the privileging of place results in the denial of history (see, for example, Dainotto's comments on Freud and Rome, 18–19). However, when one considers space as a construction, issues such as class and history (among others, such as gender and ethnicity) can be, and often are, important points of consideration on which the analysis is constructed.

18 'Ecofeminism' is a both a movement and a philosophy which critiques the patriarchal norms that effect the subjugation of nature and women; the application of this kind of environmentally conscious criticism will be discussed more fully in chapter 6. The development in the last three decades of ecologically orientated criticism (namely, Ecocriticism and Ecofeminism) has evolved into an innovative branch of literary studies that privileges the examination of spatiality and the dynamics of oppression. This approach, however, is not without its detractors: Dainotto's rejection, for instance, of literary criticism's interest in 'nature' and of 'ecological' criticism does little more than reiterate the Manichean opposition between environmentalism and Marxism: 'It might be too early to speak of a new "ecological" trend in literary studies, one whose explicit goal is that of substituting "green" politics for the "red" politics of new historicism' (12). He easily dismisses ecological criticism as symptomatic of 'the general and ubiquitous revivals of New Age mysticisms, fantasias about the planet Earth, and sociobiological euphorias' (12). Yet I would maintain that rigorous, ethically inclined Ecocriticism and Ecofeminism can and frequently do call into question all forms of domination, be they based on gender, ethnicity, class, or species, without ignoring historical considerations, and in fact deliberately engage with the interrelationship between the spatial and the temporal.

1. The Country and the City

1 As witnessed, for example, in the following statement regarding Remigio's relationship to the countryside: 'La campagna cambiava come i suoi stati

mentali; ma non gli apparteneva' (*Con gli occhi chiusi* 128) [The countryside changed along with his mental states, but it didn't belong to him]. Jeuland-Meynaud provides similar examples from Tozzi's *Novelle*, stating: 'Passi tutti dove si vede la natura, nell'esaltazione come nella disperazione, mettersi all'unisono col soggetto' (70) [These are all passages where one sees nature, both in exaltation and in desperation, uniting itself with the subject]. Jeuland-Meynaud attributes Tozzi's 'ansia mai appagata ... di stabilire collegamenti tra l'uomo e le cose circostanti' [ever unsatisfied anxiety ... for establishing connections between man and objects surrounding him] to his desire to 'evidenziare quella solidarietà basilare di una comune origine sacra' (70) [highlight that fundamental solidarity of a sacred common origin].

2 'Il nous semble en somme que l'interprétation analogique demeure problématique à plus d'un égard; et que la description comporte – en tout cas – des éléments qui résistent au sens: tous ces fragments de paysage juxtaposés, dépeints dans leurs caractéristiques concrètes et sensibles, ne se laissent pas [sic] d'évidence, ni également recouvrir d'une signification abstraite' (Fratnik 13–14) [It seems to us, in short, that the analogical interpretation remains problematic for more than one reason and that the description implies – in any case – some elements which resist meaning: all these landscape fragments which are juxtaposed, depicted in their concrete and perceptible characteristics, do not cohere in any obvious way, nor, at the same time, do they conceal an abstract significance.] (Missing elements supplied by me).

3 The common farming practice of the period was the *mezzadria*: 'L'istituto della mezzadria stimola infatti il più intensivo ma anche il più variato sfruttamento possibile della terra del singolo podere a tutela dell'autosufficienza alimentare. Si è potuto parlare in questo senso, con efficace paragone, di poderi simili ad arche di Noè, dove tutto è presente dappertutto, e dove solo l'ordine e la cura diuturna possono assicurare il buon esito, ad ogni propizia stagione, di un così diversificato organismo produttivo' (Brilli 20) [The institution of sharecropping stimulates, in fact, the most intensive but also the most varied utilization of the land of the individual farm so as to safeguard a self-sufficient food supply. For this reason farms have been referred to as Noah's arks – an appropriate comparison – where everything is present everywhere, and where only order and ongoing care can ensure a good outcome, with every propitious season, for such a diversified productive organism].

4 Critics have noted how Remigio's retreat to Nature constitutes a return to the maternal. Gioanola, for instance, explains the protagonist's relationship

to the land as well as the maternal/paternal dynamic in the text: 'La campagna è il luogo per eccellenza dell'estasi, cioè dell'appagante cancellazione della prassi, dove può avvenire lo smarrimento di sé negli aspetti accoglienti della terra, delle acque, del cielo, o almeno la dimenticanza momentanea dell'eterna persecuzione ("Gli pareva di potersi nascondere in mezzo al podere; e di non farsi mai guardare da nessuno"): *Il Podere* è tutto giocato sul contrasto tra i due sensi opposti contenuti nella stessa realtà, quello "paterno," del podere come roba, eredità, lavoro, e quello "materno" della terra, dei suoni e odori della campagna, della dolcezza delle stagioni' (Gioanola 135) [The countryside is the place of ecstasy, par excellence, that is, of the satisfying erasure of praxis, where one can lose oneself in the welcoming aspects of the land, of the water, of the sky, or at least where the momentary forgetting of eternal persecution can take place ('He felt as though he could hide in the middle of the farm; and that no one could look at him'): *Il Podere* is centred on the contrast between the two opposite meanings contained in the same reality, the 'paternal,' of the farm as material goods, inheritance, work, and the maternal, of the earth, of the sounds and smells of the countryside, of the sweetness of the seasons]. Saccone, too, makes a similar observation: 'La reazione del personaggio è caratteristica. È una fuga dalla "sfiducia," ovvero la ricerca di un rifugio: dal sospetto inquietante, addirittura terrorizzante, in cui sembrano accumularsi gli attributi superegoici di un padre padrone giudicante e perseguitante. Donde anche, all'opposto, il riparo cercato in uno spazio evidentemente materno' (Saccone, *Allegoria* 12) [The character's reaction is typical. It is an escape from 'mistrust,' or rather, it is a search for a refuge: from the disturbing, indeed terrifying, suspicion, in which the super-egoic attributes of a judgmental and persecutory father-master seem to accumulate. For this reason, in contrast, shelter is sought in a space which is clearly maternal]. Saccone then cites the same passage as an illustration. At the same time, this desire to possess the land (not solely as a physical entity, but also as a source of income) clearly has links to male desire of colonization not only of the earth, but of the female body. Thus, Tozzi's model of feminization of the landscape, despite its originality under other aspects, conforms to fairly standard patriarchal depictions of nature as equated with the female.

5 Urry summarizes what constitutes the tourist gaze: 'Minimally there must be certain aspects of the place to be visited which distinguish it from what is conventionally encountered in everyday life. Tourism results from a basic binary division between the ordinary/everyday and the extraordinary. Tourist experiences involve some aspect or element which induces

pleasurable experiences which are, by comparison with the everyday, out of the ordinary' (Urry, *Tourist Gaze* 11).
6 'Nelle novelle, la realtà è carica per Tozzi di predicati antropologici perché la relazione con le cose viene mediata dalle attività e dagli affetti specifici del soggetto' (Jeuland-Meynaud 63) [In his short stories, reality for Tozzi is loaded with anthropological predicates because the relationship with things is mediated by the activities and specific affections of the subject].
7 Debenedetti persuasively describes the different manners in which the textual patterning of animal imagery functions in *Bestie*; see 61–72.
8 Melloni attributes Tozzi's reaction of vertigo to the sublime in part, yet his analysis is less convincing in this regard. For the Sienese writer, the sensation of vertigo can be activated even by mundane surroundings (be they interiors or exteriors), not necessarily by views that would normally be classified as examples of the sublime.
9 This dynamic of disorientation as symptomatic of the disjunction between the subject and external space rings true not only for Tozzi's characters, but also for Forster's Lucy, as well as for Argento's Anna Manni.
10 'There are reasons more immediate … that keep mimicry from being taken for a defense reaction … The experiments of Judd and Foucher have definitely resolved the question: predators are not at all fooled by homomorphy or homochromy: they eat crickets that mingle with the foliage of oak trees or weevils that resemble small stones, completely invisible to man … Generally speaking, one finds many remains of mimetic insects in the stomachs of predators. So it should come as no surprise that such insects sometimes have other and more effective ways to protect themselves' (Caillois 23–5).
11 Tozzi gives his own account of his period of isolation and illness in his letters to Emma in Novale, in particular those dated 27 January 1907 (75–6), 22 March 1907 (87), 7 April 1907 (94), 12 September 1907 (149–52), and 15 September 1907 (153–7), among others.
12 '[S]ul piano biografico, la famosa "malattia" di Tozzi adolescente, caratterizzata tra l'altro da una temporanea cecità, a cui fecero seguito due anni di isolamento selvaggio, fa pensare irresistibilmente ad un attacco psicotico acuto' (Gioanola 133) [In terms of his biography, the famous 'illness' of the adolescent Tozzi, characterized by temporary blindness, which was followed by two years of savage isolation, makes one think, irresistibly, of an acute psychotic attack].
13 See Caillois 28–30.
14 Janet's *Les névroses* is listed in Geddes da Filicaia's catalogue of the author's private library (134–5). Marchi also notes the presence of this

volume in the writer's collection: 'Janet e Freud, come alla Salpêtrière, ancora assieme in un altro testo della cultura psicologica di Tozzi recuperato a Castagneto: non *L'État mental des hystériques* ... ma *Les névroses*, Flammarion 1909, in versione originale, con sezioni volta a volta distinte concernenti l'isteria e la psicastenia, le malattie di cui soffrono rispettivamente Adele e Fabio' (Marchi 65) [Janet and Freud, just like in Salpêtrière, together again in another one of Tozzi's texts on the culture of psychology found in Castagneto: not *The Mental State of Hysterics*, but rather *Les névroses* [Neuroses], Flammarion 1909, in the original version, with highlighted sections concerning hysteria and psychasthenia, the illness from which Adele and Fabio suffer, respectively]. Melosi also discusses Tozzi's bibliographical sources on psychology in the chapter 'Filosofia e scienza nella narrativa tozziana' [Philosophy and Science in Tozzi's Fiction]. Martini's volume examines Tozzi's debt to James's work in psychology and touches on Janet as well.

15 'Defined as a disturbance in the relation between self and surrounding territory, psychasthenia is a state in which the space defined by the coordinates of the organism's own body is confused with represented space. Incapable of demarcating the limits of its own body, lost in the immense area that circumscribes it, the psychasthenic organism proceeds to abandon its own identity to embrace the space beyond. It does so by camouflaging itself into the milieu. This simulation effects a double usurpation: while the organism successfully reproduces those elements it could not otherwise apprehend, in the process it is swallowed by them, vanishing as a differentiated entity. Psychasthenia helps describe contemporary experience and account for its uneasiness. Urban culture resembles this mimetic condition when it enables a ubiquitous feeling of being in all places while not really being anywhere' (Olalquiaga 1–2). Olalquiaga then analyses current examples of spatial disorientation, such as that found in the shopping mall. Clearly she has extrapolated from the core premises of Caillois's essay and is applying them elastically to her study of the postmodern condition. Soja discusses Olalquiaga's use of the term psychasthenia in *Postmetropolis*, 150–1, 330–2. I am indebted to Laura Rorato for providing me with these two bibliographical references for 'psychasthenia.'

16 In Tozzi sons characteristically practise an infraction of the Fifth Commandment, 'Honour thy Father,' an age-old struggle that Freud outlines: 'Let us consider first the relation between father and son. The sanctity which we attribute to the rules laid down in the Decalogue has, I think, blunted our powers of perceiving the real facts. We seem scarcely to

venture to observe that the majority of mankind disobey the Fifth Commandment ... The more unrestricted was the rule of the father in the ancient family, the more must the son, as his destined successor, have found himself in the position of an enemy, and the more impatient must he have been to become ruler himself through his father's death. Even in our middle-class families fathers are as a rule inclined to refuse their sons independence and the means necessary to secure it and thus to foster the growth of the germ of hostility which is inherent in their relation' (Freud 357–8).

17 In Ovid's *Metamorphoses*, for example, Daphne escapes Apollo's grasp, and her rape by him, through her transformation into a laurel (1: 525–52). In the nymph's instance it is however her father Peneus, the river god, who has brought about the conversion into the noble tree, and Apollo adopts the laurel as his symbol. Dante, too, portrays a human-plant synthesis, in canto 13 of the *Inferno*, where Pier della Vigna (the relevance of his name cannot be ignored) is punished for his suicide by being confined to the form of a plant. (*Inf* 13: 28–108). His suffering is all the more acute because after Judgment Day he will be denied reunification with his original body, a fate which underscores his humiliation, since in the Middle Ages to be associated with the vegetable kingdom – considered the lowest on the scale of existence – would have been especially degrading (as Spitzer explains in his cogent and most informative study of Pier della Vigna and his textual antecedents, including Ovid). Presumably Pier della Vigna is being punished for violence against the self, yet his ruler, Emperor Federigo II, had him imprisoned (unjustly, della Vigna maintains) for treason: thus, the subject has gone against authority in this case of hybridity, too, although unlike Tozzi's patterns of paternal hegemony, it is an issue of sovereign authority here.

18 'So old is our usage of body imagery for landscape features that the terms have been appropriated by our environmental vocabulary, and are no longer thought of as metaphor. The use of landscape as a metaphier for the human body, in contrast, is more contrived, more obviously a literary device, and therefore more vivid. Novelists, of course, may go to extremes in their search for effect, as when one heroine is made to describe her pubic hair as 'spreading over her thighs like human blight' (Simon 1980). Landscape as body is clearly an anthropomorphism. As yet we have no technical term for body as landscape, although "geomorphism" suggests itself' (Porteous 78).

19 'Le rapprochement s'impose d'autant plus que les paysages de Tozzi, ainsi réduits à leurs apparences, tendent à se fragmenter, à se désagréger et

finalement à se dissoudre dans l'atmosphère qui les enveloppe, à l'instar, précisément, de certains paysages impressionnistes. Les textes plus tardifs, surtout (composés entre 1917 et 1920), en offrent les exemples les plus parlants, à travers une série de vues de Rome' (Fratnik 85) [The parallel comes to the fore all the more in that Tozzi's landscapes, reduced in this way to their appearances, tend to fragment, to come apart and finally to dissolve in the atmosphere that envelops them, precisely in the manner of certain Impressionist landscapes. The later texts especially (composed between 1917 and 1920) offer the most telling examples of this, through a series of views of Rome].
20 'Signore del tempo, esso introduce alle dimore dei vivi e vigila sul sonno dei morti ... La chioma del cipresso appartiene al mondo della luce e del vento, ma le sue radici affondano nel regno dei morti. Ne sarebbe indizio la proverbiale frugalità e la sussistenza in ogni genere di terreno. La sua consacrazione al regno dei defunti è un retaggio delle antiche civiltà mediterranee' (Brilli 13) [Lord of time, it shows the way to the abodes of the living and watches over the sleep of the dead ... The foliage of the cypress belongs to the world of light and wind, but its roots dig deep into the realm of the dead. Its proverbial frugality and its survival in all types of terrain testify to this. Its consecration to the realm of the dead is an inheritance of ancient Mediterranean civilizations].
21 Grosz comments on the death drive as represented in Caillois's research on psychasthenia: 'In his work on mimicry, Caillois makes it clear that an insect's ability to camouflage itself does not have survival value – it does not protect the creature from attack or death, and in fact may leave it open to even more hideous and unimaginable forms of death. He cites cases of the caterpillar cut in half by pruning shears, or the insect devoured by a member of its own species who mistakes it for a leaf' (190).

2. Palazzeschi's Spaces of Difference

1 Critics seem to agree that the setting of both *La piramide* and *Stefanino* is most likely Florence (Diafani 189). Regarding the presumed location of *Stefanino*, Luigi Baldacci in 'Gli ultimi romanzi' says, 'Stefanino è un trovatello che è stato rinvenuto dalla pubblica pietà, nascosto tra le molli pieghe di una coperta rosa, sulla porta di uno storico palazzo municipale. Quale palazzo, quale città? Direi che si tratti di Firenze. Alcune allusioni discrete ma abbastanza decifrabili starebbero a provarlo. Per esempio l'arazzo rappresentante il casto Giuseppe e la moglie di Putifar in una sala di quel palazzo medesimo. Ma Firenze o no, siamo prima di tutto nella

dimensione della fiaba' (259) [Stefanino is an orphan who has been discovered by public pity, hidden between the soft folds of a pink blanket, by the door of a historic municipal building. Which building, which city? I would say it must be Florence. A few discreet but quite decipherable allusions would seem to prove this. For example, the tapestry depicting the chaste Joseph and Potiphar's wife in one of the halls of this very same building. Whether or not it is Florence, we find ourselves above all in the dimension of the fairytale].

2 'Buffe,' the feminine form of 'buffi,' is borrowed from Nicolas J. Perella and Ruggero Stefanini, who employ it in connection with the female figures in *Il codice di Perelà* (111). Ferraris provides a thorough and persuasive analysis of the *buffi* and their implications for Palazzeschi's short stories in his 'Il motivo del buffo.'

3 The original Italian text is found in Palazzeschi, *Tutte le novelle* (965); translation by Nicholas J. Perella in his 'Introduction' to Palazzeschi's *A Tournament of Misfits*, xxix.

4 Palazzeschi employs female characters for this purpose in other instances as well, for example, in *Interrogatorio della Contessa Maria*, published posthumously in 1988, where the licentious Countess narrates her daring sexual exploits. 'Lo scandaloso *Interrogatorio della Contessa Maria* era stato ben riposto in un cassetto, ma non era venuta meno l'idea di trasferire sui personaggi femminili la propria sensibilità omosessuale. Questa modalità di rappresentare l'omosessualità trova infatti nelle *Sorelle Materassi* del 1934 la sua più alta espressione' (Gnerre 75) [The scandalous *Interrogation of Countess Maria* had been well hidden in a drawer, but the idea of transferring his own homosexual sensibility on to female characters was not abandoned. This mode of representing homosexuality in fact finds its highest expression in *The Sisters Materassi* of 1934].

5 Sedgwick emphasizes the importance of the notion of difference to understanding sexuality. Her first axiom is 'People are different from each other,' a statement which initially seems self-evident, but in Sedgwick's analysis has countless ramifications for individuals' attitudes towards sexuality.

6 Somigli wonders at the fact that Palazzeschi has received less critical attention than he merits in the English-speaking world, especially given his works' potential to appeal to such critical methodologies as Queer theory: 'Al di fuori dell'italianistica, però, Palazzeschi rimane poco letto e studiato anche in quegli ambiti – e penso a … campi di ricerca di più recente formazione come i *queer studies* – in cui … l'attenzione per tematiche quali il corpo e la sessualità dovrebbero assicurargli piena cittadinanza' (178) [Outside of Italian Studies, however, Palazzeschi remains little

read and studied, even in those environments – and here I am thinking of ... areas of research of more recent development such as Queer Studies – in which ... attention to such themes as the body and sexuality should ensure him full citizenship].
7 Hirdt discusses at length the medieval literary influences on Palazzeschi's representation of Florence, which opens *Sorelle Materassi*.
8 Translations of *Sorelle Materassi* by Angus Davidson.
9 Marchi aptly notes that the novel's initial landscapes are feminized (93–4).
10 'A model of a vertically oriented universal system is created. In several instances the "top" is identified with "spaciousness" and the "bottom" with "crowding," or the "bottom" is associated with "materiality" and the "top" with "spirituality." The world of the "bottom" is the world of everyday affairs' (Lotman 218–19).
11 Wells remarks on the movement from the wider geographical area to domestic space in the novel: 'The inscriptions designating the various formal divisions of the novel are in themselves partially suggestive of the movement of perspective along which the reader is to be directed. From "Santa Maria a Coverciano" to "Sorelle Materassi" to "Remo! Remo!", and so forth until the final "Sepolte vive," the reader is gradually taken from the physical geographical context of the area surrounding Florence to the specific house which encloses the story to be retold, and then to the principal figures who furnish the eponymous center of the text. There is, then, a determined movement from exterior to interior, from outside to inside, from locus to persona' (205).
12 For Diafani, Palazzeschi's settings are, in the vast majority, urban (190–1). She neglects to take into account, however, the hybrid nature of a peripheral location such as Santa Maria a Coverciano, which defies classification as either rural or urban.
13 *Strapaese* and *Stracittà* were two literary and artistic movements which sprang up under Fascism, one espousing 'rural,' the other 'urban,' values.
14 'Sta di fatto che *Sorelle Materassi* è un'ennesima parabola morale che descrive ... l'arco di cerchio dissipazione-riparazione-dissipazione' (Febbraro 386–7) [It's a fact that *The Sisters Materassi* is the umpteenth moral parable which describes the arc of the circle dissipation-reparation-dissipation].
15 Tamburri analyses the poetics of fire in Palazzeschi, in particular in *Il codice di Perelà*; see the chapter entitled '*Il codice di Perelà*. Svelamento del codice' in *Una semiotica della ri-lettura*.
16 Giovanardi stresses the liminality of the window in *Sorelle Materassi*, aptly reading it as a metaphor for the women's own desires, and as a representation of the act of writing and literature. Yet he does not investigate further

ramifications of the permeable space of the window in terms of gender (Giovanardi 12–13).
17 I have modified Davidson's translation slightly.
18 It is not uncommon to associate the window with spectacle, as is illustrated by Crowhurst Lennard and Lennard's comments: 'Windows and balconies are an important element in public spaces for they give evidence of human presence. Providing they are scaled to human dimensions, and providing they are no higher than five stories, they allow inhabitants to participate actively in the public life of the square below. Those living in the building become an audience to the comings and goings of strangers and acquaintances; they can begin to identify frequent actors on the public stage, and enrich their understanding of the community's social networks by seeing who is meeting whom, and how the people they observe are relating to one another' (24).
19 Pullini, too, notes that the sisters 'inventano e inscenano una specie di "commedia dell'amore" ogni domenica pomeriggio, quando si ritirano nella loro stanza ... In queste occasioni lasciano affiorare una femminilità segreta' (103) [invent and perform a kind of 'comedy of love' every Sunday afternoon when they retire to their room ... On these occasions they let their secret femininity emerge].
20 Barbaro examines the influence of the theatre and the clownesque on Palazzeschi's oeuvre in her *I poeti-saltimbanchi e le maschere di Aldo Palazzeschi*.
21 Translation slightly modified.
22 'The Duce himself liked to parade his own manliness; harvesting stripped to the waist, running with his cabinet, exercising his body' (Mosse 174).
23 Marchi comments on Palazzeschi's autobiographical disguise that is effected in another text, *Interrogatorio della Contessa Maria*, composed under the Fascist regime, but published only after his death: 'E si comprende il perché dell'imbarazzo di un Palazzeschi degli anni Venti, avviato a rimeditazioni moderate e congedi, di fronte a un suo personaggio dell'anima in tutti sensi estremo, così poco riscattato in astrazione e stilizzazione da risolversi in un *en travesti* artisticamente formidabile, ma più che audace imprudente, troppo facilmente decifrabile e compromettente, da occultare: timori favoriti e quindi, come si accennava, almeno in parte indotti da un contesto storico destinato a farsi sempre più acerbamente normalizzatore come quello dell'Italia di regime' (64) [And Palazzeschi's embarrassment in the 1920s is understandable – as he was on the path of moderate re-meditations and farewells – in the face of a character of the soul which was, in all senses, extreme, so scarcely redeemed by abstraction and stylization that it turned into an artistically formidable disguise, more

imprudent than daring, too easily decipherable and compromising to be concealed: these were fears augmented and thus brought on, as mentioned before, at least in part by a historical context destined to become more and more harshly normative as was that of Italy under the regime].

3. Vasco Pratolini's Florentine Spaces of Exclusion

1 Three documentaries on Pratolini and Florence have been produced, another indicator of the author's deep-seated ties to his city, as well as being symptomatic of his involvement in the film industry: Cecilia Mangini's *Firenze di Pratolini* (1959), Nelo Risi's *La Firenze di Pratolini* (1963), and Patrizio Barbaro and Fabio Pierangeli's *La Firenze di Vasco Pratolini*, produced in 1992 for the Rai International series *L'Italia narrata* (Vannini and Grasso 13–14).
2 J. Hillis Miller comments on the significance of topographical detail: 'Landscape or cityscape gives verisimilitude to novels and poems. Topographical setting connects literary works to a specific historical and geographical time. This establishes a cultural and historical setting within which the action can take place' (6–7).
3 Alessandra Gabelli outlines the importance of the street within the novel in her article 'Un luogo di Firenze: Via del Corno nella vita e nell'opera di Vasco Pratolini' (A Florentine Place: Via del Corno in the Life and Works of Vasco Pratolini), where she delineates the genesis of *Cronache di poveri amanti* and Pratolini's interest in topographical detail.
4 Alberto Asor Rosa recognizes the importance of the vivid sketches of via del Corno and notes the references to degradation: 'E anche quando Via del Corno la fa protagonista, sono i suoi muri vecchi, le sue fogne che sfiatano, i mucchi d'immondizia sparsi lungo i muri, il suo orinatorio, i tetti che lasciano passare la pioggia, e i gerani alle finestre, i polli sugli abbaini, a riempire la pagina del loro peso di cose concrete, reali, riferibili senza difficoltà all'esperienza dei protagonisti, e pure nello stesso tempo capaci di denunciare una condizione umana e storica con maggiore efficacia di quanto non possa fare una tirata oratoria o un intenerimento lirico' (121) [And even when he makes via del Corno the protagonist, it is the street's old walls, its steaming sewers, it piles of refuse spread out along the walls, its urinal, the roofs which let the rain through, and the geraniums at the windows, the chickens on the rooftops, which fill the page with their weight of concrete, real things, easily traceable to the experience of the protagonists, and yet at the same time capable of denouncing a human, historical condition more effectively than an oratorical harangue or lyrical demonstration of compassion].

5 For more on the spatial relationship between the Signora and via del Corno, see my article 'The Fascist Body Politic and Florentine Space: The *Signora* in Vasco Pratolini's *Cronache di poveri amanti*.' The significance of local festivals to via del Corno's residents is discussed in my 'Resistance and the Carnivalesque in Vasco Pratolini's *Cronache di poveri amanti*.'
6 The eponymous cinematic adaptation was produced in 1966 and directed by Pasquale Festa Campanile.
7 Memmo's comments seem to capture appropriately Pratolini's vision of the period in the novel: 'queste esperienze si chiamano guerra, e soprattutto dopoguerra, e soprattutto il dopo del dopoguerra, il capitalismo risorgente dalle proprie ceneri, le lusinghe aggiornate della borghesia, i ricatti subdoli e crudeli di un potere politico ormai tranquillo e assestato che innalza la bandiera del "miracolo economico" ma nei fatti, poi, reprime duramente la classe operaia attraverso il clientelismo piú sfacciato e le piú odiose discriminazioni nelle assunzioni' (Memmo 118) [these experiences are called war, above all post-war, and above all post post-war, capitalism reborn from its own ashes, the new allure of the bourgeoisie, the cruel, underhanded blackmail of a political power which is by now placid and established which raises the flag of the 'economic miracle' but in actual fact harshly represses the working class through a most shameless clientelism and the worst kind of discrimination in hiring practices]. Macrí also discusses the historical setting of the novel, but less perceptively than Memmo: 'Questo romanzo scritto nel '62 riflette gli anni del graduale *boom* economico e un governo stabile con al centro la D.C., dialogo tra Confindustria e sindacati, che stabilirono un relativo autonomismo dai poteri politici (e ci salvò!), restando ibernate sacche e frange di nostalgici d'ogni banda, che, sobillati da intellettuali, esplosero con la contestazione e il terrorismo. Nel personaggio di Bruno si affermano valori rivoluzionari e resistenziali dal nucleo del sindacalismo di sinistra; e un intellettuale in veste operaia si presenta Bruno nelle sue riflessioni' (Macrí 131). [This novel was written in 1962 and reflects the years of the gradual economic boom and a stable government with the Christian Democrats at the centre, the dialogue between Confindustria (Italian Manufacturers' Association) and the unions, which established a relative autonomy from political powers (and saved us!), with pockets and fringe groups of throwbacks of all kinds in hibernation, who, incited by intellectuals, exploded with public demonstrations and terrorism. The values of revolution and resistance from the nuclei of leftist unionism are affirmed

in the character of Bruno; and in his reflections, Bruno is presented as an intellectual in worker's clothing.]
8 Cresti (apart from a rather incongruous excursus on Michelucci's architecture) examines the city's older, historic areas in Pratolini: 'Gli esempi fiorentini di Santa Croce e San Frediano offrivano a Pratolini la concreta, credibile testimonianza che il quartiere, dove la povertà "è patita con orgoglio," era invece capace di mantenere vivo il cemento di una tradizione comunitaria' (109) [The Florentine examples of Santa Croce and San Frediano offered Pratolini concrete, credible testimony that the neighbourhood where poverty 'is borne with pride,' was instead able to keep alive the glue of a tradition of community].
9 Cf. the novel's incipit – 'Qui sono nato; ora è camera mia, prima c'era il salottino' (5) [I was born here; now this is my bedroom, but before it was the living room] – where, in conversation with his mother, the narrator/protagonist begins by discussing his birth.
10 For a history of the Officine Galileo, see the exhibition catalogue *Percorsi della Memoria, Una storia, molte storie ... la Galileo* [A Trip through Memory: One Story, Many Stories ... la Galileo], by the Gruppo Lavoratori Anziani delle Officine Galileo.
11 The significance of names in the novel in fact would merit lengthier critical attention.
12 For more on the figure of the priest, see Mariarosaria Covino's *Don Giulio Facibeni: Il Padre, uomo della carità*.
13 A description is provided in Listri of the Camera del Lavoro being involved in 'la vertenza alle Officine Galileo nel 1958–59, con l'occupazione dello stabilimento, fino a quando gli operai licenziati furono in parte riassunti con l'arrivo di nuove commesse di lavoro' (Listri 77) [the dispute at the Galileo Factory in 1958–59, with the occupation of the building, until the workers who had been fired were in part rehired with the arrival of new work orders]. For a detailed description of the dispute and its ramifications, see Paoletti and Torrini, 2: 641–3, 676.
14 See, for example, Amatori and Colli's analysis of FIAT's labour politics in comparison with the national context (246–7).
15 The law of the father is a significant concern for the three Tuscan writers examined in the first three chapters. Tozzi's sons invariably feel inept in the face of their father's overbearing authority. For Palazzeschi's autobiographical works (e.g., *Stampe dell'800*), the father is either seen as a force of interdiction, or else is absent, allowing for the son to develop his Oedipal attachment to the mother. In Pratolini's case, fathers are, for the most part,

absent; in fact, most families for Pratolini do not consist of the stereotypical unit of both parents and children. In the case of *La costanza della ragione*, the factory and Millo become replacement father figures, and Bruno's relationship with both is problematic.

16 See in particular one of the final episodes of *Cronache di poveri amanti*, where Milena and Mario escape to the countryside and sleep in a field under the stars in a rural idyll that precedes his arrest.

17 Foot explains that the label emerged when these residential areas for migrant populations developed in the 1950s and early 1960s, in association with their supposed resemblance to scenes from the Korean War (46). His study of the *coree* outside Milan reveals, however, that they 'were usually marked by *good* housing and often helped integration' (47), thus indicating that the stigmatization of these zones is misrepresentative.

18 'On the level of our individual psychosexual development, the abject marks the moment when we separated ourselves from the mother, when we began to recognize a boundary between "me" and other, between "me" and "(m)other"' (Felluga). See Kristeva's essay *The Powers of Horror*.

19 In his correspondence with Alessandro Parronchi, Pratolini, at least initially, admits that he fears the novel's message may be ambiguous, a fact borne out by the vastly different critical appraisals of the work: 'Mai come questa volta, decidendomi a licenziarlo, un mio lavoro mi trova pieno di dubbio ... Sono ritornato, con le ragioni dei ragazzi d'oggi (e contro di loro e per loro) all'atmosfera del "Quartiere." Ed ho il terrore di avere sacrificato incensi a una semplicità di maniera, di essermi giocato delle verità per affermare l'irragionevolezza della ideologia, là dove si dovrebbe invece, di essa ideologia, rilevare l'insostituibilità nella vita dell'uomo. Insomma, o è chiaro che la ragione trova la sua più clamorosa (e totale) vittoria nella sconfitta – o è tutto sbagliato' (Pratolini, *Lettere a Sandro* 400). [Never has a work of mine when I am deciding to send it off left me with such feelings of doubt as this one ... I've gone back – taking on the mindset of today's young people (both for and against them) – to the atmosphere of *Il Quartiere*. And I am terrified of having chosen to burn offerings at the altar of simplicity, of having jeopardized truths in order to affirm the unreasonableness of ideology, where instead one should point out the fact that ideology is irreplaceable in man's life. Basically, either it is clear that reason finds its most resounding (and total) victory in defeat – or else the whole thing is wrong.] Critics' assessments of the text range from praise (Parronchi) to dismissal (Longobardi).

20 Pratolini's presumably sub-conscious re-inscription of Fascist dogma characterizes other texts, as seen, for instance, in *Cronache di poveri amanti*. Nerenberg and Hainsworth, among others, have both pointed out this contradiction within Pratolini's fiction.

4. The Stendhal Syndrome, or The Horror of Being Foreign in Florence

1 Tuan discusses the association of fear with urban zones in the chapter 'Fear in the City' in *Landscapes of Fear*: 'It is deeply ironic that the city can often seem a frightening place. Built to rectify the apparent confusion and chaos of nature, the city itself becomes a disorienting physical environment in which tenement houses collapse on their inhabitants, fires break out, and heavy traffic threatens life and limb. Although every street and building – and indeed all the bricks and stone blocks in them – are clearly the products of planning and thought, the final result may be a vast, disorderly labyrinth' (146–7).
2 Bruno Santini, too, in Pratolini's *La costanza della ragione*, published over a century after Stendhal's, equates Florence's centre with its past, but for Bruno the associations are entirely negative as the historic monuments for him and for Lori are essentially equated with a lack of vitality, with death, and are set in opposition to the industrial neighbourhood of Rifredi.
3 As epitomized by Lucy's falling into a typical Forsterian 'muddle' and her attempting to free herself of it. Prakash (among others) discusses the importance of the word 'muddle' in Forster in *Symbolism in the Novels of E.M. Forster*: '*A Room with a View* celebrates the victory of love and truth over 'Muddle,' a word having rich and varied meaning and connotation in Forster's novels that normally signifies some fatal obscuring of inner vision by the falsifying conventions of society' (144).
4 For the importance of 'sight' in *A Room with a View*, consult Michael L. Ross, *Storied Cities* 80–90 in particular.
5 Butler, *Butler's Lives of the Saints* 549. The choice of Lucy's name is not gratuitous; many of Forster's works reveal a knowledge of hagiography.
6 Dunkling and Gosling note that 'the name [Cecil] reached a peak of popularity around 1900' (45), precisely the period when Forster was writing *A Room with a View*.
7 George's name, too, while not related to the topos of sight, has salient connotations. As well as being the patron saint of England, St George is linked with farming and land, a connection that lends itself well to the character of the young Mr Emerson, who is often associated with nature; his surname, furthermore, probably alludes to the figure of Ralph Waldo Emerson, who wrote the well-known essay 'Nature' (1836; a linkage kindly suggested to me by Michael Ross, and also noted by Goldman, 130). Moreover, when Cecil asks Lucy if she pictures him indoors or outdoors, she replies that she only thinks of him in a room; the contrast with George is evident in this context, since the dialogue immediately precedes Cecil's unhappy attempt to kiss her in the wood, a gesture that cannot escape

comparison with George and Lucy's earlier spontaneous embrace on the Tuscan hillside amidst the violets (especially as Cecil's pince-nez becomes dislodged in the effort, a gaffe that hints again at his 'blindness').

8 Ruskin in fact favoured medieval art over that of the Renaissance. For more on the influence of art on Forster, see Meyers and Summers.
9 Buzard's article furnishes an especially insightful analysis of the role of the Baedeker in Forster and of his opus's links to tourist culture more generally.
10 Barthes points out the mixed nature of this passion of Stendhal for Italy: 'Stendhal est donc amoureux de l'Italie … Ce pluriel amoureux … est visiblement un principe stendhalien: il entraîne une théorie implicite du *discontinu irrégulier*, dont on peut dire qu'elle est à la fois esthétique, psychologique et métaphysique' (Barthes 335). [Stendhal is therefore in love with Italy … This loving plurality is obviously a Stendhalian principle: it implies an implicit theory of *irregular discontinuity*, which one can say is at once aesthetic, psychological and metaphysical.]
11 Meyers, in *Painting and the Novel*, notes Lucy's frequent connection to the heavenly (44).
12 'Mr Eager conveniently forgets that – to go no further – the stabbing occurred almost exactly on the spot where Savonarola was burnt at the stake on 23 May 1498' (Stallybrass's note to Eager's comment in his edition of Forster's *Room*, 244).
13 Landy's 'Filmed Forster' discusses the five adaptations of Forster's texts and situates them in the context of the British heritage film trend of the 1980s and 1990s.
14 In Hutchings's view, the traumatic aspects of the piazza murder scene seem discordant in the film: 'Here, the threat of Italy to bourgeois proprieties and sublimations actually makes it onto the screen, only to vanish as quickly as the fallen Italian and we are back in romance mode. Shock isn't really something that can be accommodated within the film's limpid aesthetic, it seems a species of bad taste' (223).
15 'She stopped and leant her elbows against the parapet of the embankment. He did likewise. There is at times a magic in identity of position; it is one of the things that have suggested to us eternal comradeship' (Forster, *Room* 65).
16 After describing the viewer's reaction to the pyramids of Egypt, Kant then refers to 'the bewilderment or sort of embarrassment that is said to seize the spectator on first entering St. Peter's in Rome. For here there is a feeling of the inadequacy of his imagination for presenting the ideas of a whole, in which the imagination reaches its maximum and, in the effort to extend it, sinks back into itself, but is thereby transported into an emotionally moving satisfaction' (136).

17 The Stendhal Syndrome has clearly influenced Sebald's fictional travelogue *Vertigo*, in which the narrator studies Stendhal's biography and travels to Italy, where he undergoes a mental crisis.
18 Ardis's 'Hellenism and the Lure of Italy' analyses the interplay between Ancient Greek culture and Forster's Italy, although it does not include a discussion of this particular short story. See also Flego.
19 For a (not entirely persuasive) interpretation of the role of the artworks depicted in the film, see Gallant 65–73.
20 For Rauger, Argento's film is 'una variazione costruita intorno a una celebre sequenza di *Vertigo*' (101) [a variation constructed around a famous sequence in *Vertigo*].
21 'The recurrence of androgynous representations in Argento's cinema indicates the filmmaker's interest in that which places existing and totalising gender categories under stress' (Mendik 30).
22 The reference to Veronica Lake is explicit in Argento's book *La sindrome*, where Anna communicates with her psychologist in the final stages of her madness via recorded cassettes: 'Da nascondere veramente ho solo questa maledetta cicatrice, e riesco a farlo con degli occhialoni neri che non mi levo mai, e soprattutto con una parrucca di capelli lunghi che porto spioventi sul viso, capelli biondi, tipo quell'attrice americana degli anni quaranta, la *femme fatale* … Come si chiamava? Veronica Lake, mi pare' (197). [Actually, all I have to hide is this damn scar, and I manage to do it with large dark glasses which I never remove, and above all with a long-haired wig which I wear hanging over my face, blonde hair, like that American actress from the 1940s, the *femme fatale* … What was her name? I think it was Veronica Lake.] Jones, too, has remarked on Anna's resemblance to the Hollywood star (230).
23 Asia Argento attributes her father's obsession with depicting violence against women to his matrophobia: 'The problem my father has with women can be traced back to the relationship he had with his mother. I have no idea what my grandmother did to him as a child but he has always seen her as some kind of monster. When he kills any woman in his films, he's vicariously killing my grandmother. Perhaps she was braver and stronger than him and he's been trying to emulate that ever since. I have tried to ask him questions about this but he avoids the issue and it has never been clear to me. He likes to say that women are much more fun to kill on screen than men but that's because he wants to punish them for being so much stronger than him. He has killed Daria repeatedly in his movies, my sister Fiore once and had me raped and abused. All his male lead characters are weak ones and I think that speaks volumes for his own stance on the female of the species' (Jones 272).

24 'The screen-within-the-screen arrangement only makes explicit what is perhaps universally implicit in horror: the alignment of the audience with screen victims in general, regardless of how directly or indirectly they are figured as themselves spectators' (Clover 200).
25 '"Sei bella, Anna," le dice l'assassino, mentre la mano scende sfiorando sapientemente la pelle ... "Bella come quei quadri che ti fanno star male. Io stesso sto male per quanto sei bella"' (Argento, *La sindrome* 51). ['You are beautiful, Anna,' the assassin tells her, as he lowers his hand, brushing against her skin knowledgeably ... 'Beautiful like those paintings that make you suffer. I suffer, too, because you are so beautiful.']
26 Goldman ably interprets the role of art and representation in *A Room with a View*, especially on 125–7.
27 McDonagh expresses the notion of the spectator figuratively entering Argento's cinema of gore: 'Argento's camera is alternately enthralled and repelled by ripe flesh and blood-drenched fantasy. Some viewers find it all too off-putting, and indifference is rare – it seems you either pull back from Argento's films or dive in head first' (8).
28 Cited in Jones, 228–9.
29 'La scena sublime chiede infine di ancorare le sensazioni dello spettatore all'interno del film ... Il sublime *meduseo* fa dello sguardo l'operatore indispensabile della sua espressione: è la testa di Caravaggio che affascina Anna Manni ... all'inizio di *La sindrome di Stendhal* ... che non è altro che una reazione estrema e organica alla potenza dell'immagine sublime. È questo che spiega lo svenimento di Anna davanti alla *Caduta di Icaro* di Bruegel, e che realizza allora il movimento che fonda il sublime (plongée nel *cuore* di un'immagine). Ma penetrando nell'immagine, Anna penetra anche nell'orrore. La veloce inquadratura del serial killer, che precede la plongée, appare così come l'incarnazione letterale della carica di violenza di cui sono portatrici le immagini sublimi: mélange indistricabile di bellezza (il quadro) e d'orrore (il crimine), d'attrazione e di repulsione, altrettanti paradossi sensoriali che il cinema di Argento continua a *perseguire*, ostinatamente' (Thoret 96–7). [A sublime scene wants moreover to anchor the viewer's sensations within the film ... The Medusan sublime makes the gaze the indispensable instrument of its expression: it is Caravaggio's head that fascinates Anna Manni ... at the beginning of *La sindrome di Stendhal* ... which is nothing except a reaction both extreme and physical to the power of the sublime image. This explains Anna's fainting before Bruegel's *The Fall of Icarus*, and fulfils the movement that grounds the sublime (*plongée* into the *heart* of an image). But by penetrating the image, Anna penetrates horror as well. The rapid visual shot of the serial

killer, which precedes her *plongée*, thus appears as the literal incarnation of the potential for violence of which sublime images are the bearers: the inextricable mélange of beauty (the painting) and horror (the crime), of attraction and repulsion, equally sensorial paradoxes that Argento's cinema continues to *pursue*, doggedly.]

30 'In the *Cat O'Nine Tales* the villain is schizophrenic, a condition that is linked to his genetic illness (he has XYY chromosomes). This ties in with my interest in the split mind and personality disorders. People constantly live with many personalities, and it's a theme that runs through many of my films: in *Deep Red*, in *Tenebrae* and in my latest film, *The Stendhal Syndrome*.' Argento, 'Murder in the Dark' 61.

31 See Balmain (5) and Gallant (73).

32 'In his second Mediterranean novel, *A Room with a View* (1908), Forster was more careful to dissimulate the homosexual inspiration and chose a suppressed woman as his fictional surrogate' (Pemble 162). Meyers, in '"Vacant Heart and Hand and Eye": The Homosexual Theme in *A Room with a View*,' has analysed Reverend Beebe as a character who denotes homosexuality in *A Room with a View*, but does not take Lucy into consideration as a stand-in for Forster's own sexuality. Goldman instead provides a thorough and cogent examination of women in Forster's novels, and Lane's contribution to the same volume treats Forster's sexuality.

5. 'Going Native': Tuscan Houses and Italian Others in Contemporary American Travel Writing

1 For an overview of even earlier examples of English-speaking visitors to Florence, see Attilio Brilli's 'Viaggiatori inglesi e americani nella Città del Fiore.'

2 Peter Mayle's travel memoirs include *A Year in Provence* (1991), *Toujours Provence* (1992), *Encore Provence: New Adventures in the South of France* (1999), *French Lessons: Adventures with a Knife, Fork and Corkscrew* (2001), and *Provence A–Z* (2006). He has also written several novels set in France.

3 From the title, the reader might think that Dario Castagno's *Too Much Tuscan Sun: Confessions of a Chianti Tour Guide* (2004) provides a welcome parody of the genre, and of Mayes's text in particular. Unfortunately, the tour guide's book is basically a litany of stereotypes about American tourists whom he has encountered in his work.

4 'Travel writing, it need hardly be said, is hard to define, not least because it is a hybrid genre that straddles categories and disciplines. Travel narratives run from picaresque adventure to philosophical treatise, political

commentary, ecological parable, and spiritual quest. They borrow freely from history, geography, anthropology, and social science, often demonstrating great erudition, but without seeing fit to respect the rules that govern conventional scholarship' (Holland and Huggan 8–9).

5 Jeffrey J. Folks defines Mayes, one of the writers on which this analysis concentrates, as a 'travel writer' (104), although his opinion of her work's merit is scathingly critical. See his 'Mediterranean Travel Writing: From *Etruscan Places* to *Under the Tuscan Sun.*' Russo Bullaro classifies Mayes's Italian texts as travel memoirs (7).

6 Together they have edited some of Forster's fiction as well as the Penguin anthology of gay short stories. Aside from his numerous and successful novels, Leavitt has authored two other texts about Italy: *Florence, A Delicate Case* (2002) and, again with Mark Mitchell, *Italian Pleasures* (1996).

7 Polezzi also identifies the topos of 'renewal' in Mayes: 'One of the themes bubbling just under the surface of the book is that of change and regeneration. Mayes writes the book after a traumatic divorce, and its subplot is centred on finding a new life, and a new identity' (308).

8 Russo Bullaro makes a related observation about Mayes's second travel memoir: 'It becomes increasingly obvious towards the end of *Bella Tuscany* that Mayes' essential goal is to locate and define home' (Russo Bullaro 16).

9 Polezzi has noted the region's metonymic function for Mayes: 'She exploits stereotypical, antiquarian images of 'authentic' Tuscany (and, by metonymic extension, of Italy) to fulfil the expectations of American (and other non-Italian) readers' (308).

10 Docherty, too, explicitly links the symbol of the house/home with identity: 'The concept of 'home' or familial house is essentially one which is used by people to give a sense of centralisation to experience. The home not only gives a primary sense of identity, being the social space from which one comes; it also represents a hypothetical centre from which we may deviate but to which we can return' (Docherty 69).

11 Mayes commits many linguistic errors that are common to beginners, from simple spelling mistakes (*excellente* 22 [*eccellente*], *intonoco* 76 [*intonaco*]), to difficulties with single and double consonants, to incorrect adjectival-noun agreements (*poco acqua* 47 [*poca acqua*], *molte anni* 132 [*molti anni*]), among others. To be fair, Mayes makes no pretence of having a command of the language, as she observes during a trip to Massa Marittima: 'Last overnight – the town I have chronically mispronounced. The accent, I find, is on Marit' tima. I've said Maritti' ma. Will I ever, ever learn Italian? Still so many basic errors' (185). Leavitt and Mitchell's text reveals fewer linguistic errors, but perhaps this is also due to the basic fact that their book is less than half the

length of Mayes's. Nonetheless, they, too, have difficulties with double/ single consonants (*condonno* 12 [*condono*], *Grosetto* 56 [*Grosseto*], *assagio* 119 [*assaggio*]), and adjectival-noun agreement (*foglie rosse* 61 [*fogli rosa*: the plural form for a learner's permit or temporary driver's licence]).

12 Anthropology, in turn, also owes a great deal to travel writing, and Fabian himself recognizes that the origins of anthropology as a discipline stem at least in part from travel accounts: 'Until recently anthropologists were anxious to keep autobiography separate from scientific writing. The strictures of positivism account for this, although they may have been operating indirectly. Somehow the discipline "remembers" that it acquired its scientific and academic status by climbing on the shoulders of adventurers and using their travelogues, which for centuries had been the appropriate literary genre in which to report knowledge of the Other' (87).

13 Russo Bullaro maintains that, despite these stereotypes about Tuscans, Mayes's portrayal of them is essentially innocuous, especially when compared with her comments on Sicilians, which resort to commonplaces about the Mafia. For Russo Bullaro, Mayes 'sees Tuscany through the eyes of love' (8). This is true only up to a point, since the stereotypes about Tuscans (which for Mayes become representative of all Italians), while not as blatantly offensive as those about Sicilians, are also insidious and ultimately damaging, as is illustrated by numerous examples in her texts.

14 I have examined Mayes's use of Etruscan culture in her stereotyping of present-day Italians in my essay 'The Myth of the Etruscans in Travel Literature in English.' See also my 'Tuscan Environments and Italian Identities in Gary Paul Nabhan and Frances Mayes.'

15 This (albeit ambivalent) attraction towards the Italian Other recalls Barthes's comments on Stendhal's 'reverse racism,' that is, his exaltation of Italy and Italians' difference.

16 Lengthy reportage of the 'subaltern's' speech in contemporary travel narratives set in central Italy is relatively rare. One refreshing exception, however, is Gary Paul Nabhan's *Songbirds, Truffles, and Wolves: An American Naturalist in Italy* (1993), wherein ample textual space is devoted to relaying the direct speech of Italians whom the writer encounters (although clearly their words are mediated via the author).

17 Incidentally, the four walls are a significant concept in the titles of several novels and travel books set in Central Italy as well, such as W. Somerset Maugham's *Up at the Villa* (1941), Teresa Crane's *The Italian House* (1996), William Trevor's *My House in Umbria* (1991), or Lisa St Aubin de Terán's *A Valley in Italy: Confessions of a House Addict* (1994).

18 I have borrowed the expression from Ashcroft, Griffiths, and Tiffin, *The Empire Writes Back: Theory and Practice in Post-Colonial Literatures* (1989), 135.
19 Mayes considers her ties to the house to be both affective and physical ('This house, every brick and lock, will be as known to me as my own or the loved one's body' 95). Clearly, the writer is cognizant of the house's many associations, as she cites Bachelard's core text *The Poetics of Space* shortly after the above statement (95–6). The French philosopher's influence on Mayes's romanticized construction of the domestic sphere, which emphasizes dreams and memory, is evident.
20 It must also be noted that houses undoubtedly act as indicators of the owner's social standing: 'Fairly obviously, the size, style, and location of one's home is – at least in part – a function of the house-holder's economic status.... [D]ecisions regarding house purchase, and about what to do with the house thereafter, are as likely to be determined by an individual's sense of social identity and ideological aspirations as by personal whimsy or pragmatic needs' (Dolan 71).
21 Many thanks to Mark Chu for his help in looking into the various television offerings of this nature.
22 This perhaps should not be particularly surprising, as 'commercial and personal choices are so embedded in the domestic environment that it would be difficult to find a better context in which to explore the interweaving of consumer interests and the manufacturing of preference' (Shove 131).
23 I am grateful to Gabriella Romani for this observation.

6. The Tuscan Countryside: Nature and the (Non)Domestic in Elena Gianini Belotti

1 Belotti's own interest in the area of Trequanda is testified by her authoring a guide to the local town, *Trequanda e dintorni* (1997).
2 To date, little scholarly criticism exists on Belotti's oeuvre. The chapter 'Ripening and Completion in Women's Old-Age Novels' in Cavigioli's *Women of a Certain Age* examines in part *Apri le porte all'alba*. Carol Lazzaro-Weis also devotes a section of her essay 'Women's Histories, Women's Stories: The Italian Case' to Belotti's *Prima della quiete*, as a text representative of recent feminist historical writing.
3 'L'espace de la femme âgée dans Elena Gianini Belotti.'
4 The farmland outside Rome was awarded to his family at a modest rent in recognition of his brother's service in the First World War, as is narrated in Belotti's *Pane amaro*.

5 'L'esodo di massa ha certamente due componenti causali: l'incapacità della forma mezzadrile a seguire il generale ritmo d'incremento della produttività agricola e la "rivelazione" dell'anacronismo dei rapporti socio-culturali dominanti nelle campagne toscane. La percezione, soggettiva e collettiva, di queste contraddizioni viene filtrate da "teorie" molto spesso inadeguate e "datate," per cui il processo di trasformazione, che si svolge praticamente tutto nel breve arco di trent'anni, ci si presenta vestito coi panni di razionalizzazioni economiche e politiche che non colgono le cause efficienti del fenomeno' (Becattini 908). [The mass exodus certainly has two causes: the incapacity of the form of the *mezzadria* to follow the general rhythm of an increase in agricultural productivity and the 'revelation' of the anachronism of the dominant socio-cultural relationships in the Tuscan countryside. The subjective and collective perception of these contradictions is filtered by 'theories' that are often inadequate and 'dated,' and for this reason, the transformation process, which all takes place basically in the brief space of thirty years, is presented to us dressed in the cloth of economic and political rationalizations that do not capture the effective causes of the phenomenon.]
6 Mayes, in contrast, fantasizes about the former occupants of the house, inventing the figure of the *nonna* [grandmother] and the kinds of foods she might have prepared with produce from the garden. Clearly, Mayes's property originally belonged to more affluent owners than Belotti's; nonetheless, Mayes's propensity to idealize is strong.
7 This dedication to environmental preservation emerges in Belotti's guidebook *Trequanda e dintorni* as well, where much of the text extols the area's natural beauty and one section, 'Piccolo breviario ecologico per gli ospiti' (Short Ecological Breviary for Visitors], even provides tips for minimizing the ecological impact of tourism in the area.
8 Baker describes the phenomenon and cites Elizabeth Lawrence's comments on Konrad Lorenz's explanation of neoteny: '[Lorenz] proposes that the physical configuration of a high and slightly bulging forehead, large brain case in proportion to the face, big eyes, rounded cheeks, and short, stubby limbs call forth an adult nurturing response to such a "lovable" object, moving people to feelings of tenderness. The same positive reactions are elicited by animals who exhibit these juvenile traits' (Baker 181).
9 In another example, a young cow gives birth and Belotti reads the animal's running away from her offspring as a rejection of the maternal impulse. This observation is in keeping with Belotti's poetics, as motherhood is a particularly complex, and in some ways contradictory, theme in most of her works. Her oeuvre indicates a search for alternative forms of maternity,

yet this interest in substitute modes of motherhood possibly points to a certain ambivalence about mothers (and motherhood?) more generally. Indeed, the narrator, when she revisits her own mother's image in childhood memory in *Voli*, depicts her as uncaring, unaffectionate, and overly strict. In one instance, the author recalls how her dislike for cats stems from her own mother's favouring her feline pet, showing it more affection that she did her own daughter (31). The mother figure is commonly perceived in such negative terms in other works by Belotti as well, in particular *Pimpì oselì* (1995) and *Apri le porte all'alba*.

10 After much internal debate, however, she is less accommodating in this (earlier) instance of swallows attempting to nest in her house; she feels she cannot live with a bird's nest above her kitchen table and decides to shut the swallows out.

11 The issue of being a female landowner in a rural area as breaking some local code is also present in Annie Hawes's *Extra Virgin* (2001), which, although set in Liguria, is a similar kind of narrative to Mayes's. Hawes and her sister buy an inexpensive olive farm and the author recounts life among the locals, who frequently wonder openly about the lack of a male presence on the farm.

12 For more on this subject, see my 'Subverting Stereotypes of Aging in Elena Gianini Belotti's *Adagio un poco mosso*.'

13 Belotti's commitment to denouncing Tuscany's environmental decline is found in other writings as well, in particular in 'Amore e rabbia,' where she makes a case for preserving the region's beauty: 'Se il patrimonio principale di questi luoghi è la bellezza, ragiono, solo difendendola con le unghie e coi denti e conservandola con la massima cura, ci si assicura per lungo tempo il benessere economico, visto che è la bellezza ad attrarre coloro che arrivano qui. È a costoro che si vendono i prodotti locali – vino, olio, salumi, formaggi, tartufi, terrecotte – i quali hanno ripreso lena negli ultimi anni; sono loro ad affittare le case, a occupare gli alberghi e gli agriturismi, a frequentare i negozi, i caffé, i ristoranti. Ma quando la bellezza viene appannata, l'attrazione inevitabilmente svanisce. Se questi luoghi incantati saranno sempre più deturpati dal cemento e dall'asfalto, finiranno per assumere l'anonimo squallore di certi quartieri cittadini, per cui tanto varrà restarsene a casa propria, col sicuro vantaggio di non spendere un soldo' (14). [If the principal patrimony of these places is beauty, I reason, then only by defending it tooth and nail and preserving it with the utmost care, can we ensure economic well-being, seeing as it is beauty that draws those who come here. It is to them that local products are sold – wine, oil, cured meats, cheeses, truffles, terracotta ceramics – products that have regained strength

in recent years; they are the ones who rent the houses, who occupy the hotels and the holiday farmhouses, who frequent the shops, the cafés, the restaurants. But when the beauty is obscured, the attraction inevitably vanishes. If these enchanted places continue to be disfigured more and more by cement and asphalt, they will end up taking on the anonymous squalour of certain urban neighbourhoods, in which case one might just as well stay at home, with the definite advantage of not spending a cent.]

Afterword

1 The Tuscan settings of this and various other modern and contemporary films and advertisements are described in Bologni's *Ciak in Toscana* (2000).

Works Cited

Adamson, Walter L. *Avant-garde Florence*. Cambridge: Harvard UP, 1993.
Amatori, Franco, and Andrea Colli. *Impresa e industria in Italia dall'Unità a oggi*. Venice: Marsilio, 1999.
Ardis, Ann. 'Hellenism and the Lure of Italy.' In *The Cambridge Companion to E.M. Forster*. Ed. David Bradshaw. Cambridge: Cambridge UP, 2007. 62–76.
Argento, Dario. 'Murder in the Dark.' *Sight and Sound* 6.9 (1996): 61.
– *La sindrome*. Milan: Bompiani, 1996.
– *La sindrome di Stendhal*. 1996.
Ashcroft, Bill, Gareth Griffiths, and Helen Tiffin. *The Empire Writes Back: Theory and Practice in Post-Colonial Literatures*. London: Routledge, 1989.
Asor Rosa, Alberto. *Vasco Pratolini*. Rome: Edizioni Moderne, 1958.
Assunto, Rosario. *Il paesaggio e l'estetica*. Naples: Giannini, 1973.
Bachelard, Gaston. *The Poetics of Space*. Trans. John E. Stilgoe. Boston: Beacon P, 1994.
Baker, Steve. *Picturing the Beast: Animals, Identity and Representation*. Manchester: Manchester UP, 1993.
Bal, Mieke. *Introduction to the Theory of Narrative*. Trans. Christine Van Boheemen. Toronto: U of Toronto P, 1985.
Baldacci, Luigi. 'Gli ultimi romanzi.' In *Palazzeschi oggi: Atti del convegno Florence, 6/8 novembre 1976*. Ed. Lanfranco Caretti. Milan: Il Saggiatore, 1978. 255–65.
Ballini, Pier Luigi, et al. *La cultura a Firenze tra le due guerre*. Florence: Bonechi, 1991.
Balmain, Collette. 'Female Subjectivity and the Politics of "Becoming Other": Dario Argento's *La sindrome di Stendhal* (*The Stendhal Syndrome*, 1996).' *kinoeye* 2.12 (2002): 1–7. Accessed 6 January 2008, at http://www.kinoeye.org/02/12/balmain12.php.

Barbaro, Marta. *I poeti saltimbanchi e le maschere di Aldo Palazzeschi*. Pisa: Edizioni ETS, 2008.
Barthes, Roland. 'On échoue toujours à parler de ce qu'on aime.' In *Le bruissement de la langue*. Paris: Seuil, 1984. 333–42.
Barzanti, Roberto. 'Senso ed immagine della città in Federigo Tozzi.' *Bullettino senese di storia patria* 90 (1984): 267–86.
Becattini, Giacomo. 'Riflessioni sullo sviluppo socio-economico della Toscana in questo dopoguerra.' In *Storia d'Italia. Le regioni dall'Unità a oggi. La Toscana*. Ed. Giorgio Mori. Turin: Einaudi, 1986. 901–24.
Bertolucci, Bernardo. *Io ballo da sola* [Stealing Beauty]. 1996.
Bertoncini, Giancarlo. *Vasco Pratolini*. Rome: Edizioni dell'Ateneo, 1987.
Bhabha, Homi K. 'On the Irremovable Strangeness of Being Different.' In 'Four Views on Ethnicity.' *PMLA* 113 (1998): 34–39.
Bilenchi, Romano. *Conservatorio di Santa Teresa*. 1940. Milan: Garzanti, 1991.
Birdwell-Pheasant, Donna, and Denise Lawrence-Zúñiga. 'Introduction: Houses and Families in Europe.' In *House Life: Space, Place and Family in Europe*. Ed. Donna Birdwell-Pheasant and Denise Lawrence-Zúñiga. Oxford and New York: Berg, 1999. 1–35.
Blanton, Casey. *Travel Writing: The Self and the World*. London: Routledge, 2002.
Boccioni, Umberto, et al. 'La pittura futurista: Manifesto tecnico.' In *Filippo Tommaso Martinetti e il futurismo*. Ed. Luciano De Maria. Milan: Mondadori, 1973, 2000. 23–6.
Bologni, Maurizio. *Ciak in Toscana*. Florence: Le Lettere, 2000.
Brilli, Attilio. *Lo spirito della campagna toscana*. Milan: Silvana, 1992.
– 'Viaggiatori inglesi e americani nella Città del Fiore.' In *Firenze dei grandi viaggiatori*. Ed. Franco Paloscia. Casale Monferrato [AL]: Abete, 1993. 51–82.
Butler, Alban. *Butler's Lives of the Saints*. Westminster, MD: Christian Classics, 1956.
Butler, Judith. *Gender Trouble: Feminism and the Subversion of Identity*. New York and London: Routledge, 1999.
Buzard, James Michael. 'Forster's Trespasses: Tourism and Cultural Politics.' *Twentieth Century Literature* 34.2 (1988): 155–79.
Caillois, Roger. 'Mimicry and Legendary Psychasthenia.' Trans. John Shepley. *October* 31 (1984): 16–32.
Calamandrei, Piero. *Inventario della casa in campagna*. 1941. Montepulciano (SI): Le Balze, 2002.
Cassola, Carlo. 'Alla ricerca di Federigo Tozzi.' In Federigo Tozzi, *I romanzi*. Ed. Glauco Tozzi. Florence: Vallecchi, 1973. xxi–lxxii.
– *Paura e tristezza*. 1970. Milan: BUR, 1997.
– *La ragazza di Bube*. 1960. Milan: BUR, 1998.

– *Il taglio del bosco*. 1954. Milan: BUR, 1993.
Castagno, Dario, with Robert Rodi. *Too Much Tuscan Sun: Confessions of a Chianti Tour Guide*. Guilford, CT: Globe Pequot P, 2004.
Castellana, Riccardo. 'Procedimenti analogici e costruzione del 'correlativo oggettivo' nelle descrizioni tozziane.' In *Tozzi: La scrittura crudele. Atti del Convegno internazionale*. Ed. Maria Antonietta Grignani. Pisa and Rome: Istituti Editoriali e Poligrafici Internazionali, 2003. In *Moderna* 4.2 (2002): 59–76.
Cavigioli, Rita C. *Women of a Certain Age: Contemporary Italian Fictions of Female Aging*. Madison-Teaneck, NJ: Fairleigh Dickinson UP, 2005.
Cesarini, Paolo. *Tutti gli anni di Tozzi*. Montepulciano (SI): Le Balze, 2002.
Cibrario, Benedetta. *Rossovermiglio*. Milan: Feltrinelli, 2007.
Cieraad, Irene. 'Dutch Windows: Female Virtue and Female Vice.' In *At Home: An Anthropology of Domestic Space*. Ed. Irene Cieraad. Syracuse: Syracuse UP, 1999. 31–52.
Clifford, James. *Routes: Travel and Translation in the Late Twentieth Century*. Cambridge and London: Harvard UP, 1997.
Cloke, Paul, Chris Philo, and David Sadler. *Approaching Human Geography: An Introduction to Current Theoretical Debates*. London: Paul Chapman, 2001.
Clover, Carol. *Men, Women, and Chainsaws: Gender in the Modern Horror Film*. London: BFI, 1992.
Costantini, Anthony. 'Il paesaggio nella narrativa del primo Pratolini.' *Ipotesi 80* 27 (1989): 75–90.
Covino, Mariarosaria. *Don Giulio Facibeni: Il Padre, uomo della carità*. Florence: Edizioni Medicea, 1996.
Crane, Teresa. *The Italian House*. London: Warner, 2000.
Crang, Mike, and Nigel Thrift, eds. *Thinking Space*. London and New York: Routledge, 2000.
Cresti, Carlo. 'Vasco Pratolini e l'architettura: La città, il quartiere, la strada, la casa.' In *Convegno internazionale di studi su Vasco Pratolini. Atti*. Ed. Piero Bigongiari et al. Florence: Polistampa, 1995. 105–12.
Cresswell, Tim. *Place: A Short Introduction*. Oxford: Blackwell, 2004.
Crowhurst Lennard, Suzanne H., and Henry L. Lennard. *Public Life in Urban Places*. Southampton, NY: Gondolier, 1984.
Crowther, Paul. *The Kantian Sublime: From Morality to Art*. Oxford: Clarendon P, 1989.
Dainotto, Roberto. *Place in Literature: Regions, Cultures, Communities*. Ithaca and London: Cornell UP, 2000.
Debenedetti, Giacomo. *Il romanzo del Novecento*. Milan: Garzanti, 1971.

de Certeau, Michel. *The Practice of Everyday Life*. Trans. Steven Rendall. Berkeley/Los Angeles/London: U of California P, 1984.
Diafani, Laura. 'Le città di Palazzeschi.' In *Palazzeschi europeo. Atti del Convegno Internazionale di Studi, Bonn-Colonia, 30–31 maggio 2005*. Ed. Willi Jung and Gino Tellini. Florence: Società Editrice Fiorentina, 2007. 185–204.
Docherty, Thomas. *On Modern Authority: The Theory and Condition of Writing, 1500 to the Present Day*. Sussex / New York: Harvester P / St Martin's P, 1987.
Dolan, John A. '"I've Always Fancied Owning Me Own Lion": Ideological Motivations in External House Decoration by Recent Homeowners.' In *At Home: An Anthropology of Domestic Space*. Ed. Irene Cieraad. Syracuse: Syracuse UP, 1999. 60–72.
Donald, James. 'The Fantastic, the Sublime and the Popular; Or, What's at Stake in Vampire Films?' In *Fantasy and the Cinema*. Ed. James Donald. London: BFI, 1989. 233–51.
Doran, Phil. *The Reluctant Tuscan: How I Discovered My Inner Italian*. London: Virgin, 2005.
Duncan, Derek. *Reading and Writing Italian Homosexuality: A Case of Possible Difference*. Aldershot, Hampshire, and Burlington, VT: Ashgate, 2006.
Dunkling, Leslie, and William Gosling, *Everyman's Dictionary of Names*. London and Melbourne: J.M. Dent and Sons, 1983.
Dusi, Isabella. *Bel Vino: A Year of Sundrenched Pleasure among the Vines of Tuscany*. London: Pocket, 2004.
– *Vanilla Beans and Brodo: Real Life in the Hills of Tuscany*. London: Simon and Schuster, 2001.
Fabian, Johannes. *Time and the Other: How Anthropology Makes Its Object*. New York: Columbia UP, 1983.
Febbraro, Paolo. *La tradizione di Palazzeschi*. Rome: Gaffi, 2007.
Felluga, Dino. 'Modules on Kristeva: On the Abject.' In *Introductory Guide to Critical Theory*. Purdue University. Last updated, 28 Nov. 2003. Accessed 25 April 2007, at http://www.cla.purdue.edu/english/theory.
Ferraris, Denis. 'Il motivo del buffo nella novellistica palazzeschiana.' In *L'opera di Aldo Palazzeschi. Atti del Convegno Internazionale*, Florence, 22–4 February 2001. Ed. Gino Tellini. Florence: Olschki, 2002. 323–39.
'The 50 Most Beautiful People in the World.' *People Magazine*, 9 May 1994: 54–151.
Finocchiaro Chimirri, Giovanna. '*La costanza della ragione* di Vasco Pratolini.' In *Studi in onore di Carmelina Naselli* 2. Catania: Università di Catania, 1968, 137–53.
Flego, Fabio. 'Il mito italiano di E.M. Forster.' *Miscellanea di studi sociolinguistici* 2.4 (1988): 107–25.

Folks, Jeffrey J. 'Mediterranean Travel Writing: From *Etruscan Places* to *Under the Tuscan Sun.*' *Papers on Language and Literature* 40.1 (2004): 102–12.
Fonnesu, Iolanda, and Leonardo Rombai, with Pietro Piussi. *Letteratura e paesaggio in Toscana: Da Pratesi a Cassola*. Florence: Centro Editoriale Toscano, 2004.
Foot, Jonathan. 'Revisiting the *Coree*: Self-construction, Memory and Immigration on the Milanese Periphery, 1950–2000.' In *Italian Cityscapes. Culture and Urban Change in Contemporary Italy*. Eds. Robert Lumley and John Foot. Exeter: U of Exeter P, 2004. 46–60.
Forster, E.M. *The Life to Come and Other Stories*. London: Penguin, 1989.
– *A Passage to India*. Ed. Pankaj Mishra. London: Penguin, 2005.
– *A Room with a View*. Ed. Oliver Stallybrass. London: Penguin, 1990.
Foucault, Michel. 'Of Other Spaces.' *Diacritics* 16.1 (1986): 22–7.
Fratnik, Marina. *Paysages: Essai sur la description de Federigo Tozzi*. Florence: Olschki, 2002.
Freud, Sigmund. *The Interpretation of Dreams*. London: Penguin, 1991.
Gabelli, Alessandra. 'Un luogo di Florence: Via del Corno nella vita e nell'opera di Vasco Pratolini.' *Forum Italicum* 38.2 (2004): 468–90.
Gallant, Chris. 'The Art of Allusion: Painting, Murder and the "Plan Tableau."' In *Art of Darkness: The Cinema of Dario Argento*. Ed. Chris Gallant. Godalming, Surrey: FAB P, 2001. 65–73.
Garber, Marjorie. *Sex and Real Estate: Why We Love Houses*. New York: Anchor Books, 2000.
Geddes da Filicaia, Costanza. *La biblioteca di Federigo Tozzi*. Florence: Le Lettere, 2001.
Gelley, Alexander. 'Setting and Sense of World in the Novel.' *Yale Review* 62 (1973): 186–201.
George, Don. 'Frances Mayes and the Riches of Tuscany.' *Salon*, Accessed 30 Oct. 2002, at http://www.salon.com/travel/bag/1999/04/14/mayes/index1.html.
Gervais, Paul. *A Garden in Lucca: Finding Paradise in Tuscany*. New York: Hyperion, 2000.
Gianini Belotti, Elena. *Adagio un poco mosso*. Milan: Feltrinelli, 1993.
– *Amore e pregiudizio: Il tabù dell'età nei rappori sentimentali*. Milan: Mondadori, 1988.
– 'Amore e rabbia.' In *Tracce di Toscana*. Ed. Fiorenza Giovannini. Florence: Regione Toscana, Consiglio regionale, 2006. 11–25.
– *Apri le porte all'alba*. Milan: Feltrinelli, 1999.
– *Che razza di ragazza*. Milan: Savelli, 1979.
– *Cortocircuito*. Milan: Rizzoli, 2008.
– *Dalla parte delle bambine*. Milan: Feltrinelli, 2002.

– *Il fiore dell'ibisco*. Milan: Rizzoli, 1985.
– *Non di sola madre*. Milan: Rizzoli, 1983.
– *Pane amaro*. Milan: Rizzoli, 2006.
– *Pimpì oselì*. Milan: Feltrinelli, 1995.
– *Prima della quiete: Storia di Italia Donati*. Milan: Rizzoli, 2003.
– *Prima le donne e i bambini*. 1980. Milan: Feltrinelli, 1998.
– *Trequanda e dintorni*. San Quirico d'Orcia: Editrice Donchisciotte, 1997.
– *Voli*. Milan: Feltrinelli, 2001.
Gioanola, Elio. *Psicanalisi, ermeneutica e letteratura*. Milan: Mursia, 1991.
Giovanardi, Stefano. *La critica e Palazzeschi*. Bologna: Cappelli, 1975.
Giuttari, Michele, and Carlo Lucarelli. *Compagni di sangue*. Florence: Le Lettere, 1998.
Gnerre, Francesco. *L'eroe negato: Omosessualità e letteratura nel Novecento italiano*. Milan: Baldini & Castoldi, 2000.
Goldman, Jane. 'Forster and Women.' In *The Cambridge Companion to E.M. Forster*. Ed. David Bradshaw. Cambridge: Cambridge UP, 2007. 120–37.
Grignani, Maria Antonietta, ed. *Tozzi: La scrittura crudele. Atti del Convegno Internazionale*, Siena, 24–6 October 2002. In *Moderna* 4.2 (2002), Pisa and Roma: Istituti Editoriali e Poligrafici Internazionali, 2003.
Grosz, Elizabeth. *Space, Time, and Perversion*. New York and London: Routledge, 1995.
Gruppo Lavoratori Anziani delle Officine Galileo. *Percorsi della Memoria: Una storia, molte storie ... la Galileo*. Florence: Alinari, 2000.
Guida d'Italia: Toscana. Touring Club Italiano. Milan: Touring Editore,1997.
Hainsworth, Peter. 'Fascism in Fiction: Pratolini Reconsidered.' *Italian Studies* 55 (2000): 121–37.
Hampshire, David. *Buying a Home in Italy*. London: Survival Books.
Harris, Thomas. *Hannibal*. New York: Dell, 2000.
Harvey, David. *Justice, Nature and the Geography of Difference*. Oxford: Blackwell, 1996.
Hawes, Annie. *Extra Virgin: Amongst the Olive Groves of Liguria*. London: Penguin, 2001.
Hirdt, Willi. 'Superbia punita. Su *Sorelle Materassi*.' In *L'opera di Aldo Palazzeschi. Atti del Convegno Internazionale*, Florence, 22–4 February 2001. Ed. Gino Tellini. Florence: Olschki, 2002. 341–55.
Holland, Patrick, and Graham Huggan. *Tourists with Typewriters: Critical Reflections on Contemporary Travel Writing*. Ann Arbor, MI: U of Michigan P, 2000.
Holloway, Lewis, and Phil Hubbard. *People and Place: The Extraordinary Geographies of Everyday Life*. Harlow: Pearson Education, 2001.

Hubbard, Phil, Rob Kitchin, and Gill Valentine, eds. *Key Thinkers on Space and Place*. London: Sage, 2004.
Hulme, Peter. 'Travelling to Write (1940–2000).' In *The Cambridge Companion to Travel Writing*. Ed. Peter Hulme and Tim Youngs. Cambridge: Cambridge UP, 2002. 87–101.
Hutchings, Peter J. 'A Disconnected View: Forster, Modernity and Film.' In *E.M. Forster*. Ed. Jeremy Tambling. Basingstoke and New York: Palgrave, 1995. 213–28.
Ivory, James. *A Room with a View*. 1985.
Jeuland-Meynaud, Maryse. *Lettura antropologica della narrativa di Federigo Tozzi*. Rome: Bulzoni, 1991.
Jones, Alan. *Profondo Argento: The Man, the Myths and the Magic*. Godalming, Surrey: FAB P, 2004.
Kant, Immanuel. *Critique of the Power of Judgment*. Ed. Paul Guyer. Trans. Paul Guyer and Eric Matthews. Cambridge: Cambridge UP, 2000.
Kirby, Kathleen M. *Indifferent Boundaries: Spatial Concepts of Human Subjectivity*. New York and London: Guilford, 1996.
Knopp, Lawrence. 'Sexuality and Urban Space: A Framework for Analysis.' In *Mapping Desire*. Ed. David Bell and Gill Valentine. London and New York: Routledge, 1995. 149–61.
Kristeva, Julia. *Powers of Horror: An Essay on Abjection*. Trans. Leon S. Roudiez. New York: Columbia UP, 1982.
Landy, Marcia. 'Filmed Forster.' In *The Cambridge Companion to E.M. Forster*. Ed. David Bradshaw. Cambridge: Cambridge UP, 2007. 235–53.
Lane, Christopher. 'Forsterian Sexuality.' In *The Cambridge Companion to E.M. Forster*. Ed. David Bradshaw. Cambridge: Cambridge UP, 2007. 104–19.
Lanuzza, Stefano. *Firenze degli scrittori del Novecento*. Naples: Alfredo Guida, 2001.
Lasansky, D. Medina. *The Renaissance Perfected: Architecture, Spectacle, and Tourism in Fascist Italy*. University Park: Pennsylvania State UP, 2004.
Lazzaro-Weis, Carol. 'Women's Histories, Women's Stories: The Italian Case.' In *Women's Writing in Western Europe*. Ed. Adalgisa Giorgio and Julia Waters. Newcastle: Cambridge Scholars Publishing, 2007. 312–30.
Leavitt, David. *Florence, A Delicate Case*. London: Bloomsbury, 2002.
Leavitt, David, and Mark Mitchell. *In Maremma: Life and a House in Southern Tuscany*. Washington: Counterpoint, 2001.
– *Italian Pleasures*. San Francisco: Chronicle, 1996.
Listri, Pier Francesco. *Dizionario di Firenze*. Florence: Le Lettere, 1998.
Longobardi, Fulvio. *Vasco Pratolini*. Milan: Mursia, 1984.
Lotman, Jurij. *The Structure of the Artistic Text*. Trans. Gail Lenhoff and Ronald Vroon. Ann Arbor, MI: U of Michigan P, 1977.

Luti, Giorgio, *Cronache dei fatti di Toscana: Storia e letteratura tra Ottocento e Novecento*. Florence: Le Lettere, 1996.
Lynch, Kevin. *The Image of the City*. Cambridge, MA, and London: MIT P, 1973.
Macrí, Oreste. *Pratolini: Romanziere di 'Una storia italiana.'* Florence: Le Lettere, 1993.
Magherini, Graziella. *La sindrome di Stendhal*. Florence: Ponte alle Grazie, 1989.
Manzini, Gianna. *Tempo innamorato*. 1928. Milan: Mondadori, 1943.
Marabini, Claudio. 'Pratolini e Firenze.' In *Le città dei poeti*. Turin: Società Editrice Internazionale, 1976. 105–10.
Marchegiani Jones, Irene, and Thomas Haeussler, eds. *The Poetics of Place: Florence Imagined*. Florence: Olschki, 2001.
Marchi, Marco. *Federigo Tozzi: Ipotesi e documenti*. Genoa: Marietti, 1993.
– *Palazzeschi e altri sondaggi*. Florence: Le Lettere, 1996.
Martini, Martina. *Tozzi e James: Letteratura e psicologia*. Florence: Olschki, 1999.
Massey, Doreen. *for space*. London: Sage, 2005.
Maté, Ferenc. *The Hills of Tuscany: A New Life in an Old Land*. New York: Delta, 1998.
Maugham, W. Somerset. 1941. *Up at the Villa*. New York: Vintage, 2000.
Mayes, Frances. *Bella Tuscany: The Sweet Life in Italy*. New York: Broadway Books, 1999.
– *Bringing Tuscany Home*. New York: Broadway Books, 2004.
Mayes, Frances, and Edward Mayes. *In Tuscany*. New York: Broadway Books, 2000.
– *Shrines: Images of Italian Worship*. New York: Doubleday, 2006.
– *Under the Tuscan Sun: At Home in Italy*. New York: Broadway Books, 1996.
– *A Year in the World*. New York: Broadway Books, 2006.
Mayle, Peter. *Encore Provence: New Adventures in the South of France*. London: Penguin, 2000.
– *French Lessons: Adventures with a Knife, Fork and Corkscrew*. New York: Random House, 2002.
– *Provence A–Z*. London: Profile, 2006.
– *Toujours Provence*. London: Pan Books, 1992.
– *A Year in Provence*. London: Penguin, 2000.
McDonagh, Maitland. *Broken Mirrors / Broken Minds: The Dark Dreams of Dario Argento*. New York: Citadel, 1994.
Melloni, Giorgio. 'La scrittura come "Vertigine della dissoluzione": Una proposta di lettura di *Con gli occhi chiusi* di Federigo Tozzi.' *Strumenti critici* 11.1 (1996): 23–50.
Mellor, Mary. *Feminism and Ecology*. New York: New York UP, 1997.

Melosi, Laura. *Anima e scrittura: Prospettive culturali per Federigo Tozzi*. Florence: Le Lettere, 1991.
Memmo, Francesco Paolo. *Pratolini*. Florence: La Nuova Italia, 1977.
Mendik, Xavier. 'A (Repeated) Time to Die: The Investigation of Primal Trauma in the Films of Dario Argento.' In *Crime Scenes: Detective Narratives in European Culture since 1945*. Ed. Anne Mullen and Emer O'Beirne. Amsterdam-Atlanta: Rodopi, 2000. 25–36.
Meyers, Jeffrey. *Painting and the Novel*. Manchester: Manchester UP, 1975.
– '"Vacant Heart and Hand and Eye": The Homosexual Theme in *A Room with a View*.' *English Literature in Transition* 13 (1970): 181–92.
Miller, J. Hillis. *Topographies*. Stanford: Stanford UP, 1995.
Mitchell, W.J.T. 'Preface to the Second Edition of *Landscape and Power*: Space, Place, and Landscape.' In *Landscape and Power*. Ed. W.J.T. Mitchell. Chicago: Chicago UP, 2002. vii–xii.
Mori, Giorgio. 'Dall'unità alla guerra: Aggregazione e disgregazione di un'area regionale.' In *Storia d'Italia. Le regioni dall'Unità a oggi. La Toscana*. Ed. Giorgio Mori. Turin: Einaudi, 1986. 3–88.
Mosse, George. *Nationalism and Sexuality: Middle-Class Morality and Sexual Norms in Modern Europe*. Madison: U of Wisconsin P, 1985.
Nabb, Magdalen. *The Monster of Florence*. London: HarperCollins, 1996.
Nabhan, Gary Paul. *Songbirds, Truffles, and Wolves: An American Naturalist in Italy*. London: Penguin, 1993.
Nerenberg, Ellen. *Prison Terms: Representing Confinement During and After Italian Fascism*. Toronto: U of Toronto P, 2001.
Newby, Eric. *A Small Place in Italy*. London: Lonely Planet, 1994.
Nye, David E. *American Technological Sublime*. Cambridge, MA, and London: MIT P, 1994.
Olalquiaga, Celeste. *Megalopolis: Contemporary Cultural Sensibilities*. Minneapolis and London: U of Minnesota P, 1992.
Oliver, Jamie. *Jamie's Italy*. London: Michael Joseph, 2005.
Oliver, Kelly, ed. *The Portable Kristeva*. New York: Columbia UP, 1997.
Ondaatje, Michael. *The English Patient*. New York: Knopf, 1996.
Ovid. *Metamorphoses*, I. Trans. Frank Justus Miller. Cambridge: Harvard UP, 1977.
Palazzeschi, Aldo. 'Ho sognato Firenze.' *Firenze e il mondo* 1 (1948): 5–8.
– 'Il paesaggio.' In *Dopo il diluvio: Sommario dell'Italia contemporanea*. Ed. Dino Terra. Milan: Garzanti, 1947. 161–7.
– *The Sisters Materassi*. Trans. Angus Davidson. New York: Doubleday, 1953.
– *Tre imperi ... mancati. Cronaca (1922–45)*. Florence: Vallecchi, 1945.
– *Tutte le novelle*. Ed. Luciano De Maria. Milan: Mondadori, 1991.
– *Tutti i romanzi*, I. Ed. Gino Tellini. Milan: Mondadori, 2004.

- *Tutti i romanzi*, II. Ed. Gino Tellini. Milan: Mondadori, 2005.
Paloscia, Franco, ed. *Firenze dei grandi viaggiatori*. Casale Monferrato: Abete, 1993.
Paoletti, Paolo, and Paola Torrini. *Firenze Anni '50*, II. Florence: Bonechi, 1991.
Parker, Allan. *Ciao, Tuscany*. London: Penguin, 2001.
- *Seasons in Tuscany: A Tale of Two Loves*. London: Penguin, 2000.
Parronchi, Alessandro. 'Introduzione.' In Vasco Pratolini, *La costanza della ragione*. Milan: Mondadori, 1974. v–xiii.
Pemble, John. *The Mediterranean Passion: Victorians and Edwardians in the South*. Oxford: Clarendon P, 1987.
Perella, Nicolas J. 'Introduction.' In Aldo Palazzeschi, *A Tournament of Misfits: Tall Tales and Short*. Trans. Nicolas J. Perella. Toronto: U of Toronto P, 2005. xi–xliii.
Perella, Nicolas J., and Ruggero Stefanini. 'Aldo Palazzeschi's Code of Lightness.' *Forum Italicum* 26.1 (1992): 94–120.
Perry Levine, June. 'Two Rooms with a View: An Inquiry into Film Adaptation.' *Mosaic* 22 (1989): 67–84.
Pike, Burton. *The Image of the City in Modern Literature*. Princeton: Princeton UP, 1981.
Place, Janey. 'Women in Film Noir.' In *Women in Film Noir*. Ed. E. Ann Kaplan. London: BFI, 1980. 35–67.
Plumwood, Val. *Feminism and the Mastery of Nature*. London and New York: Routledge, 1993.
Polezzi, Loredana. 'Did Someone Just Travel All Over Me? Travel Writing and the Travelee ...' In *Seuils et Traverses: Enjeux de l'écriture du voyage*, II. Ed. Jean-Yves Le Disez and Jan Borm. Brest: Centre de Recherche Bretonne et Celtique, 2002. 303–12.
Porteous, J. Douglas. *Landscapes of the Mind: Worlds of Sense and Metaphor*. Toronto: U of Toronto P, 1990.
Prakash, Lakshmi. *Symbolism in the Novels of E.M. Forster*. Delhi: Seema Pub, 1987.
Pratolini, Vasco. *La costanza della ragione*. Milan: Mondadori, 1974.
- *Lettere a Sandro*. Ed. Alessandro Parronchi. Florence: Edizioni Polistampa, 1992.
- *Romanzi I*. Milan: Mondadori, 1993.
Pratt, Jeff. *The Rationality of Rural Life: Economic and Cultural Change in Tuscany*. Chur, Switzerland: Harwod Academic Publishers, 1994.
Pratt, Mary Louise. *Imperial Eyes: Travel Writing and Transculturation*. London and New York: Routledge, 1992.

Preston, Douglas, and Mario Spezi. *The Monster of Florence: A True Story.* London: Virgin Books, 2009.
Pullini, Giorgio. *Aldo Palazzeschi.* Milan: Mursia, 1972.
Rauger, Jean-François. 'Dall'introspezione alla fede ritrovata. Gli anni '90.' In *L'eccesso della visione: Il cinema di Dario Argento.* Ed. Giulia Carluccio, Giacomo Manzoli, and Roy Menarini. Turin: Lindau, 2003. 99–113.
Riggins, Stephen Harold. 'The Rhetoric of Othering.' In *The Language and Politics of Exclusion: Others in Discourse.* Ed. S.H. Riggins. London: Sage, 1997. 1–20.
Rocca, Tony. *Catching Fireflies: Capturing the Dream of a Tuscan Vineyard.* London: Century, 2004.
Romani, Valerio. *Il Paesaggio: Teoria e pianificazione.* Milan: FrancoAngeli, 1994.
Ross, Michael L. *Storied Cities: Literary Imaginings of Florence, Venice and Rome.* Westport, CT: Greenwood P, 1994.
Ross, Silvia. 'L'espace de la femme âgée dans Elena Gianini Belotti.' In *Actes des Journées d'étude 'Écrire au féminin,' 13 mai 2000 et 12 mai 2001 –CERCLI* (Rennes: Presses Universitaires de Rennes, forthcoming).
– 'The Fascist Body Politic and Florentine Space: The *Signora* in Vasco Pratolini's *Cronache di poveri amanti.*' *Italian Studies* 60.1 (2005): 60–70.
– 'The Myth of the Etruscans in Travel Literature in English.' In *Myths of Europe.* Ed. Richard Littlejohns and Sara Soncini. Amsterdam and New York: Rodopi, 2007. 263–73.
– 'Resistance and the Carnivalesque in Vasco Pratolini's *Cronache di poveri amanti.*' *Italian Culture* 16 (1998): 183–96.
– 'Subverting Stereotypes of Aging in Elena Gianini Belotti's *Adagio un poco mosso.*' *Italica* (2007): 422–37.
– 'Tuscan Environments and Italian Identities in Gary Paul Nabhan and Frances Mayes.' In *Arts et Identité Régionale – D'un Sud à l'autre: Des rives de la Méditerranée au golfe du Mexique.* Ed. Paul Carmignani and Tony Jappy. Cahiers de l'Université de Perpignan 32 (2001): 171–85.
Rossi, Aldo. *Modelli e scrittura di un romanzo tozziano: Il podere.* Padua: Liviana, 1972.
Rushdie, Salman. *The Enchantress of Florence.* London: Jonathan Cape, 2008.
Russo Bullaro, Grace. 'Frances Mayes' *Bella Tuscany* and the Reconfiguration of Self and Home.' *Essays in Arts and Science* 34.1 (2005): 7–19.
Saccone, Eduardo. *Allegoria e sospetto: Come leggere Tozzi.* Naples: Liguori, 2000.
– *Conclusioni anticipate.* Naples: Liguori, 1988.
St Aubin de Terán, Lisa. *A Valley in Italy: Confessions of a House Addict.* London: Penguin, 1995.
Sarup, Madan. 'Home and Identity.' In *Travellers' Tales: Narratives of Home and Displacement.* Ed. George Robertson, Melinda Mash, Lisa Tickner, Jon Bird,

Barry Curtis, and Tim Putnam. London and New York: Routledge, 1994. 93–104.

Sassoon, Donald. *Contemporary Italy*. London and New York: Longman, 1986.

Savellini, Paolo Gori, ed. *Firenze nella cultura italiana del Novecento. Atti del convegno di Firenze*, 5–7 December 1990. Florence: Festina Lente, 1993.

Schippisi, Ranieri. 'Il paesaggio di Tozzi.' *Humanitas* 6.1 (1951): 194–208.

Scott, Ridley. *Hannibal*. 2001.

Sebald, W.G. *Vertigo*. Trans. Michael Hulse. London: Harvill P, 1999.

Sedgwick, Eve Kosofsky. *Epistemology of the Closet*. Berkeley and Los Angeles: U of California P, 1990.

Sharp, Joanne P. 'Writing over the Map of Provence: The Touristic Therapy of *A Year in Provence*.' In *Writes of Passage: Reading Travel Writing*. Ed. James Duncan and Derek Gregory. London and New York: Routledge, 1999. 200–18.

Shove, Elizabeth. 'Constructing Home: A Crossroads of Choices.' In *At Home: An Anthropology of Domestic Space*. Ed. Irene Cieraad. Syracuse: Syracuse UP, 1999. 130–43.

Sibley, David. *Geographies of Exclusion: Society and Difference in the West*. London and New York: Routledge, 1995.

Smith, H., 'Holy City Visitors God-Struck.' *Herald Sun*, 1 October 1994.

Smouts, Marie-Claude. 'The Region as the New Imagined Community.' In *Regions in Europe*. Ed. Patrick Le Galès and Christian Lequesne. London and New York: Routledge, 1998. 30–8.

Socco, Carlo. *Il paesaggio imperfetto: Uno sguardo semiotico sul punto di vista estetico*. Turin: Tirrenia, 1998.

Soja, Edward W. *Postmetropolis: Critical Studies of Cities and Regions*. Oxford: Blackwell, 2000.

Somigli, Luca. 'Il saltimbanco nel Nuovo Mondo (con qualche capatina in Gran Bretagna): Palazzeschi e la cultura anglo-americana.' In *L'arte del saltimbanco: Aldo Palazzeschi tra due avanguardie*. Ed. Luca Somigli and Gino Tellini. Florence: Società Editrice Fiorentina, 2008. 161–79.

Spender, Matthew. *Within Tuscany: Reflections on a Time and Place*. London: Penguin, 1993.

Spini, Giorgio, and Antonio Casali. *Florence*. Rome-Bari: Laterza, 1986.

Spitzer, Leo. 'Speech and Language in *Inferno* XIII.' In *Dante: A Collection of Critical Essays*. Ed. John Freccero. New York: Ridge P / Random House, 1965. 78–101.

Stendhal. *Rome, Naples et Florence*. Ed. Pierre Brunel. [Paris]: Gallimard, 1987.

Stone, Wilfred. *The Cave and the Mountain: A Study of E.M. Forster*. London: Oxford UP, 1966.

Summers, C.J. 'The Meaningful Ambiguity of Giotto in *A Room with a View.*' *English Literature in Transition: 1880–1920* 30.2 (1987): 165–75.
Tabucchi, Antonio. *Gli Zingari e il Rinascimento: Vivere da rom a Florence*. Milan: Feltrinelli, 1999.
Tamburri, Anthony Julian. *Una semiotica della ri-lettura: Guido Gozzano, Aldo Palazzeschi, Italo Calvino*. Florence: Franco Cesati, 2003.
Thoret, Jean-Baptiste. 'La percezione attraverso la pelle. Gli anni '80.' In *L'eccesso della visione: Il cinema di Dario Argento*. Ed. Giulia Carluccio, Giacomo Manzoli, and Roy Menarini. Turin: Lindau, 2003. 79–98.
Tozzi, Federigo. *Novale*. Ed. Glauco Tozzi. Florence: Vallecchi, 1984.
– *Opere*. Ed. Marco Marchi. Milan: Mondadori, 1987.
Tozzi, Glauco. 'I luoghi tozziani di Siena.' *Terra di Siena* 4 (1960): 32–7.
Trevor, William. *My House in Umbria*. London: Penguin, 2000.
Tuan, Yi-Fu. *Dominance and Affection: The Making of Pets*. New Haven and London: Yale UP, 1984.
– *Landscapes of Fear*. Oxford: Basil Blackwell, 1979.
– *Space and Place: The Perspective of Experience*. Minneapolis and London: U of Minnesota P, 1977, 2003.
UNESCO, 'World Heritage List.' Accessed 2 April 2009. At http://whc.unesco.org/en/list/.
Urry, John. *Consuming Places*. London: Routledge, 1995.
– *The Tourist Gaze: Leisure and Travel in Contemporary Societies*. London: Sage, 1990.
Vannini, Andrea, and Mirko Grasso. *Firenze di Pratolini: Un documentario di Cecilia Mangini*. Lecce: Kurumny, 2007.
Vannucci, Marcello. *L'avventura degli stranieri in Toscana*. Aosta: Musumeci, 1981.
– *Storia di Firenze*. Translated as *The History of Florence*. Charles Lambert, trans. Rome: Newton Compton, 1988.
Wells, Byron R. 'Narrative Design and the Role of the Reader in Aldo Palazzeschi's *Sorelle Materassi*.' *Forum Italicum* 20.2 (1986): 198–208.
Williams, Raymond. *The Country and the City*. Oxford: Oxford UP, 1973.
Wilson, Thomas M., and Hastings Donnan. 'Nation, State and Identity at International Borders.' In *Border Identities: Nation and State at International Frontiers*. Ed. Thomas M. Wilson and Hastings Donnan. Cambridge: Cambridge UP, 1998. 1–30.

Index

abjection: in *La costanza della ragione*, 71, 82, 83–4, 86–87, 188n18; in place, 5; on via del Corno, 68
Adamson, Walter L., 173n10
aging: Belotti's analysis of women and, 160; Bruno's mother in *La costanza della ragione*, 86; spinsters in *Sorelle Materassi*, 14, 51, 53, 62
alterity: in *La costanza della ragione*, 71, 84; cultural in travel writers, 120; Fabian's theories on, 124–5; and identity, 8, 11, 167; Materassi sisters', 45, 66; sexual, 44, 63, 119; and space, 4, 13, 165, 168; and the Stendhal Syndrome, 14–15, 90; sublime and, 15, 31, 108, 119, 164; in Tozzi, 24; in *Voli*, 153, 158–9. *See also* Other; otherness
Amatori, Franco, and Andrea Colli, 187n4
animals: assimilation of, in Caillois, 34, 42; in Belotti, 15, 143, 144, 148, 150–5, 161–3; Greek immigrants, as in *La costanza della ragione*, 81–2; Materassi sisters as, 65; neoteny and, 197nn8,9; in Tozzi, 28, 43, 178n7

Ardis, Ann, 191n18
Argento, Asia, 110, 191n23
Argento, Dario, 90, 168, 191nn20,21, 192nn27,29, 193n30; *La sindrome* (novel) 191n22, 192n25; *La sindrome di Stendhal* (film) 15, 16, 31, 91, 95, 104, 110–19, 164, 178n9
Arno River, 5, 33, 103–4, 112
Ashcroft, Bill, Gareth Griffiths, and Helen Tiffin 196n18
Asor Rosa, Alberto, 185n4
Assunto, Rosario, 174n14

Bachelard, Gaston, 151–2, 196n19
Baker, Steve, 197n8
Bal, Mieke, 169
Baldacci, Luigi, 181–2n1
Ballini, Pier Luigi, et al., 173n10
Balmain, Collette, 115, 193n31
Barbaro, Marta, 184n20
Barthes, Roland, 94, 190n10, 195n15
Barzanti, Roberto, 19
Becattini, Giacomo, 172n4, 197n5
Belotti, Elena Gianini. *See* Gianini, Elena Belotti
Bertolucci, Bernardo, 165
Bertoncini, Giancarlo, 71, 84–5

Bhabha, Homi K., 119
Bilenchi, Romano, 166
Birdwell-Pheasant, Donna, and Denise Lawrence-Zúñiga, 132–3
Blanton, Casey, 121
Boccaccio, Giovanni, 5, 6, 47, 93
Boccioni, Umberto, 40–1
Bologni, Maurizio, 199n1
border: between body and outside world in Tozzi, 36–7; between inside and outside, 17, 153; difficulty of distinguishing, 4, 171n1; and window, 51
borderline, the abject and, 87
Brilli, Attilio, 176n3, 181n20, 193n1
Butler, Alban, 189n5
Butler, Judith, 54–5, 57
Buzard, James Michael, 190n9

Caillois, Roger, 34–7, 42, 178nn10,13, 179n15, 181n21
Calamandrei, Piero, 166
Cassola, Carlo, 19, 166
Castagno, Dario, with Robert Rodi, 193n3
Castellana, Riccardo, 24–5
Cavigioli, Rita C., 196n2
Cesarini, Paolo, 24
Chianti, 120, 123, 139
Chiantishire, 120, 165
Cibrario, Benedetta, 166
Cieraad, Irene, 51, 52
city: centre of Florence, 14–15; and fear, 189n1; and Greek community in Pratolini, 82; hero's exclusion in, 24–5; landmarks and legibility of, 76–7; in Pratolini, 70; postmodern, 37; and the sublime in Florence, 90–1; versus country, 12–13, 14, 20, 44, 51, 78–80, 153, 156, 174–5n16; and vertigo, 27–8. *See also* urban
Clifford, James, 133
Cloke, Paul, Chris Philo, and David Sadler, 174n15
closet: Palazzeschi's self and, 46, 62; Remo and the space of, 57; Sedgwick and Duncan on, 59–60; and space, 59, 60
Clover, Carol, 114, 116–17, 192n24
colonization, 120, 139, 154, 158, 163, 165, 177n4
Cortona, 12, 16, 123, 130, 131, 137, 172n5
Costantini, Anthony, 70
country: and Belotti, 142, English-speakers' settlement of, 120; exodus from, 197n5; house restoration in countryside, 123, 137, 164; idealized, 15; idyll in Pratolini, 188n16; in Tozzi, 20–4, 175–6n1, 176–7n4; Tuscan countryside, 7, 138, 166; versus city, 12–13, 14, 20, 44, 51, 78–80, 153, 156, 174–5n16. *See also* rural
Covino, Mariarosaria, 187n12
Crane, Teresa, 195n17
Crang, Mike, and Nigel Thrift, 173n12
Cresti, Carlo, 70, 187n8
Cresswell, Tim, 173n12
Crowhurst Lennard, Suzanne H., and Henry L. Lennard, 184n18
Crowther, Paul, 91

Dainotto, Roberto, 175nn17,18
Dante, 5, 6, 22, 47, 92–3, 94, 104, 180n17
Debenedetti, Giacomo, 24, 178n7
de Certeau, Michel 9, 174n13

Diafani, Laura, 181n1, 183n12
difference: 11, 12, 182n5; cultural, 119; and Mayes, 130; and Palazzeschi, 14, 16, 44–7, 48, 53, 54, 66, 165; and Pratolini, 67, 82–3, 89; and Stendhal's 'reverse racism,' 94; and stereotype, 128; and Tozzi, 24, 25–6, 43
Docherty, Thomas, 194n10
Dolan, John A., 196n20
domestic space: 15; as confining in Belotti, 158; in *Sorelle Materassi*, 183n11. *See also* home; house; space
Donald, James, 118
Doran, Phil, 121
Duncan, Derek, 56–7, 59–60
Dunkling, Leslie, and William Gosling, 95, 189n6
Duomo (Santa Maria del Fiore, Florence), 76, 107
Dusi, Isabella, 121

Ecocriticism, 175n18
Ecofeminism, 143–4, 175n18
environment: and body, 13; degradation of, 143–4, 160–2; human 4, 9, 10; preservation of in Belotti, 197n7, 198n13
ethnicity: and alterity, 14, 84, 89, 119, 164; and Ecocriticism, Ecofeminism, 175n18; hybrid identity and, 8; and oppressed groups, 118; and the Other, 11, 14, 15, 67, 82; and spatial construction, 175n17

Fabian, Johannes, 124–6, 128, 131, 156, 195n12
Fascism, 62, 68, 89, 166, 183n13

Febbraro, Paolo, 49, 60, 183n14
Felluga, Dino, 188n2
Ferraris, Denis, 182n2
Finocchiaro Chimirri, Giovanna, 70, 75
Flego, Fabio, 191n18
Florence (Firenze): and Argento, 110–14; and art, 15, 90; conflict and, 104, 168; effect on visitors, 15, 94–5, 107–8; and Forster, 31, 95–7, 99–105, 109–10; history of, 5–6; and the horrific, 15, 167; outskirts, 14; and Palazzeschi, 47–9, 165; and Pratolini, 67–71, 76–7, 78–82, 88–9; and Stendhal, 92–4; and Stendhal Syndrome, 90–2; the sublime, 119; and Tozzi, 20, 25
Folks, Jeffrey J., 131, 194n5
Fonnesu, Iolanda, and Leonardo Rombai, with Pietro Piussi, 171n3
Foot, Jonathan, 188n17
foreign: anxiety and the, 119; culture, 109, 121, 141; house, 53, 133, 138; invasion in Argento, 112; reverse racism, 94; tourists, 90; versus native, 11–12; writers in Tuscany, 3, 110, 123, 129, 165, 166
Forster, E.M.: Baedeker, 190n9; Florence, 90, 168; Italy, 191n18; Lucy Honeychurch as stand-in for author's sexuality, 65, 118–19, 193n32; Lucy and Italian otherness, 119, 141; muddle, 189n3; names, 189nn5,6,7; *A Passage to India* and cultural clash, 109; *A Room with a View*, 15, 16, 26, 95–106, 108–10, 116, 120, 132, 141, 142, 164, 167, 178n9, 190nn8,12, 13,15

Foucault, Michel. *See* heterotopia, Foucauldian
Fratnik, Marina, 19, 22, 39–40, 176n2, 181–2n19
Freud, Sigmund, 100, 175n17, 178–9n14, 179–80n16
Futurism, 7, 40–1, 173n10

Gabelli, Alessandra, 70, 185n3
Gallant, Chris, 191n19, 193n31
Garber, Marjorie, 133–4, 140
Geddes da Filicaia, Costanza, 178n14
Gelley, Alexander, 17
gender: alterity and, 164; in Argento, 114–16, 118–19, 191n21; in Belotti, 143, 157–60; Butler on performativity of, 54–7; in Cassola, 166; difference and, 11; Ecofeminism and, 175n18; in Manzini, 166; in Palazzeschi, 44, 49, 51–7, 59, 61, 183–4n16; performative, 14; place and, 12; in Pratolini, 67, 71; space and, 175n17
geography: human, 173–4n12, 174n15; Tuscany's, 3, 4–5; writers and Tuscan, 171n3
Gervais, Paul, 121
Gianini Belotti, Elena: *Apri le porte all'alba*, 143–4, 196n2; Ecofeminism,143–4; ecology and Tuscan countryside, 160–3; emigration, 143; house reconstruction narrative, 15–16, 17, 142; landscape, nature, and animals, 148–55; spaces of fear and alterity, 155–60; Tuscan farmhouse, 144–8; *Voli*, 144–63; women's issues, 142
Gioanola, Elio, 36–7, 176–7n4, 178n12
Giovanardi, Stefano, 183–4n16

Giuttari, Michele, and Carlo Lucarelli, 168
Gnerre, Francesco, 46, 57, 182n4
Goldman, Jane, 105, 119, 189n7, 192n26, 193n32
Grignani, Maria Antonietta, 19
Grosz, Elizabeth, 35–6, 181n21
Gruppo Lavoratori Anziani delle Officine Galileo, 187n10

Hainsworth, Peter, 188n20
Harris, Thomas, 168
Harvey, David, 11
Hawes, Annie, 198n11
heterotopia, Foucauldian, 14, 80–1, 89
Hirdt, Willi, 183n7
Holland, Patrick, and Graham Huggan, 129, 193–4n4
Holloway, Lewis, and Phil Hubbard, 174n12
home: and Belotti, 152, 194n8; and house, 51, 132–3, 194n10; identity, 123, 132–8; improvement, 146; incarceration in, 59, 64–5; and Mayes, 127; second, 140; and social status, 196n20; and rebirth, renewal, 141. *See also* domestic space; house; villa
horror: blood, 106; female body and, 85–7; Kristeva, 188n18; movie, 16, 104, 110, 111, 113–14, 116–18, 192nn24,29; sublime and, 16, 90–1, 117
house: and animals, 153–4; in book titles, 195n17, 151–4; and consumerism in Mayes, 134–7, 140–1; history, 129; and home, 51, 132–3, 194n10; and identity, 16, 130–1, 132–8, 140–1, 158, 194n10; and

Mayes, 196n19; in Palazzeschi, 47, 49–51, 53, 64–5; as prison, 64–5; restoration, 15, 16–17, 142; socio-economic status, 17, 196n20; as toppling in Tozzi, 24, 28; in Tuscany, 120, 122–3, 144–8, 150, 162. *See also* domestic space; home; villa
Hubbard, Phil, Rob Kitchin, and Gill Valentine, 174n12
Hulme, Peter, 121–2
Hutchings, Peter J., 105, 190n14

Ivory, James, 15, 90, 91, 105–6

Jeuland-Meynaud, Maryse, 176n1, 178n6
Jones, Alan, 191nn22,23

Kafka, Franz, 24
Kant, Immanuel, 91, 107, 190n16
Kirby, Kathleen M., 31, 35
Knopp, Lawrence, 46–7
Kristeva, Julia, 80, 188n18

landmark(s), 165, absence of, 80, in Florence, 6, 7, 14, 16, 26, 47, 76, 90, 165, 167
landscape: in Belotti, 147, 148, 150, 162; Belotti and animals in, 148–50; of Florence, 119, 168; humans and, 4, 19; idealized, 5, 22; literary, 8; in Palazzeschi, 47, 183n7; place, space, and, 8–10; in Pratolini, 70, 75, 80; sublime, 91; theory, 174n14; in Tozzi, 19–20, 22, 23, 26, 28, 36–8, 177n4; Tuscan, 18, 42, 165, 167, 172n4; and verisimilitude, 185n2
Landy, Marcia, 190n13

Lane, Christopher, 193n32
Lanuzza, Stefano, 173n11
Lasansky, D. Medina, 172n6
Lazzaro-Weis, Carol, 196n2
Leavitt, David, and Mark Mitchell: authorial identity, 129, 131–2; colonization, 154, 163; identity and home, 132–4, 137–8, 140–1, 164; *In Maremma: Life and a House in Southern Tuscany*, 122–41; Italians as Others, 123–8; Italy as timeless, 128–9; linguistic errors, 194n11; Maremma as American West, 138–40; rebirth in Tuscany, 110, 141; restoration of Tuscan house, 15, 16–17, 144; romanticized Tuscany, 150
Listri, Pier Francesco, 187n13
local(s): government, 4; integration into local culture, 129–32; life among the, 122, 163; and outsider, 168; population, Fabian on, 124; population in travelogues, 122; prejudice towards, 160; residents, 11, 155–6; speech of absent in travelogues, 141; stereotyping of, 16, 164–5; struggle in Pratolini's *Il Quartiere*, 68; versus national, 171n2; wildlife, 16
Loggia dei Lanzi, 16, 25–6, 100–1, 102
Longobardi, Fulvio, 188n19
Lotman, Jurij, 48, 164, 183n10
Luti, Giorgio, 173n11
Lynch, Kevin, 76

McDonagh, Maitland, 192n27
Machiavelli, Niccolò, 5, 93
Macrí, Oreste, 186n7
Magherini, Graziella, 15, 90, 94–5, 98–9, 105, 106–8, 109, 111, 112

Manzini, Gianna, 166
Marabini, Claudio, 88
Marchegiani Jones, Irene, and Thomas Haeussler, 173n11
Marchi, Marco, 45, 49, 56, 57, 178–9n14, 183n9, 184n23
Maremma, 16, 123, 127, 138–40, 166
marginalization: alterity, space and, 67, 68, 71, 78, 81; difference and, 24; and heterotopias, 14; and Other, 12; in Palazzeschi, 45, 66; in Pratolini, 16, 80, 81; and Rom, 168; wasteland, 88
Martini, Martina, 179n14
Massey, Doreen, 174n12
Maté, Ferenc, 121
Maugham, W. Somerset, 195n17
Mayes, Frances: authorial identity, 129–31; colonization, 154; consumerism and house, 134–7, 140–1; idealization of Tuscan villa and countryside, 145–6, 147, 150; identity and home, 132–8, 140–1, 164, 194n8, 196n19; Italians as Others, 123–8; Italy as timeless, 128–9; linguistic errors, 194–5n11; Maremma as American West, 138–40; rebirth in Tuscany, 110, 141, 194n7; restoration of Tuscan house, 15, 16, 17, 144; as travel writer, 194n5; *Under the Tuscan Sun: At Home in Italy*, 15, 122–41
Mayle, Peter, 120, 128, 193n2
Melloni, Giorgio, 29, 178n8
Mellor, Mary, 143
Melosi, Laura, 29, 179n14
Memmo, Francesco Paolo, 186n7
Mendik, Xavier, 191n21
Meyers, Jeffrey, 97–8, 190nn8,11, 193n32

Miller, J. Hillis, 185n2
miracolo economico (Economic Miracle), 7, 14, 69, 74, 78, 88, 186n7
Mitchell, W.J.T., 9–10
modernity, 13, 22, 43, 78, 88
Mori, Giorgio, 4, 172n5
Mosse, George, 184n22

Nabb, Magdalen, 168
Nabhan, Gary Paul, 167, 195n116
nature: and animals in Belotti, 15, 17, 142, 148–55, 160–3; attempt to connect with in Tozzi, 23, 175–6n1, 176–7n4; Calamandrei and, 166, Ecofeminism and, 175n18; and George in *A Room with a View*, 189–90n7; human/nature assimilation, or psychasthenia, 34; human/nature relationship, 5; nature/culture dualism 12; as persecutor in Tozzi, 24; in Pratolini, 79; sublime in, 90–1; versus city in Tuan, 189n1
Nerenberg, Ellen, 188n20
Newby, Eric, 121
Nye, David E., 91, 105

Olalquiaga, Celeste, 37, 179n15
Oliver, Jamie, 135
Oliver, Kelly, 87
Ondaatje, Michael, 120, 167
Other, the: ambivalence towards, 128–32; animal, 16, 153–4, 162; in Belotti, 143, 155, 159; dominant culture and, 168; in Forster, 119; heterotopias and, 80; in Ivory, 105–6; in Nabhan, 167; in Pratolini, 67, 71, 82–3, 87, 89; Self and, 11–12, 31, 113, 121, 163; 'sociologizing' of,

118; in Tozzi, 43; travel writing and, 123–8, 141; Tuscan, 165. *See also* alterity; otherness

otherness: Belotti's own, 16; ethnic, 15; female in Argento, 118; in Forster, 109, 141; Italian in travel writers, 122, 123–8; Palazzeschi and, 45; Pratolini and, 89; Stendhal Syndrome as response to, 90, 91. *See also* alterity; Other, the

Ovid, 180n17

Palazzeschi, Aldo (Aldo Giurlani): *buffi*, 45–6, 182n2; closet space, 57–62; country versus city, 16, 49, 183nn12,13; difference and sexuality, 14, 44–7; Florence, 47–9, 165; Futurists, 7; gender and sexuality as labile, 44; house, 49–51, 64–5; law of the father, 187n15; Materassi Sisters/women as stand-in for author, 45–6, 119, 182n4, 184–5n23; performance, 62–4, 184nn19,20; queer theory, 182–3n6; *Sorelle Materassi*, 14, 44–66, 183nn11,14; window, 17, 51–7, 153, 166, 183–4n16

Palazzo Vecchio, 16, 25–6, 68–9, 100, 103–4

Paloscia, Franco, 173n11

Paoletti, Paolo, and Paola Torrini, 187n13

Parker, Allan, 121

Parronchi, Alessandro, 69, 188n19

Pemble, John, 193n31

Perella, Nicolas J., 182n3; and Ruggero Stefanini, 182n2

performance, 14, 44, 45, 51, 55–7, 62–3, 184n19

Perry Levine, June, 100, 105

Piazza della Signoria, 11, 16, 25, 31, 67, 100–1, 102, 103–4, 105, 110, 111, 112, 114

Pike, Burton, 24

place: definitions of, 173n12; ethical engagement with place, 148, 162; ethnic minorities, 82; as menacing in Tozzi, 16, 20; the Other and, 11–12, 80, 155, 165, 168; people and, 8; personal, 8; socio-economic history of in Belotti, 146; and space, 4, 8, 9–11, 13, 132, 165, 169, 173–4n12, 174n13; stereotypes and, 15, 18, 165; subjectivity and, 10, 165; 'Terrible Place' in horror films, 114; textual portrayals of, 5, 16, 17, 19, 20 165, 167; and toponymy, 16. *See also* space

Place, Janey, 118

Plumwood, Val, 12, 143–4

Polezzi, Loredana, 194nn7,9

Porteous, J. Douglas, 39, 180n18

Prakash, Lakshmi, 189n3

Pratolini, Vasco: (body)spaces of abjection, 83–7; *La costanza della ragione*, 14, 67, 69–89, 188n19; *Cronache di poveri amanti*, 67, 68–9, 166; documentaries on, 185n1; factory space, 73–8; Fascist dogma, 188n20; and Florence, 88–9, 90; Florence as setting, 67–8, 187n8; Florentine cultural circles, 7; in-between zones, marginalization, and difference, 78–83; industrial suburbs of Florence, 16, 69–70; law of the father, 187–8n15; *miracolo economico*, 186–7n15; *Il Quartiere*, 67–8, 165–6; via del Corno, 185nn3–4, 186n5

Pratt, Jeff, 146

Pratt, Mary Louise, 158
Preston, Douglas, and Mario Spezi, 168
psychasthenia, legendary: Caillois and definition of, 34–5; death drive and, 181n21; in Grosz, 35–6; Olalquiaga on, 179n15; Soja on, 179n15; subject and surroundings, 13; and Tozzi, 31–43, 179n14; and vertigo in Tozzi, 20
Pullini, Giorgio, 60, 184n19

Rauger, Jean-François, 191n20
region: definition of, 4, 171n2; as metonymic for Italy, 194n9; regional novel, 13, 175n17; textual depiction of, 8, 164; Tuscany, 3–5, 18
Rifredi, 14, 69–70, 71, 73–7, 81–2, 88–9, 168, 189n2
Riggins, Stephen Harold, 12, 128, 131, 132
Rocca, Tony, 121
Romani, Valerio, 174n14
Ross, Michael L., 100, 102, 173n11, 189n7
Ross, Silvia, 186n5, 195n14, 196n3, 198n12
Rossi, Aldo, 22
rural: commune in Williams, 174n16; environment in Belotti, 15, 144, 163; environment in Mayes and Leavitt/Mitchell, 15, 16, 120, 141, 150; environment in Tozzi, 20–4; Europe, travel in, 127–8; female landowners, 159, 198n11; idyll in Pratolini, 188n16; life in Maremma in Cassola, 166; migration from rural Tuscany, 146; picturesque rural Tuscany in Cibrario, 166; property in Belotti, 150; versus urban, 12–13, 14, 43, 49, 70, 78–80, 183nn12,13. *See also* country
Rushdie, Salman, 3
Russo Bullaro, Grace, 126, 194nn5,8, 195n13

Saccone, Eduardo, 22, 43, 177n4
St Aubin de Terán, Lisa, 195n17
Santa Croce, 16, 31, 67, 69, 93–4, 96, 97, 99, 101–2, 103, 187n8
Sarup, Madan, 123
Sassoon, Donald, 74
Savellini, Paolo Gori, 173n11
Schippisi, Ranieri, 19
Scott, Ridley, 168
Sebald, W.G., 191n17
Sedgwick, Eve Kosofsky, 59, 182n5
setting: criticism on Tozzi, 19; Ondaatje, 167; pathetic fallacy and, 20; relationship with character, 32; space, place and, 169; in Tozzi, 20; Tuscan, 12
sexuality: in Argento, 113–18; difference and, 11; in Forster, 109, 118–19, 193n32; in Palazzeschi, 14, 17, 44–7, 52–66, 119, 182nn4,5, 182–3n6; in Pratolini, 14, 72, 83–9
Sharp, Joanne P., 127–8
Shove, Elizabeth, 196n22
Sibley, David, 82, 83
Siena: architecture, 172n5; and Tozzi, 7, 16, 19–20, 24, 27–9, 166
Smith, H., 108
Smouts, Marie-Claude, 171n2
Socco, Carlo, 174n14
Soja, Ed, 37, 179n15
Somigli, Luca, 182n6
space: alterity and, 4, 13, 165, 168; assimilation to, 34–6, 42; difference

and, 14, 44, 46–7; domestic, 15, 158, 183n11; and exclusion, 82–3, 89; Futurism and, 40–1; gender/sexuality and space, 52, 54–5, 59–60, 166, internal, 85; liminal/in-between, 44, 51, 80, 183–4n16; marginalization and, 67, 68, 71, 78, 81; perception of, 19, 34; and place, 4, 8, 9–11, 13, 132, 165, 169, 173–4n12, 174n13; public, 141; thematized, 169. *See also* place

Spender, Matthew, 121

Spini, Giorgio, and Antonio Casali, 173n8

Spitzer, Leo, 180n17

Stendhal (Marie-Henri Beyle): and Florence, 16, 92–4, 103–4, 106, 168; origin of Stendhal Syndrome, 91; otherness, 90, 195n15; passion for Italy, 190n10; *Rome, Naples et Florence*, 91, 92–4, 97, 101–2, 103–4, 110; Santa Croce, 31, 93–4, 96, 97, 101–2; sensual reaction to art, 31, 101, 113; sublime and otherness, 31, 119, 164

Stendhal Syndrome: Argento, 110–12; and art and spectatorship, 116–17; cultural and sexual alterity and, 164; description of, 14–15; Magherini's definition of, 90; in media, 92; oppressive architecture and, 106–8; as psychological watershed, 109; Sebald and, 191n17; sublime and otherness and, 90–1; tourists in Florence and, 94, 108

stereotype: and ambivalence, 128; Castagno, 193n3; Mayes and Italy, 130–1; Mayes and Leavitt/Mitchell on Italian Others, 123–8, 141, 165, 195n13; on place and inhabitants, 17–18; Tabucchi on Florence, 168; travel writing on Italy, 15

Stone, Wilfred, 171n2

sublime: and alterity, 15, 31, 108, 119, 164; Burke and terror, 90–1; Florentine architecture, 16; horror, 105, 112, 117,192–3n29; Lucy Honeychurch and, 99, 105; mathematical, 107; terrible, 168; Tozzi, 178n8; urban, 90–1; vertigo, 106–7

suburb: heterotopia in Pratolini, 89; in Palazzeschi, 48; in Pratolini, 14, 16, 67, 70–1, 78–80; in Tabucchi, 168; Williams on, 175n16

Summers, C.J., 190n8

Tabucchi, Antonio, 168

Tamburri, Anthony Julian, 183n15

terror, 11, 90

Thoret, Jean-Baptiste, 116, 117, 192n29

Tozzi, Federigo: alienation, 14; *Bestie*, 20, 27–9, 34, 42, 178n7; *Con gli occhi chiusi*, 20, 27, 36, 38, 39, 175–6n1; descriptions in, 19–20; illness, 178–9n14; landscapes, 180–1n19; law of the father, 179–80n16, 187n15; literary groups, 6–7; *Novale*, 24, 38, 178n11; pre-Freudian psychology, 178–9n14; *Il podere*, 20, 21–4, 41–2, 176–7n4; psychasthenia, legendary, 31–42, 44, 166, 175–6n1, 178n7; retreat to nature, 176–7n4; *Ricordi di un impiegato*, 20, 25–6, 27, 31–3; rural and urban environments, 20–6; subject and his/her surroundings, 13, 19;

urban location, 16; vertigo, 13, 26–31, 106, 178n8
Tozzi, Glauco, 19
travel writing: Blanton on, 121; clichés in, 122; definition of, 121–2; 193–4n4, 195n12; home-away opposition in, 133; hybridity of genre, 141; and identity, 129–32; settlement literature as sub-genre of, 129; on Tuscany, 15, 167
Trequanda, 17, 142, 153, 196n1, 197n7
Trevor, William, 195n17
Tuan, Yi-Fu, 10, 152, 189n1
Tuscany (Toscana): 'authentic,' 146; and beauty, 11; consumerist attitude towards, 140–1; critical works on, 173n11; environmental decline, 198n13; 'exotic,' 134; foreigners and, 120, 165, 173n9; geographical region, 4–5; geography and literature, 171n3; historic significance, 5–8; idealized/romanticized, 15, 126–8; literary depictions of, 13, 164–5; migration in, 146; rebirth/renewal trope, 110, 122–3; restoration of house, 15; as setting, 16; significance of, 3–4; as timeless/slow, 126–8; travel writing on, 120–1; 'Tuscan aesthetic,' 135; urban-rural in Tozzi, 43

Uffizi, 110, 111, 112–13, 117, 125
UNESCO, 172n5
urban: development in Tuscany, 5; environment, 9; landmarks in Florence, 167–8; locations in Tozzi, 16, 24–6, 26–9; peripheries in Pratolini, 75–8; settings in Palazzeschi, 183n12; society and animals, 152; sublime in Florence, 90–1; versus rural, 12–13, 14, 43, 49, 70, 78–80; zones and fear, 189n1. *See also* city
Urry, John, 26, 128, 135–6, 177–8n5

Vannini, Andrea, and Mirko Grasso, 185n1
Vannucci, Marcello, 173nn8,9
vertigo: elicited by place, 20; Kirby on, 35; Lucy Honeychurch and, 106; in Tozzi, 13, 16, 26–31, 32–3, 42, 43, 106, 178n8
villa: house in Belotti versus Mayes, 145–6; in literature on Italy, 195n17; in travel writing, 120; Tuscan, in Cibrario, 166; Tuscan, as emblematic, 5, 11; Tuscan, restored, 164. *See also* home

Wells, Byron R., 183n11
window: Cieraad on, 51–2; as liminal in Belotti, 153; as liminal in Palazzeschi, 14, 44, 153, 183–4n16; Manzini and, 166; in Materassi Sisters' house, 50–1; sensation of falling from in Tozzi, 27–8, 32–3, 42; spectacle, 184n18; as symbol of sexuality in Palazzeschi, 17, 51–7; view from Uffizi, 112
Williams, Raymond, 19, 174–5n16
Wilson, Thomas M., and Hastings Donnan, 171n1

www.ingramcontent.com/pod-product-compliance
Lightning Source LLC
Chambersburg PA
CBHW030316080526
44584CB00012B/582